D1536764

JUDICIAL CLERKSHIPS: LEGAL METHODS IN MOTION

LexisNexis Law School Publishing Advisory Board

William Araiza
Professor of Law
Brooklyn Law School

Lenni B. Benson
Professor of Law & Associate Dean for Professional Development
New York Law School

Raj Bhala
Rice Distinguished Professor
University of Kansas, School of Law

Ruth Colker
Distinguished University Professor & Heck-Faust Memorial Chair in Constitutional Law
Ohio State University, Moritz College of Law

David Gamage
Assistant Professor of Law
UC Berkeley School of Law

Joan Heminway
College of Law Distinguished Professor of Law
University of Tennessee College of Law

Edward Imwinkelried
Edward L. Barrett, Jr. Professor of Law
UC Davis School of Law

David I. C. Thomson
LP Professor & Director, Lawyering Process Program
University of Denver, Sturm College of Law

Melissa Weresh
Director of Legal Writing and Professor of Law
Drake University Law School

JUDICIAL CLERKSHIPS: LEGAL METHODS IN MOTION

Aliza Milner
Professor of Legal Writing
Syracuse University College of Law

 LexisNexis®

ISBN: 978-1-4224-7756-4

Library of Congress Cataloging-in-Publication Data

Milner, Aliza.
Judicial clerkships : legal methods in motion / Aliza Milner.
    p. cm.
Includes index.
ISBN 978-1-4224-7756-4 (perfect bound) 1. Law clerks--United States--Handbooks, manuals, etc. I. Title.
KF8771.M55 2011
347.73'016--dc22
                                                                            2010053855

This publication is designed to provide accurate and authoritative information in regard to the subject matter covered. It is sold with the understanding that the publisher is not engaged in rendering legal, accounting, or other professional services. If legal advice or other expert assistance is required, the services of a competent professional should be sought.

LexisNexis and the Knowledge Burst logo are registered trademarks and Michie is a trademark of Reed Elsevier Properties Inc., used under license. Matthew Bender and the Matthew Bender Flame Design are registered trademarks of Matthew Bender Properties Inc.

Copyright © 2011 Matthew Bender & Company, Inc., a member of the LexisNexis Group. All Rights Reserved.

No copyright is claimed in the text of statutes, regulations, and excerpts from court opinions quoted within this work. Permission to copy material exceeding fair use, 17 U.S.C. § 107, may be licensed for a fee of 25¢ per page per copy from the Copyright Clearance Center, 222 Rosewood Drive, Danvers, Mass. 01923, telephone (978) 750-8400.

NOTE TO USERS

To ensure that you are using the latest materials available in this area, please be sure to periodically check the LexisNexis Law School web site for downloadable updates and supplements at www.lexisnexis.com/lawschool.

Editorial Offices
121 Chanlon Rd., New Providence, NJ 07974 (908) 464-6800
201 Mission St., San Francisco, CA 94105-1831 (415) 908-3200
www.lexisnexis.com

MATTHEW◆BENDER

(2011–Pub.3302)

FOREWORD

Lawyers have been heard to say: "There is the trial I planned, the trial I tried, and the trial I wished I tried." Such comparisons abound in life, but for judicial clerks, they may also apply to their time working for judges: the clerkships they hoped for, those they experienced, and those they wished they had. Professor Milner's book can help make the law clerk experience live up to the hopes of those graduates who start their careers at a judge's side.

A clerkship is a time to participate in meaningful public service with a chance for some even to influence judges in properly ruling on and deciding cases. Clerking for a judge can also be a look behind the stage curtain and inside the judge's chambers to where so many disputes are resolved on motions before trial, at trial, or later on appeal. For the general public and many lawyers, these court dynamics are shrouded in mystery. Clerks cannot only see firsthand and up-close just how court process works, but also view from the inside just how nuanced judges' decisions are.

The relationship between judges and law clerks is more like a short-term marriage, or more precisely, like a short-term adoption of an adult by an older lawyer. The experience can be more valuable and meaningful, both for the clerk and for the judge, if there is a good fit and the clerk knows what to do and how to do it well. Professor Milner was my clerk for many years and I never had a better one. She is a gifted writer who demonstrated mature judgment and an excellent grasp of the law while she adjusted well in the cloister where an appellate judge works daily with a small staff. She is highly equipped to pass on her experience to others who aspire to clerk and who want to get the most out of their service. Following her advice can help assure that when the clerkship is over, clerks look back with pride and a sense of fulfillment as they begin their careers at the bar.

Andrew L. Sonner,
Associate Judge, Maryland Court of Special Appeals

INTRODUCTION

By the third semester in law school, I knew I wanted to apply for clerkships because the job offered intellectual challenges, collaborative work, and a clear civic purpose. And clerk I did, for three judges, over seven years. It was my good fortune to serve in the chambers of Judge Alan M. Wilner on the Court of Appeals of Maryland, Judge Andrew L. Sonner on the Court of Special Appeals of Maryland, and Patrick L. Woodward on the Court of Special Appeals of Maryland. Each of these judges taught me how to think about cases and draft legal analysis. The administrative assistants in chambers, particularly Donetta Swick, and my co-clerks also taught me how to work together to create a product of which we all could be proud.

As I began teaching the judicial drafting course at Syracuse University College of Law, I sought to introduce my students to the invigorating thinking and writing that happens in chambers. This book is a product of those efforts. It is organized in three parts. The first part introduces clerkships by probing some of the controversies that swirl around the position, as well as by describing the work that law clerks perform in appellate and trial courts. The second part covers appellate clerkships, first examining the foundational principles of scope of review and *stare decisis*, before turning to the drafting and editing process for majority and minority opinions. The message I hope to relay is that careful thinking is a prerequisite to any writing.

Part three of the book addresses trial court clerkships. It begins with a discussion of fact and law and how these wayward concepts show themselves in motions for summary judgment. It continues with an example of the kind of statutory law that trial courts apply on a regular basis. Part three ends with a chapter on drafting orders, judgments, and findings of fact and conclusions of law. Here too, my purpose is to demonstrate both the analytical skills and the drafting skills that law clerks employ.

The primary sources for this book are opinions and orders from state and federal courts. Most of the citations and footnotes in these documents have been deleted. Some of the text has been omitted as well, as indicated by asterisks, ellipses, or brackets. Each chapter also includes notes and questions to provoke discussion, as well as suggested further reading to satisfy the curious reader. I chose and edited the material and structured the chapters with the goal of creating a book that would serve equally well as a textbook in a "clerking" course as it would a desk reference in a judicial clerkship or internship.

Thanks to the strong team of Legal Communication and Research faculty at Syracuse University College of Law and all the students at the law school who motivate me to teach as best I can. Special thanks to Ian Gallacher and Andrew Greenberg for checking in on me. I am also grateful to the three judges who hired me for what could be the best legal job there is (aside from teaching). Judge Sonner, in particular, has become a mentor to me in life and law. He demonstrates that

INTRODUCTION

intelligence and grace are complementary, and he taught me that laughter in chambers increases productivity. I am one among his many admirers.

Most of all, this book would not have been written without my family's support. My parents and my sisters are part of everything I do. My daughters delight and sustain me. Thank you, Ariella and Sarah, for being patient. My husband Daniel encouraged me to take on this project and stood by me throughout its development. He gave advice, read chapters, brought nourishment, and pulled me away from the computer at just the right time. Daniel is the love of my life, and the book is dedicated to him.

TABLE OF CONTENTS

PART I	**WELCOME TO THE COURTHOUSE: AN INTRODUCTION TO CLERKING**	**1**

Chapter 1	**CLERKS AND CONTROVERSY: AN EVOLVING HISTORY**	**3**

I.	INTRODUCTION	3
II.	CONTROVERSIES	4
A.	What Do Our Laws Require of Judges?	4
B.	What Does *Stare Decisis* Demand?	4
C.	How Many Hours Should There Be in a Judge's Work Day?	6
III.	CONCLUSION	7
	NOTES AND QUESTIONS	7
IV.	SUGGESTED FURTHER READING	8

Chapter 2	**INSIDE CHAMBERS: WHAT JUDICIAL CLERKS DO**	**11**

I.	INTRODUCTION	11
II.	APPELLATE COURT CHAMBERS	11
A.	Case Assignment	11
B.	From Briefs to Opinions	12
C.	Types of Opinions	14
D.	Precedential Effect	15
	Anastasoff v. United States	16
	Hart v. Massanari	18
E.	Oral Argument	21
F.	Petitions for Certiorai	22
G.	The Sum of Its Parts	22
	NOTES AND QUESTIONS	22
III.	TRIAL COURT CHAMBERS	23
A.	Case Assignment	23
B.	Pleadings and Motions	23
C.	Discovery	23
D.	Trials	24
E.	The Sum of Its Parts	24

TABLE OF CONTENTS

	State v. North	24
	NOTES AND QUESTIONS	27
IV.	SUGGESTED FURTHER READING	27

| **PART II** | **FOUNDATIONAL PRINCIPLES FOR APPELLATE COURT LAW CLERKS** | **29** |

| **Chapter 3** | **SCOPE OF REVIEW: THE SELF-CONSCIOUS APPELLATE COURT** | **31** |

I.	INTRODUCTION	31
II.	STANDARDS OF REVIEW	32
A.	*De Novo* Review	32
	Whitson v. Stone County Jail	32
	NOTES AND QUESTIONS	35
B.	Abuse of Discretion	36
	Herrington v. Ford Motor Co., Inc.	36
	Ham v. State	39
	NOTES AND QUESTIONS	40
C.	Clearly Erroneous	41
	Knight v. Knight	41
	NOTES AND QUESTIONS	47
	EXERCISE	48
III.	PRESERVATION DOCTRINE	49
IV.	THE SELF-CONSCIOUS APPELLATE COURT: A CASE STUDY	51
	Oesby v. State	51
	NOTES AND QUESTIONS	62
V.	SUGGESTED FURTHER READING	62

| **Chapter 4** | **UNRAVELING THE THREADS OF *STARE DECISIS*** | **65** |

I.	INTRODUCTION	65
II.	*STARE DECISIS* IN ACTION	65
	Citizens United v. Fed. Elec. Comm'n	66
	NOTES AND QUESTIONS	84
	EXERCISE	86
III.	SUGGESTED FURTHER READING	86

TABLE OF CONTENTS

Chapter 5   **SCIENCE AND ART: DRAFTING APPELLATE**
                  OPINIONS 87

I.   INTRODUCTION 87
        Johnson v. Tennis 87
        NOTES AND QUESTIONS 94
II.   ELEMENTS OF AN APPELLATE OPINION 95
   A.   Introductory Paragraph 95
        EXERCISE 95
   B.   Review of the Facts 96
        NOTES AND QUESTIONS 98
   C.   Legal Analysis 98
      1.   Accuracy 99
      2.   Clarity 100
           NOTES AND QUESTIONS 101
   D.   Mandate 102
III.   NITTY-GRITTY QUESTIONS AND ANSWERS 103
   A.   *How should I refer to the parties in an appellate opinion?* 103
   B.   *How should I refer to courts in an appellate opinion?* 103
   C.   *Must I include all the facts provided in the briefs and the trial court's*
        order? 104
   D.   *Should I include citations in the fact section?* 104
   E.   *What verb tense should I use in the draft opinion?* 105
   F.   *Must I answer all the questions presented in the briefs?* 105
   G.   *Should I address all the arguments that the parties raise?* 105
   H.   *What should I draft first, the factual review or the legal analysis?* .. 106
IV.   THREE TECHNIQUES FOR IMPROVED WRITING 106
   A.   Topic Sentences 106
   B.   Transitional Phrases 107
   C.   Effective Use of Quotations 108
V.   SUGGESTED FURTHER READING 110

Chapter 6   **A DIVIDED BENCH: DISSENTS AND**
                  CONCURRENCES 113

I.   INTRODUCTION 113
II.   CASE STUDY 114
        Pinkney v. State 114
        NOTES AND QUESTIONS 143

TABLE OF CONTENTS

III.   SUGGESTED FURTHER READING 143

Chapter 7   CLERKING: THE BEAUTY IS IN THE DETAILS . . . 145

I.   INTRODUCTION 145
II.   STEP-BY-STEP CLERKING 145
          EXERCISES 147
III.   SUGGESTED FURTHER READING 148

**PART III   FOUNDATIONAL PRINCIPLES FOR TRIAL COURT
                   LAW CLERKS 149**

Chapter 8   A PRIMER ON LAW AND FACT 151

I.   INTRODUCTION 151
   A.   Fact 151
   B.   Inference 151
   C.   Finding of Fact 152
   D.   Law 152
   E.   Conclusion of Law 153
   F.   Appellate Review: Connecting the Dots 153
          NOTES AND QUESTIONS 154
          EXERCISE 155
II.   SUMMARY JUDGMENT 156
          Tedone v. H.j. Heinz Co. 156
          NOTES AND QUESTIONS 165
          EXERCISE 165
III.   SUGGESTED FURTHER READING 166

Chapter 9   WORKING WITH STATUTES 167

I.   INTRODUCTION 167
II.   PRACTICE 167
          PARENTS DUTY TO SUPPORT CHILD 168
          CHILD SUPPORT STANDARDS 172

TABLE OF CONTENTS

Chapter 10   **DRAFTING IN THE TRIAL COURTS: THE LONG AND SHORT OF IT** **173**

I.   INTRODUCTION 173

II.   ORDERS 173

   A.   Three Examples 173

           Pellegrini v. L A Fitness Sports Club LLC 174

           Lips v. Univ. of Cincinnati Coll. of Med. 174

           NOTES AND QUESTIONS 177

   B.   Drafting Guidelines 177

     1.   Introductory Paragraph 178

     2.   Review of the Facts 178

     3.   Legal Analysis 179

     4.   Disposition 179

           NOTES AND QUESTIONS 179

III.   JUDGMENTS 179

           Serrano v. Austin 180

IV.   FINDINGS OF FACT AND CONCLUSIONS OF LAW 180

           Carter v. United States 181

           NOTES AND QUESTIONS 187

V.   SUGGESTED FURTHER READING 187

PART I

WELCOME TO THE COURTHOUSE: AN INTRODUCTION TO CLERKING

Chapter 1

CLERKS AND CONTROVERSY: AN EVOLVING HISTORY

I. INTRODUCTION

These days, admiration and suspicion shroud judicial clerkships in equal measure. For every law clerk who praises the wisdom and grace of a mentoring judge, there is a detractor who suggests judges have become lazy with their entrusted state power. For every judge who relies openly on a law clerk's drafting skills, another judge fiercely defends the writing of his or her own decisions. And while commentators scrutinize judicial clerkships and question their efficacy, law students continue to prize them, ever faithful in the education and prestige they promise.

Public attention has fed these dichotomies. Indeed, a widening stream of books, law review articles, and newspaper articles describe clerkships and purport to reveal the division of labor between judges and clerks. Most of the commentary concerns the U.S. Supreme Court, even though, by and large, Americans experience the judicial system at their local state or federal court. Law clerks working in these local chambers influence personal encounters with litigation to a far greater extent. Nonetheless, the U.S. Supreme Court continues to receive more attention, perhaps because it hears high-profile cases, hires clerks from prestigious law schools, and nine justices create a manageable sample size for the study of clerkships. Often, we are left to extrapolate from the experience in the U.S. Supreme Court to the other federal courts and state courts.

This chapter reviews three contemporary controversies regarding the division of labor in chambers. The controversies speak to the aspirations and practicalities of our judicial system. Where do you stand on each of the controversies? What further information do you need to take a position?

II. CONTROVERSIES

A.   What Do Our Laws Require of Judges?

A primary controversy is whether judges may lawfully delegate any part of their responsibilities to law clerks. Judges, after all, whether appointed or elected, are public officials, whereas law clerks are government employees. Judges are accountable to the public they serve, whereas law clerks are anonymous and accountable to their judges only. Moreover, voters and elected officials choose judges for their professional, personal, and political experience. What does the public even know about a law clerk's qualifications? Proponents of these arguments condemn any meaningful delegation of judicial function from a known, accountable, public official to an unknown, untested, government employee.

In response, commentators, including many judges and former law clerks, characterize the judge-clerk relationship as a principal-agent relationship. Judges, the argument goes, may safely delegate their work to law clerks because agents serve the principals' interests. The law clerk's work product is always an extension of the judge's initiative, so there is no improper delegation of the judicial function. Clerks may enhance, but cannot replace, robed decision-making.

Emphasizing the agency nature of clerks, commentators further note that law clerks serve at the pleasure of their judges. Moreover, conversations in chambers are strictly confidential. These conditions allow judges to think out loud about their cases and test their analysis before deliberating with colleagues. "A law clerk's opinions or suggestions often result in a more careful search for the means by which a just decision should be reached. This sounding board function often compels a judge to consider alternatives that might otherwise have been ignored or considered inadequately." J. Daniel Mahoney, *Law Clerks: For Better or for Worse?*, 54 BROOK. L. REV. 321, 342 (1988).

B.   What Does *Stare Decisis* Demand?

Another emerging controversy concerns whether law clerks' involvement in decision-making, particularly their drafting of orders and opinions, impairs *stare decisis*. Law clerks usually are recent law school graduates, and most of the time, they did not practice law before their clerkships. Does inexperience lead to faulty logic? Consider Judge Richard Posner's assessment:

> The law clerk will be reluctant to confess to the judge or even to himself that the outcome that the judge told him to write up will not write (and he may think it due to his own inexperience), while the judge, by not writing will be spared a painful confrontation with the inadequacy of the

reasoning that supports his decision. . . . The Judge does not know the opinion will not write, and the law clerk will not tell him.

Richard A. Posner, *Judges'Writing Styles (And Do They Matter?)*, 62 U. Chi. L. Rev. 1421, 1448 (1995). And consider this prediction: "[D]ecisions in cases where clerks write are probably worse than decisions in cases where judges write. By worse I mean that they are less likely to reach the heart of the matter at issue, and less likely to be useful to persons who might be in analogous positions in the future." David McGowan, *Judicial Writing and the Ethics of the Judicial Office*, 14 GEO. J. LEGAL ETHICS 509, 556 (2001).

Moreover, even if the law clerks' logic is correct, because they are new to judicial writings, they may look for model orders or opinions that are clean, but lacking style. Again, consider Judge Posner's remarks:

> Law clerks often prepare for their job by reading a bunch of their boss's old opinions (sometimes the judge tells them to do this), and then model their own style on that of the opinions they read. By this process, a chambers style, not perhaps very distinctive but distinctive enough to be recognizable, does indeed evolve. All that shows, however, is that style can be a corporate characteristic.

Richard A. Posner, *Judges'Writing Styles (And Do They Matter?)*, 62 U. Chi. L. Rev. 1421, 1425 (1995). If you believe that most law clerks, as compared to judges, are inferior writers, then you might worry that the opinions and orders issued today are likewise substandard.

But what if a law clerk's draft is merely the starting point to the final, written decision? Some judges freely revise and edit law clerks' drafts to reflect their independent thoughts and writing styles. Judge Abner Mikva explained:

> I always found that I didn't care who did the first draft. Some of the time I had the clerks do the first draft. Sometimes I'd write the first draft. But I wanted to make sure that I still felt enthusiastic about the opinion and fresh enough by the time it got to the final draft. That's where my work counted.

WILLIAM DOMNARSKI, FEDERAL JUDGES REVEALED 187 (2009).

Still, for those concerned about law clerks' effect on *stare decisis*, this is a small comfort because the law clerk's draft structures the analysis with subtle, but indelible effect. For these observers, writing is an active pursuit, but editing is eternally passive.

On the other hand, many judges are comfortable having their law clerks draft orders and opinions, because they prioritize the final judgment over the language of the opinion leading up to the judgment. For example, Judge Patricia Wald has written:

The judge's essence is in determining the result in an individual case, the grounds for reaching it, and drawing out from his superior wisdom and life experience its implications for future cases. If the clerk can take that essence and find precedent to support it, add some insights of her own, and put it all into a coherent literary for[m], easily understood by an ordinary reader, nothing is lost and much gained.

Patricia M. Wald, *Rhetoric and Results*, 62 U. CHI. L. REV. 1371, 1384 (1995).

Commentators on this side of the *stare decisis* controversy emphasize that judges file decisions under their signature, and they alone are accountable if the decisions are faulty. These commentators also perceive greater vigor in the judges' review and editing of law clerks' drafts, because, once again, the judges understand that the contents of the writings will reflect on their competency, not that of their law clerks. As one former clerk remarked, "we always knew whose name was on the presidential commission and who had been confirmed by the Senate." Stephen L. Wasby, *Clerking for an Appellate Judge: A Close Look*, 5 SETON HALL CIRCUIT REV. 19, 84 (2008).

Also, judges and law clerks who have enjoyed a strong working relationship praise collaborative writing. Building an opinion from two minds, they say, doubles the analytical input and produces a final product that is greater than the sum of what each person contributed. For example, remembering his judge's mentoring and collegiality, a former clerk explained:

Judge Jones would gather with his two law clerks around a table for an hour or more to parse every paragraph, word-for-word and line-by-line. With pride of authorship removed as an impediment, the three of us enjoyed wordsmithing because words are tools, and crafting remains creative regardless of who holds the toolbox.

Douglas E. Abrams, *Judges and Their Editors*, 3 Alb. Gov't L. Rev. 392, 397 (2010).

C.   How Many Hours Should There Be in a Judge's Work Day?

Finally, a third debate about how judges meet their responsibilities in chambers is whether the burgeoning dockets across state and federal courts justify an increased delegation of judicial writing to law clerks. The idea is that judges simply are overwhelmed with the volume of cases assigned to them, which leaves them with two choices: delegate writing to law clerks and finish cases in a timely fashion, or write the orders and opinions themselves and submit cases much later than attorneys and litigants expect. Although we may dislike both choices, at least law clerks' efforts sustain a timely and efficient administration of justice. Proponents of this position often point out that any meaningful change in how judges meet their responsibilities must include the hiring of more judges.

Not surprisingly, other court observers do not agree that the dockets have grown so much as to justify the delegation of essential judicial functions. They suggest that the perception of swelling dockets is largely exaggerated. Moreover, individual judges have spoken out to confirm that whatever the assignment of cases, they write their own opinions. And if they are able, should not their colleagues be likewise able?

III. CONCLUSION

These three controversies are timely and worthy of attention. The arguments suggest that the judiciary is under strain, its administration of justice is imperfect, and judges are not performing all of the responsibilities of judging. At the same time, it would be a mistake to allow these controversies to obscure the benefits that judicial clerkships provide for judges, law clerks, and the legal profession as a whole.

At the very least, judges bring practical knowledge and experience to the relationship, as well as absolute accountability for any errors in the final decision. Law clerks bring enthusiasm, fresh thinking, and updated research and writing skills. In a strong working relationship, they will capitalize on what each of them brings to the process, with wisdom and innovation complementing one another to produce quality decision-making. Also, the legal profession as a whole benefits when judges, as leaders of the profession, share their knowledge with clerks, the newest members of the profession. Few legal jobs traverse the generational divide as regularly, or as successfully.

NOTES AND QUESTIONS

1.   In *Tafari v. McCarthy*, No. 9:07-CV-654, 2010 WL 2044705, *54 (N.D. N.Y., May 24, 2010), the judge included the following footnote: "My thanks to Kara J. Krueger, a second year student at Syracuse University College of Law, for her assistance in researching and drafting the Report-Recommendation on Defendants' motion for summary judgment." Is it appropriate for judges to thank their law clerks in written orders or opinions? Is it deceitful for them *not* to include such acknowledgments? What are the risks of these acknowledgements? Judge Gerald Lebovits discourages them because they "make[] it appear that someone other than the judge decided the case." Gerald Lebovits, *Judges' Clerks Play Varied Roles in the Opinion Drafting Process*, N.Y. Sт. B.J., July/Aug. 2004, at 34, 38.

2.   At least one commentator has proposed including rules in codes of judicial ethics that require judges to write their own opinions. *See* David McGowan,

Judicial Writing and the Ethics of the Judicial Office, 14 GEO. J. LEGAL ETHICS 509, 555 (2001). Do you agree with that proposal? What should dictate the habits of opinion-writing — laws or customs? How might such provisions be enforced?

3.   Are the cases delegated to law clerks representative of the complete panoply of cases before the court? Penelope Pether has suggested otherwise. According to her research, at least in the federal courts of appeals, law clerks and staff attorneys are more likely to process appeals concerning civil rights, post-conviction relief, and employment discrimination. Moreover, they ordinarily handle appeals from *pro se* litigants. Penelope Pether, *Sorcerers, Not Apprentices: How Judicial Clerks and Staff Attorneys Impoverish U.S. Law*, 39 ARIZ. ST. L.J. 1, 27-28 (2007). Are you troubled by this differentiation of cases?

4.   Most judicial clerkships are one-year long. Some judges, particularly on the federal courts, hire clerks for two years and stagger their hiring so that each year there is one returning clerk and one new clerk. In contrast, a sizeable minority of judges now hire permanent law clerks, who remain in chambers for years, if not decades. Do you think the division of labor differs in chambers that employ permanent clerks, as opposed to temporary clerks? Are permanent clerks a good idea?

IV.   SUGGESTED FURTHER READING

Douglas E. Abrams, *Judges and Their Editors*, 3 ALB. GOV'T L. REV. 392 (2010).

WILLIAM DOMNARSKI, FEDERAL JUDGES REVEALED (2009).

Gerald Lebovits et al., *Ethical judicial Opinion Writing*, 21 GEO J. LEGAL ETHICS 237 (2008).

Gerald Lebovits, *Judges' Clerks Play Varied Roles in the Opinion Drafting Process*, N.Y. ST. B.J., July/Aug. 2004, at 34, 38.

Stefanie A. Lindquist, *Bureaucratization and Balkanization: The Origins and Effects of Decision-making Norms in the Federal Appellate Courts*, 41 U. RICH L. REV. 659 (2007).

J. Daniel Mahoney, *Law Clerks: For Better or for Worse?*, 54 BROOK. L. REV. 321 (1988).

David McGowan, *Judicial Writing and the Ethics of the Judicial Office*, 14 GEO. J. LEGAL ETHICS 509 (2001).

Penelope Pether, *Sorcerers, Not Apprentices: How Judicial Clerks and Staff Attorneys Impoverish U.S. Law*, 39 ARIZ. ST. L.J. 1 (2007).

Richard A. Posner, *Judges' Writing Styles (And Do They Matter?)*, 62 U. CHI. L. REV. 1421 (1995).

Rick A. Swanson & Stephen L. Wasby, *Good Stewards: Law Clerks Influence in State High Courts*, 29 JUST. SYS. J. 24 (2008).

Patricia M. Wald, *Rhetoric and Results*, 62 U. CHI. L. REV. 1371 (1995).

Stephen L. Wasby, *Clerking for an Appellate Judge: A Close Look*, 5 SETON HALL CIRCUIT REV. 19 (2008).

Chapter 2

INSIDE CHAMBERS: WHAT JUDICIAL CLERKS DO

I. INTRODUCTION

Most likely, day one of your clerkship is not day one of your judge's judgeship. It certainly is not day one of the court for which you are clerking. Instead, years of judging will have produced schedules and routines for the smooth administration of justice. Your first responsibility is to learn these schedules and routines, both within your judge's chambers and, more generally, in the court for which you are clerking.

This chapter summarizes the primary responsibilities of judicial law clerks, looking first at appellate court chambers and then at trial court chambers. By the end of the chapter, you should understand what a clerkship entails and the purpose that law clerks serve in our judicial system. You may also refine your opinions about the controversies introduced in Chapter One. Admittedly, this chapter can provide only a rough sketch of how clerkships proceed because individual judges vary in what they expect from their law clerks and how they manage their chambers. Also, important institutional differences exist between federal and state courts, appellate and trial courts, and intermediate appellate courts and courts of last resort. Nonetheless, this introduction at least will prepare you to appreciate whatever distinctions you discover in particular judicial chambers.

II. APPELLATE COURT CHAMBERS

A. Case Assignment

Appellate courts generally operate on a monthly calendar. The courts set certain days of each month for oral argument and conferencing between the judges, which in turn set the pace for the work that is done in chambers. The process begins with apportionment of the docket among the judges on the bench. On courts of last resort, all of the judges hear all of the oral arguments. For intermediate appellate courts, however, the judges ordinarily sit in panels of three, hearing only a portion of the court's monthly oral arguments.

Appeals are divided evenly among the judges on the court. Imagine, for example, that an appellate court of last resort comprising seven judges hears seventeen cases each month. Each judge will author two or three opinions from that month of argument. For an intermediate appellate court of thirteen judges that processes one hundred appeals every month, each judge will author nine or ten opinions per month.

You may be surprised to learn that some appellate courts apportion cases to particular judges in advance of oral argument. The judges thus participate in oral argument knowing the cases for which they will author opinions. Pre-assignment of cases is more common on intermediate appellate courts, as compared to courts of last resort, though you will find the practice at both tiers. Also, keep in mind that litigants and the general public are not privy to the pre-assignment lists. Why do you think these lists are not disclosed?

When the cases are not assigned in advance of oral argument, judges assign them during the conference following oral argument. Many courts follow the model of the U.S. Supreme Court, authorizing the chief judge, if he or she is in the majority, to assign cases to particular authors. If the chief judge is not in the majority, the most senior judge in the majority will designate the author.

Once judges learn their assignments for a given month, they return to chambers and divide the workload among themselves and the law clerk(s). Two or more law clerks may divide the cases based upon their interests and skills, as well as the amount of work anticipated for each case. Between the judges and law clerks, the division of labor is more various, as the following section explains.

B.   From Briefs to Opinions

When cases are assigned in advance, most judges will expect their law clerks to perform some degree of work on the cases before oral argument. First, a law clerk should understand fully the court's authority to adjudicate disputes. For each assigned case, the law clerk must ensure that personal and subject matter jurisdiction exist, that the appeal is timely, and that the judge and law clerk have no conflict of interest with the case. If these prerequisites are met, considerations move to the substance of the assigned cases. Chapter Three's discussion of scope of review and Chapter Four's discussion of *stare decisis* explain the analytical work that goes into resolving appeals.

Beyond reading the briefs, judges may ask their law clerks to conduct preliminary research or to prepare bench memoranda. The preliminary research includes reading the important cases that the parties have highlighted in their briefs and independently searching for authority that the parties did not, but should have, included. A bench memorandum summarizes the contents of the briefs, including the question(s) presented, the most important facts of the dispute, the standard of review on appeal, and the authority upon which the parties rely. Some judges may also want to learn their law clerks' estimation of the merits of the appeal, as well as their suggestions for questions that should be asked at oral argument.

Many judges forgo the formality of a written bench memorandum in favor of a live-action discussion about the upcoming cases. These discussions usually prove illuminating, as law clerks discern how their reading of the cases paralleled or diverged from their judges' reading of the same material. Learning how a judge approaches a legal question is a priceless experience for any lawyer, but it is especially meaningful for a new lawyer.

If cases are not assigned in advance of oral argument, the law clerks generally read the briefs for the scheduled arguments and conduct whatever legal research the judge requests. Then, after oral argument, the process begins of ensuring the court's authority to judge, analyzing the appellate arguments, writing bench memoranda, and meeting with the judge to discuss the assigned cases.

The next step in the process is drafting the opinion, for which practices vary from court to court and chamber to chamber. Many, and probably most, appellate judges ask their law clerks to write first drafts for at least some, and possibly all, of the judicial opinions that the judges author. Some judges, particularly on intermediate appellate courts where the monthly dockets are large, will reserve one case each month to draft on their own, assigning the remaining cases to the law clerks. Nonetheless, the common element in all appellate chambers is the steady tide of drafting and editing, writing and re-writing. Chapter Five offers guidelines for drafting appellate opinions.

Eventually, the judge will decide that the opinion is just about ready for circulation to the other judges on the panel. The judge may arrange for a "line-by-line," whereby the judge, law clerks, administrative assistant, and interns sit together to review the opinion for form and substance. It helps if someone reads the opinion aloud, as the others follow attentively. The purpose of this group study is to reveal any weakness in the opinion, whether of accuracy or clarity. If your judge is a mentor, line-by-lines will leave a lasting impression with you. For example, Douglas Abrams, describing the line-by-line process in his clerkship, explained:

> Both clerks knew that Judge Jones had the final say, but we also knew that he genuinely valued our input because he gracefully accepted both praise and critique. One clerk's articulated concern was sufficient to give him pause about something he had written, but he also followed an informal "Rule of Two": where both clerks expressed the same concern, he paid particularly close attention to whether other readers similarly situated might later feel the same way. Even when Judge Jones rejected an editorial suggestion and assumed the role of teacher to explain why, we had no reason for future reluctance because he extended every

courtesy worthy of our status as fellow professionals, even if professionals considerably less experienced than he.

Douglas E. Abrams, *Judges and Their Editors*, 3 ALB. GOV'T L. REV. 392, 398 (2010).

Following the line-by-line, the opinion is "clerked." Clerking is a fine-tooth combing through the opinion to ferret out any errors in fact, law, grammar, and citation. Chapter Seven details the clerking process.

Now the opinion is ready for circulation to the other judges on the panel, who may suggest further corrections. Thus, by the time the opinion is presented for a vote at the next monthly conference of the judges, it has been read and revised many times. Once the court votes to accept the opinion, it is filed with the clerk of the court and issued to the litigants, and if the opinion holds precedential value, it is submitted for publication.

C.   Types of Opinions

The two broad categories of opinions are majority and minority opinions. A majority opinion may be signed, meaning that one judge is identified as its author, or the opinion may be unsigned, meaning that all of the judges have adopted the opinion as their own, although a single person in fact wrote the opinion. A *per curiam* opinion is an unsigned opinion that incorporates the reasoning of all the presiding judges. It carries strong precedential value because "it is a joint disposition of the case without any reservations or exceptions." JOYCE J. GEORGE, JUDICIAL OPINION WRITING HANDBOOK 324 (5th ed. 2007). What kinds of cases do you imagine merit *per curiam* disposition?

A memorandum opinion is also unsigned, but it differs from a *per curiam* opinion in depth. Whereas a *per curiam* opinion, just like a signed opinion, involves a full explanation of how the governing law applies to the facts of the case, a memorandum opinion offers only a cursory explanation of the same. "It is addressed to the parties, it is brief, and it does not require information for reader orientation . . . . Usually, it is written when the existing law is clear as to its effect upon the particular case." *Id.* at 325. Memorandum opinions ordinarily are not published.

The second category of opinions, minority opinions, includes dissents and concurrences. The distinguishing factor between dissents and concurrences is whether the writing judge agrees with the final outcome of the majority opinion. A judge who disagrees with the majority's reasoning and judgment dissents from the opinion. A judge, however, who disagrees with some portion of the majority's reasoning, but who ultimately agrees with the judgment, concurs in the result. Chapter six discusses minority opinions, and the following chart illustrates the relationship between the different types of opinions.

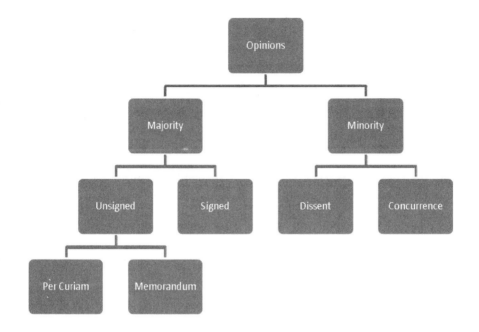

D.   Precedential Effect

Appellate courts may further distinguish opinions between those that have precedential value and those that do not. All of the opinions that a court of last resort files has precedential value. An intermediate appellate court, however, may designate an opinion as not having precedential value if there is controlling authority directly on point that dictates the outcome of the appeal and the opinion does not advance *stare decisis* in a meaningful way.

Non-precedential opinions are filed with the clerk of the court and carry the same force of law for the litigants as precedential opinions. They will not, however, influence the advocacy of future litigants, or inform the reasoning of future judges the way that precedential opinions do. First, they may not be easy to find. Second, even if some non-precedential opinions are published, local court rules may prohibit litigants from citing to them in their briefs or at oral argument. The following chart illustrates the relationship between the precedential effect and publication of opinions.

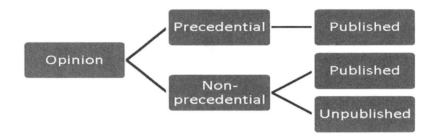

Noteworthy, under Federal Rule of Appellate Practice 32.1(a), courts of appeals cannot "prohibit or restrict the citation of federal judicial opinions, orders, judgments, or other written dispositions that have been: (i) designated as 'unpublished,' 'not for publication,' 'non-precedential,' 'not precedent,' or the like; and (ii) issued on or after January 1, 2007." Although the rule allows for citation of non-precedential opinions, it does not prescribe the value that federal courts must give to these decisions. Judges have debated the issue, and not just in secondary sources. Compare the following two excerpts from published opinions. What is your position?

ANASTASOFF v. UNITED STATES
223 F.3d 898, *vacated on other grounds*, 235 F.3d 1054 (8th Cir. 2000)

Richard S. Arnold, Circuit Judge

* * *

Although it is our only case directly in point, Ms. Anastasoff contends that we are not bound by *Christie* because it is an unpublished decision and thus not a precedent under 8th Circuit Rule 28A(i). We disagree. We hold that the portion of Rule 28A(i) that declares that unpublished opinions are not precedent is unconstitutional under Article III, because it purports to confer on the federal courts a power that goes beyond the "judicial."

* * *

Inherent in every judicial decision is a declaration and interpretation of a general principle or rule of law. *Marbury v. Madison*, 5 U.S. 137 (1803). This declaration of law is authoritative to the extent necessary for the decision, and must be applied in subsequent cases to similarly situated parties. These principles, which form the doctrine of precedent, were well established and well regarded at the time this nation was founded. The Framers of the Constitution considered these principles to derive from the nature of judicial power, and intended that they would limit the judicial power delegated to the courts by Article III of the Constitution. Accordingly, we conclude that 8th Circuit Rule 28A(i), insofar as it would allow us to avoid the precedential effect of our prior decisions, purports to expand the judicial power beyond the bounds of Article III, and is therefore unconstitutional. That rule does not, therefore, free us from our duty to follow this Court's decision in *Christie*.

* * *

Before concluding, we wish to indicate what this case is not about. It is not about whether opinions should be published, whether that means printed in a book or available in some other accessible form to the public in general. Courts may decide, for one reason or another, that some of their cases are not important enough to take up pages in a printed report. Such decisions may be eminently practical and defensible, but in our view they have nothing to do with the authoritative effect of any court decision. The question presented here is not whether opinions ought to be published, but whether they ought to have precedential effect, whether published or not. We point out, in addition, that "unpublished" in this context has never meant "secret." So far as we are aware, every opinion and every order of any court in this country, at least of any appellate court, is available to the public. You may have to walk into a clerk's office and pay a per-page fee, but you can get the opinion if you want it. Indeed, most appellate courts now make their opinions, whether labeled "published" or not, available to anyone on line. This is true of our Court.

Another point about the practicalities of the matter needs to be made. It is often said among judges that the volume of appeals is so high that it is simply unrealistic to ascribe precedential value to every decision. We do not have time to do a decent enough job, the argument runs, when put in plain language, to justify treating every opinion as a precedent. If this is true, the judicial system is indeed in serious trouble, but the remedy is not to create an underground body of law good for one place and time only. The remedy, instead, is to create enough judgeships to handle the volume, or, if that is not practical, for each judge to take enough time to do a competent job with each case. If this means that backlogs will grow, the price must still be paid. At bottom, rules like our Rule 28A(i) assert that courts have the following power: to choose for themselves, from among all the cases they decide, those that they will follow in the future, and those that they need not. Indeed, some forms of the non-publication rule even forbid citation. Those courts are saying to the bar: "We may have decided this question the opposite way yesterday, but this does not bind us today, and, what's more, you cannot even tell us what we did yesterday." As we have tried to explain in this opinion, such a statement exceeds the judicial power, which is based on reason, not *fiat*.

* * *

HART v. MASSANARI
266 F.3d 1155 (9th Cir. 2001)

KOZINSKI, CIRCUIT JUDGE

* * *

The question raised by *Anastasoff* is whether one particular aspect of the binding authority principle — the decision of which rulings of an appellate court are binding — is a matter of judicial policy or constitutional imperative. We believe *Anastasoff* erred in holding that, as a constitutional matter, courts of appeals may not decide which of their opinions will be deemed binding on themselves and the courts below them. For the reasons explained, the principle of strict binding authority is itself not constitutional, but rather a matter of judicial policy. Were it otherwise, it would cast doubt on the federal court practice of limiting the binding effect of appellate decisions to the courts of a particular circuit. Circuit boundaries — and the very system of circuit courts — are a matter of judicial administration, not constitutional law. If, as *Anastasoff* suggests, the Constitution dictates that every "declaration of law . . . must be applied in subsequent cases to similarly situated parties," then the Second Circuit would have no authority to disagree with a ruling of the Eighth Circuit that is directly on point, and the first circuit to rule on a legal issue would then bind not only itself and the courts within its own circuit, but all inferior federal courts.

Another consequence of *Anastasoff*'s reasoning would be to cast doubt on the authority of courts of appeals to adopt a body of circuit law on a wholesale basis, as did the Eleventh Circuit in *Bonner*, and the Federal Circuit in *South Corp.* Circuits could, of course, adopt individual cases from other circuits as binding in a case raising a particular legal issue. But adopting a whole body of law, encompassing countless rules on matters wholly unrelated to the issues raised in a particular case, is a very different matter. If binding authority were a constitutional imperative, it could only be created through individual case adjudication, not by a decision unconstrained by the facts before the court or its prior caselaw.

Nor is it clear, under the reasoning of *Anastasoff*, how courts could limit the binding effect of their rulings to appellate decisions. Under *Anastasoff*'s reasoning, district court opinions should bind district courts, at least in the same district, or even nationwide. After all, the Constitution vests the same "judicial Power" in all federal courts, so *Anastasoff* 's conclusion that judicial decisions must have precedential effect would apply equally to the thousands of unpublished decisions of the district courts.

No doubt the most serious implication of *Anastasoff* 's constitutional rule is that it would preclude appellate courts from developing a coherent and internally consistent body of caselaw to serve as binding authority for themselves and the courts below them. Writing an opinion is not simply a matter of laying out the facts and announcing a rule of decision. Precedential opinions are meant to govern not merely the cases for which they are written, but future cases as well.

In writing an opinion, the court must be careful to recite all facts that are relevant to its ruling, while omitting facts that it considers irrelevant. Omitting relevant facts will make the ruling unintelligible to those not already familiar with the case; including inconsequential facts can provide a spurious basis for distinguishing the case in the future. The rule of decision cannot simply be announced, it must be selected after due consideration of the relevant legal and policy considerations. Where more than one rule could be followed — which is often the case — the court must explain why it is selecting one and rejecting the others. Moreover, the rule must be phrased with precision and with due regard to how it will be applied in future cases. A judge drafting a precedential opinion must not only consider the facts of the immediate case, but must also envision the countless permutations of facts that might arise in the universe of future cases. Modern opinions generally call for the most precise drafting and re-drafting to ensure that the rule announced sweeps neither too broadly nor too narrowly, and that it does not collide with other binding precedent that bears on the issue. Writing a precedential opinion, thus, involves much more than deciding who wins and who loses in a particular case. It is a solemn judicial act that sets the course of the law for hundreds or thousands of litigants and potential litigants. When properly done, it is an exacting and extremely time-consuming task.

It goes without saying that few, if any, appellate courts have the resources to write precedential opinions in every case that comes before them. The Supreme Court certainly does not. Rather, it uses its discretionary review authority to limit its merits docket to a handful of opinions per justice, from the approximately 9000 cases that seek review every Term. While federal courts of appeals generally lack discretionary review authority, they use their authority to decide cases by unpublished — and nonprecedential — dispositions to achieve the same end: They select a manageable number of cases in which to publish precedential opinions, and leave the rest to be decided by unpublished dispositions or judgment orders. In our circuit, published dispositions make up approximately 16 percent of decided cases; in other circuits, the percentage ranges from 10 to 44, the national average being 20 percent.

That a case is decided without a precedential opinion does not mean it is not fully considered, or that the disposition does not reflect a reasoned analysis of the issues presented. What it does mean is that the disposition is not written in a way that will be fully intelligible to those unfamiliar with the case, and the rule of law is not announced in a way that makes it suitable for governing future cases. As the Federal Judicial Center recognized, "the judicial time and effort essential for the development of an opinion to be published for posterity and widely distributed is necessarily greater than that sufficient to enable the judge to provide a statement so that the parties can understand the reasons for the decision." An unpublished disposition is, more or less, a letter from the court to parties familiar with the facts, announcing the result and the essential rationale of the court's decision. Deciding a large portion of our cases in this fashion frees us to spend the requisite time drafting precedential opinions in the remaining cases.

Should courts allow parties to cite to these dispositions, however, much of the time gained would likely vanish. Without comprehensive factual accounts and precisely crafted holdings to guide them, zealous counsel would be tempted to seize upon superficial similarities between their clients' cases and unpublished dispositions. Faced with the prospect of parties citing these dispositions as precedent, conscientious judges would have to pay much closer attention to the way they word their unpublished rulings. Language adequate to inform the parties how their case has been decided might well be inadequate if applied to future cases arising from different facts. And, although three judges might agree on the outcome of the case before them, they might not agree on the precise reasoning or the rule to be applied to future cases. Unpublished concurrences and dissents would become much more common, as individual judges would feel obligated to clarify their differences with the majority, even when those differences had no bearing on the case before them. In short, judges would have to start treating unpublished dispositions — those they write, those written by other judges on their panels, and those written by judges on other panels — as mini-opinions. This new responsibility would cut severely into the time judges need to fulfill their paramount duties: producing well-reasoned published opinions and keeping the law of the circuit consistent through the en banc process. The quality of published opinions would sink as judges were forced to devote less and less time to each opinion.

Increasing the number of opinions by a factor of five, as *Anastasoff* suggests, doesn't seem to us a sensible idea, even if we had the resources to do so. Adding endlessly to the body of precedent — especially binding precedent — can lead to confusion and unnecessary conflict. Judges have a responsibility to keep the body of law "cohesive and understandable, and not muddy[ ] the water with a needless torrent of published opinions." Cases decided by nonprecedential disposition generally involve facts that are materially indistinguishable from those of prior published opinions. Writing a second, third or tenth opinion in the same area of the law, based on materially indistinguishable facts will, at best, clutter up the law books and databases with redundant and thus unhelpful authority. Yet once they are designated as precedent, they will have to be read and analyzed by lawyers researching the issue, materially increasing the costs to the client for absolutely no legitimate reason. Worse still, publishing redundant opinions will multiply significantly the number of inadvertent and unnecessary conflicts, because different opinion writers may use slightly different language to express the same idea. As lawyers well know, even small differences in language can have significantly different implications when read in light of future fact patterns, so differences in phrasing that seem trivial when written can later take on a substantive significance.

The risk that this may happen vastly increases if judges are required to write many more precedential opinions than they do now, leaving much less time to devote to each. Because conflicts — even inadvertent ones — can only be resolved by the exceedingly time-consuming and inefficient process of en banc review, an increase in intracircuit conflicts would leave much less time for us to devote to normal panel opinions. Maintaining a coherent, consistent and intelligible body of caselaw is not served by writing more opinions; it is served by taking the time to make the precedential opinions we do write as lucid and consistent as humanly possible.

* * *

E.   Oral Argument

Appellate courts hear oral arguments for several days each month. Typically, the judges conference after oral arguments to discuss the cases, divine the judges' preliminary leanings, and to designate who will write the opinions, if that has not already been determined. Although appellate judges often remark that oral argument rarely changes the outcome of an appeal, they are just as likely to remark that oral argument may clarify legal argument or elucidate the overarching theory of a case. A good oral argument also may shape the organization of the court's written opinion. Moreover, especially for courts of last resort, oral argument may generate a *sua sponte* discussion of law that the briefs do not discuss. It is worthwhile, then, for law clerks to attend oral argument as often as possible. Beyond benefitting your work product in the clerkship, when you regularly observe oral arguments, you learn which styles are persuasive and which styles only frustrate the judges. These lessons are likely to carry through your professional life.

Note that not all appeals include oral argument. Many courts maintain a docket of appeals that are decided on the briefs only. Appellant may request a case be considered without oral argument, or the court may so designate, after reading the briefs. What considerations do you imagine are involved in requesting, or deciding, that an appeal be considered without oral argument?

F.   Petitions for Certiorai

Courts of last resort choose which cases they will hear on appeal. Hopeful litigants present these courts with petitions for certiorari, which the courts may grant or deny. Some judges may ask their law clerks to read, comment, or draft memoranda on the petitions for certiorari, while others will not involve their law clerks in the process at all.

G.   The Sum of Its Parts

Appellate clerkships revolve around the monthly calendar of oral argument. A clerk might begin the work day revising a draft opinion for a case assigned last month and end the day finishing a bench memorandum for a case on next month's docket. Moreover, an appellate clerkship is comprised of independent work, such as reading, writing, and editing, as well as group activities, such as line-by-line, oral argument, and conversations with the judge. Under the best circumstances, an appellate clerkship is a collegial enterprise, whereby all the employees in chambers work toward the shared goal of producing opinions that are accurate and clear.

NOTES AND QUESTIONS

1.   What personality traits do you think make for a successful appellate law clerk? If you were an appellate judge, what would you look for in hiring a clerk?

2.   Consider all the ways that appellate cases are distinguished from one another, including whether oral argument will be heard for a given appeal, whether an opinion is designated as precedential, and whether an opinion is published. Why have courts developed these distinctions? Do they enhance or hinder the administration of justice? In answering these questions, consider Judge Patricia Wald's characterization of the customary tone adopted in non-precedential opinions:

> Often the Scroogelike verbiage sounds a complaining tone: "You shouldn't be bothering us"; "how many times do we have to tell you?" The style is typically banal: boilerplate nostrums. The message comes through clearly to the losing party: "You never had a real chance, and we have gone to the least possible trouble to tell you why."

Patricia M. Wald, *The Rhetoric of Results and the Results of Rhetoric: Judicial Writings*, 62 U. CHI. L. REV. 1371, 1373 (1995).

III.   TRIAL COURT CHAMBERS

A.   Case Assignment

Statutes and rules set the jurisdiction of trial courts, and usually, jurisdiction is distinguished based upon the amount in controversy in civil disputes and the severity of the charge in criminal prosecutions. Moreover, within a trial court, cases may be tracked based on subject matter, for example, criminal prosecutions, family law or complex civil litigation. Ordinarily the administrative judge of the court is responsible for assigning cases.

B.   Pleadings and Motions

Trial court law clerks assist their judges in nearly every aspect of adjudication. To begin with, law clerks review pleadings as they are filed to ensure personal and subject matter jurisdiction. Also, they may ascertain whether any conflict of interest exists. Law clerks may also be asked to review the propriety of service of process in a civil case or the sufficiency of the indictment in a criminal matter.

Following the pleadings, as motions are filed, law clerks conduct legal research, draft memoranda, and discuss the claims with their judges. Chapters Eight and Nine explain the analytical exercises that trial court judges and clerks perform. Summary judgment motions comprise a bulk of the motions heard in trial courts. You may also recall from your studies of civil procedure that motions attacking jurisdiction, venue, named parties, and the sufficiency of the complaint ordinarily must be filed within a certain period of time after the complaint is filed. Other motions, such as for amending the pleadings, adding named parties, or excluding evidence may be filed later in the course of litigation. In a criminal prosecution, the sufficiency of the evidence may be challenged, as well.

To manage the motions that accumulate regularly, trial judges customarily dedicate certain days of each month for hearings on motions. This practice is known as "motions day." The law clerk may be tasked with scheduling the hearings for motions day, researching the particular motions in advance of the hearings, keeping notes during the hearings, and drafting orders to resolve the controversies presented. Chapter Ten offers guidelines for drafting orders and judgments.

C.   Discovery

In civil litigation, discovery comprises another large category of activity. Court rules, such as Federal Rule of Civil Procedure 26, set out the standards for discovery, as well as the requirements for any discovery conferences that judges must convene. Several methods of discovery exist today, and the scope of discovery in civil litigation is broad. Accordingly, discovery often leads to motions for disclosure or motions to keep matters undisclosed, as well as motions asking for additional time to respond to a request. Judges may ask their law clerks to process any or all of these motions. Moreover, law clerks may attend discovery conferences as a note taker or as an active mediator.

D.   Trials

You may not have predicted that law clerks do not routinely attend the complete trials over which their judges preside. Instead, they are often busy in chambers keeping abreast of pleadings, motions, and scheduling demands. Nonetheless, if questions arise during trial that require legal research, judges will turn to their law clerks. When written documents are needed, such as jury instructions or verdict forms, law clerks may pen the first drafts. Also, in civil bench trials, law clerks may help compose findings of facts and conclusions of law, which is a topic of Chapter Ten.

In criminal proceedings, if a guilty verdict is returned, law clerks may review the sentencing guidelines and any pre-sentencing reports that have been prepared. A judge may also ask a law clerk to draft a statement of reasons for the sentence the judge decides to impose.

E.   The Sum of Its Parts

The preceding sketch outlines the reading, research, and writing of trial court clerkships. What gives color and dimension to these jobs is the regular human contact that clerks have with the bench, the bar, courthouse personnel, litigants, and the general public. Communication is constant, testing a clerk's professionalism every minute of the work day. Although proceedings in the trial court ordinarily run smoothly, emotion can erupt because important concerns, such as liberty or the custody of children, are at stake. These eruptions test the mettle of even the steadiest judges and law clerks. The following opinion specifically concerns the parameters of a trial judge's power to issue an order of contempt, but more broadly, it illustrates the emotional intensity of trial court proceedings.

STATE v. NORTH
978 A.2d 435 (Vt. 2009)

SKOGLUND, J.

Defendant appeals from the district court's order of contempt. He claims the district court abused its discretion by holding him thrice in contempt and imposing three consecutive sentences of five to six months, one for each contemptuous statement. We affirm in part and reverse in part.

The relevant facts are undisputed. On June 5, 2007, the Chittenden District Court imposed an effective sentence of three to twenty years for obtaining property by false pretenses or tokens in violation of 13 V.S.A. § 2002 and passing bad checks in violation of 13 V.S.A. § 2022. As defendant was being led from the courtroom, the following exchange occurred:

DEFENDANT: Go fuck yourself, Your Honor.

COURT: Bring him back here please. Bring him back here. I'm holding the Defendant in contempt of Court. He'll serve an additional five to six months for contempt of Court for cursing at the judge.

DEFENDANT: Go fuck yourself —

COURT: Okay. That's another five to six months for contempt of Court consecutive. Do you want to keep going, Mr. North?

DEFENDANT: [unclear]

COURT: Another five to six months. Fifteen to eighteen months consecutive, in addition to the three to twenty years.

On June 7, 2007, pursuant to its summary contempt authority under Vermont Rule of Criminal Procedure 42(a), the district court issued a signed order of contempt reciting the preceding exchange, clarifying that in his third statement, defendant called a member of the court's family a vulgar, obscene name, and imposing 3 five-to-six-month sentences, one for each infraction, each consecutive to any other sentence imposed. This appeal followed.

* * *

Defendant's first claim is that the second and third allegedly contemptuous statements should have been referred to another judge for nonsummary proceedings because his personal attack distorted the court's judgment and caused it to lose "that calm detachment necessary for fair adjudication." We disagree.

Under the Vermont Rules of Criminal Procedure, criminal contempt is punishable in two ways. "A criminal contempt may be punished summarily if the judge certifies that he saw or heard the conduct constituting the contempt and that it was committed in the actual presence of the court." This kind of contempt is commonly referred to as direct contempt. Alternatively, contempt not punishable under summary proceedings may be punished upon notice and hearing under Rule 42(b). In this more formal procedure, "[i]f the contempt charged involves disrespect to or criticism of a judge, that judge is disqualified from presiding at the trial or hearing except with the defendant's consent."

Although nonsummary proceedings for contempt involving disrespect to or criticism of a judge may require referral to another judge, we have rejected the notion that all direct contempts involving personal insults must be referred to another judge for proceedings pursuant to Rule 42(b). In *Allen*, we reasoned that "[a] rule requiring that all flagrant personal insults be responded to only after delay would undermine the court's dignity and its authority." Furthermore, we explained that because a judge is not "merely an individual," but rather "represents the authority of the law," when "a single remark insults both the individual judge personally and the sovereign authority that the judge represents, the personal aspect does not require use of the delayed procedure of [Rule] 42(b)." We cautioned, however, that "because there is always the possibility that a personal insult will cause the trial judge to lose that calm detachment necessary for fair adjudication, this Court must be ever watchful for distortion of the judge's sound discretion."

A trial court abuses its discretion by punishing a personally insulting direct contempt summarily, rather than referring it to another judge for nonsummary proceedings, when the record shows that the court harbored personal feelings against the contemnor or where the contempt is so severely insulting that we must assume such feelings exist. See *United States v. Meyer* ("[O]nce a judge has been personally attacked in such a manner that a judge of ordinary sensibilities might naturally be expected to harbor marked personal feelings against the attacker, the law must assume that such feelings exist.") Because the severity of the contempt at issue in this case did not exceed that which we expect trial courts to meet with professionalism and self-restraint, and because we see no evidence that the court lost its composure, we hold that the court acted within its discretion in punishing defendant's contempts summarily.

Defendant's second claim is that the court's question, "Do you want to keep going, Mr. North?" invited his final statement and thus rendered it noncontemptuous. Although we would not condone a court taunting a contemnor by imposing punishment and inviting further discourse in the same breath, in this case the court's question served more as a warning than an invitation.

"The historic power of summary contempt grew out of the need for judicial enforcement of order and decorum in the courtroom and to compel obedience to court orders." By longstanding tradition, courts are empowered "to impose silence, respect, and decorum[ ] in their presence," and we have long recognized that the "power to punish for contempt is indispensable to the proper discharge of [courts'] duties." Courts have broad discretion in summary contempt, but discretion has its limits. "Absolute discretion, like corruption, marks the beginning of the end of liberty."

Several jurisdictions have taken the position that otherwise contemptuous statements are not punishable when invited by the court. The Louisiana Supreme Court has held that a statement in " 'response to a question by the judge which seemed to invite and encourage further verbal sparring' is not contemptuous." The Maryland Court of Special Appeals held that a judge may not find a defendant guilty of contempt after engaging in a dialogue that may provoke the defendant to commit the contempt. These cases, however, presented more egregious provocation, invitation, and encouragement than the current case.

In *Bullock*, the court responded to the defendant's third "fuck you" with: "No, you, Mr. Bullock. Three counts in direct contempt of court consecutive, 18 months. Do you want to go for two years?" By beginning the retort with "No, you, Mr. Bullock," the court provoked the defendant by insulting him directly. Here, the court made no such insult. In *Johnson*, the court responded to the defendant's multiple vulgar, contemptuous statements by asking "What's wrong with you?" and proceeding to hold him in contempt ten consecutive times. That open-ended question explicitly invited and encouraged further dialogue. Here, in contrast, the court's yes-or-no question was a warning.

Because the court did not provoke, invite, or encourage the defendant's contemptuous statements, it acted within its discretion in punishing them.

* * *

NOTES AND QUESTIONS

1.   *State v. North* suggests that in trial court proceedings, we have simultaneous interests in demonstrating respect for the court's authority while also protecting an individual's freedom from the power of the state. Did the appellate court find the correct balance between these interests in *North*? Why did it matter to the appellate court whether the judge had provoked the defendant?

2.   The court in *State v. North* noted the "calm detachment," "professionalism," and "self restraint" expected of trial judges. What other personality traits make for an effective trial judge? And considering the responsibilities of a trial court law clerk, what personality traits are desirable for that position, as well?

3.   May a law clerk disqualify a judge from presiding over a case? The short answer is yes. A law clerk's conflict of interest with a particular case may transfer to his or her judge, because "[c]lerks are privy to the judge's thoughts in a way that neither parties to the lawsuit nor his most intimate family members may be." *Hall v. Small Bus. Admin.*, 695 F.2d 175, 179 (5th Cir. 1983). This is why it is important for law clerks to reveal any potential conflict of interests to their judges. *See* John Paul Jones, *Some Ethical Considerations for Judicial Clerks*, 4 Geo. J. Legal Ethics 771 (1991).

IV.   SUGGESTED FURTHER READING

Douglas E. Abrams, *Judges and Their Editors*, 3 Alb. Gov't L. Rev. 392 (2010).

William Domnarski, Federal Judges Revealed (2009).

Sidney S. Eagles, Jr., *Address from Chief Judge Eagles*, 35 IND. L. REV. 457 (2002).

Gerald Lebovits, *Judges' Clerks Play Varied Roles in the Opinion Drafting Process*, N.Y. ST. B.J., July/Aug. 2004, at 34.

Stefanie A. Lindquist, *Bureaucratization and Balkanization: The Origins and Effects of Decision-making Norms in the Federal Appellate Courts*, 41 U. RICH L. REV. 659 (2007).

J. Daniel Mahoney, *Foreword Law Clerks: For Better or Worse?*, 54 BROOK. L. REV. 321 (1988).

Todd C. Peppers et al., *Inside Judicial Chambers: How Federal District Court Judges Select and Use Their Law Clerks*, 71 ALB. L. REV. 623 (2008).

Penelope Pether, *Constitutional Solipsism: Toward a Thick Doctrine of Article III Duty; or Why the Federal Circuits' Nonprecedential Status Rules Are (Profoundly) Unconstitutional*, 17 WM. & MARY BILL RTS. J. 955 (2009).

Alexander M. Sanders, Jr., *Everything You Always Wanted to Know About Judges but Were Afraid to Ask*, 49 S.C. L. Rev. 343 (1998).

David R. Stras, *The Supreme Court's Gatekeepers: The Role of Law Clerks in the Certiorari Process*, 85 TEX. L. REV. 947 (2007).

Stephen L. Wasby, *Clerking for an Appellate Judge: A Close Look*, 5 SETON HALL CIRCUIT REV. 19 (2008).

Charles R. Wilson, *How Opinions Are Developed in the United States Court of Appeals for the Eleventh Circuit*, 32 STETSON L. REV. 247 (2003).

PART II

FOUNDATIONAL PRINCIPLES FOR APPELLATE COURT LAW CLERKS

Chapter 3

SCOPE OF REVIEW: THE SELF-CONSCIOUS APPELLATE COURT

I. INTRODUCTION

Before an appellate court considers the merits of a dispute, it first determines the parameters of its authority to intervene with the trial court's decision. In other words, it must determine the scope of its review. Consider the following excerpt from an appellate opinion that reviewed a trial court's response to an alleged violation of a discovery rule:

> As the Court of Appeals has stated, "[d]iscovery questions generally involve a very broad discretion that is to be exercised by the trial courts. Their determinations will be disturbed on appellate review only if there is an abuse of discretion." Further, although factual findings of the trial court are not upset unless clearly erroneous, the question whether a discovery violation occurred under the Maryland Rules is reviewed *de novo*. "Where a discovery rule has been violated, the remedy is, 'in the first instance, within the sound discretion of the trial judge. The exercise of that discretion includes evaluating whether a discovery violation has caused prejudice.' "

In re Caitlin N., 994 A.2d 454, 466(Md. Ct. Spec. App. 2010).

Even if you are unfamiliar with the phrases above, such as "broad discretion" and "clearly erroneous," you probably understand that these phrases limit the appellate court's review of what happened in the trial court in specific, demonstrative ways. Moreover, you likely appreciate from this paragraph that the appellate court will consider the factual findings of the trial court differently than it will consider the trial court's conclusion about whether the facts constituted a discovery violation. Indeed, in appellate practice, not all questions are equal, and this renders the appellate courts fiercely self-conscious. Over and over again they ask, "Should we offer our opinion?" and "Are there limits to what we can consider on appeal?"

When you have finished reading this chapter, you should be able to identify the most common expressions of the self-conscious appellate court, that is, the most frequent ways that appellate courts define the scope of their review. The chapter examines the *de novo*, abuse of discretion, and clearly erroneous standards of review, as well as the preservation doctrine.

Statutes, rules, and common law govern the scope of review. Though application of these laws often is simple and well-rehearsed, a sizable minority of cases present complicated questions. In every instance, therefore, think carefully about the scope of the court's review. And have faith that your understanding of the scope of review will improve with each case. As you master these principles, you likely will gain a deeper appreciation for the balanced interchange between trial and appellate courts in our system of judging. Indeed, each judicial tier has specialized knowledge and expertise. In respecting the standards of review, we hope to capitalize on this knowledge and expertise.

II. STANDARDS OF REVIEW

The standard of review dictates the degree of deference that the appellate court will afford the decision of the trial court. When the appellate court provides no deference to the previous decision-maker, its review is unrestrained. When, however, the appellate court provides deference to the previous decision-maker, it strives to limit its involvement in the case with practiced discipline. If you were bringing an appeal, would you prefer that the court exercise high or low deference to the trial court's decision?

Educate yourself on the specific rules governing the scope of review in your jurisdiction. You might spend some quality time with a treatise on point, or conduct basic legal research. Also, as you read opinions, attend to the ways that the author has defined the scope of review. Was it stated up front, or was it implied? Was there any disagreement about the scope of review, or just as to the merits of the case?

A. *De Novo* Review

The *de novo* standard of review allows the appellate court to review the trial court's decision anew, without any deference. It is often described as "plenary review." This standard is reserved for questions of law.

WHITSON v. STONE COUNTY JAIL
602 F.3d 920 (8th Cir. 2010)

BEAM, CIRCUIT JUDGE.

[Penny Whitson was a prisoner in the Stone County Jail. She alleged that a male prisoner raped her while they were being transported to another facility. *Pro se*, Whitson filed a claim under 42 U.S.C. § 1983 against the two transporting prison officials, alleging, in part, that they violated the Eight

Amendment when they failed to protect her from the rape. The trial court granted the defendants' motion for summary judgment because "the attack was a complete surprise to even Whitson herself, [so] the defendants necessarily lacked the required knowledge of a substantial risk of harm sufficient to support a claim under § 1983." *Whitson v. Stone County Jail*, 602 F.3d 920, 922 (8th Cir. 2010). Whitson appealed with representation by counsel.]

* * *

II. DISCUSSION

We review a grant of summary judgment *de novo*. "Summary judgment is proper when the evidence viewed in the light most favorable to the nonmoving party presents no genuine issue of material fact and the moving party is entitled to judgment as a matter of law."

A. Constitutional Violation and Qualified Immunity

Because being subjected to violent assault is not "part of the penalty that criminal offenders [must] pay for their offenses," "[t]he Eighth Amendment imposes a duty on the part of prison officials to protect prisoners from violence at the hands of other prisoners." . . . "In order to establish an Eighth Amendment failure-to-protect claim, a plaintiff must show that the prison official was deliberately indifferent to a 'substantial risk of serious harm.' " In doing so, a prisoner must satisfy two requirements, one objective and one subjective. The first requirement tests whether, viewed objectively, the deprivation of rights was sufficiently serious; i.e., whether the inmate "is incarcerated under conditions posing a substantial risk of serious harm." The second requirement is subjective and requires that the inmate prove that the prison official had a "sufficiently culpable state of mind." In prison conditions claims, which include the failure-to-protect allegations before us, the subjective inquiry regarding an official's state of mind is one of " 'deliberate indifference' to inmate health or safety." An official is deliberately indifferent if he or she actually knows of a substantial risk and fails to respond reasonably.

The biggest quandary in this case is that both the defendants and the district court fixated on Whitson's state of mind as to whether Leach would assault her that morning — a fact that is mostly irrelevant to our analysis. For example, in its determination as to whether an Eighth Amendment violation occurred at all, the district court concluded that defendants' actions did not constitute a failure to protect because the defendants lacked the required knowledge of a substantial risk of serious harm. In doing so, the court adopted the defendants' argument that "[i]n order to prevail in this case, plaintiff must show that she placed defendants on notice of a specific threat to her, and that they failed to take appropriate measures to protect her from the risk of attack." The district court gave decisive weight to *Whitson*'s subjective knowledge as to whether this attack would occur, stating that because Whitson first reported the rape about an hour after it occurred, and testified that the incident was a complete surprise to her, "the defendants . . . lacked the required knowledge of a substantial risk." But, Whitson's failure to give advance notice of the unanticipated rape is inconclusive as to the defendants' subjective knowledge. A prison official may not "escape liability for deliberate indifference by showing that, while he was aware of an obvious, substantial risk to inmate safety, he did not know that the complainant was especially likely to be assaulted by the specific prisoner who eventually committed the assault."

* * *

Turning to a credible analysis, then, we first note that the objective inquiry as to whether the risk of assault was sufficiently serious for Eighth Amendment purposes is not before us. The district court made no finding whatever on this first element of the Eighth Amendment analysis. Given the facts advanced, however — inaccessibility of the rear cage, lack of visual contact with the victim and the aggressor by the remotely located supervisor, Leach's inadequate restraints, an overarching noise level and an almost total lack of supervision or observation during transport — it is virtually certain that the objective requirement is met in this case. Even so, we recognize that we cannot make this a fact-specific determination at this time, but the district court will be able to do so (and should do so) upon remand.

We now evaluate the subjective requirements of an Eighth Amendment violation. The district court, as earlier stated, gave conclusive weight to Whitson's failure to notify the defendants of a risk of harm. This failure to notify, however, has little to do with a correct conclusion. The pivotal issue in this regard deals with whether the defendants had a sufficiently culpable state of mind. Assuming the truth of her allegations, as we must, Whitson has sufficiently stated a "deliberate indifference" claim. Whitson "may establish [defendants'] awareness by reliance on any relevant evidence." She claims that this rape was foreseeable: two inmates of the opposite sex were isolated and placed next to each other in the back of a dark van; there was loud music; and the officers did not adequately observe, nor were they particularly concerned about, the nefarious goings — on in the second caged compartment, which was accessible only from the rear of the vehicle. Whitson alleges that by failing to provide adequate attention to security during transfers of this nature where male and female inmates are placed in a remote compartment where the safety, security and welfare of the female inmate were not and could not be adequately maintained, the defendants were deliberately indifferent to a risk of harm to her. This claim does not arise from Leach's attack per se, but arises from Whitson's "allegation that defendants were deliberately indifferent to a known substantial risk that such an attack would occur." Thus, a factfinder could (and Whitson says should) conclude that the situation in which Whitson was placed demonstrated deliberate indifference to a substantial risk to her safety.

* * *

The defendants place themselves firmly within the myopic view that what Whitson knew the morning of the attack is crucial and they refuse to budge from this limited scope. This is fatal to their case, at least at this stage of the proceedings. What Whitson knew about Leach, while not wholly irrelevant, is nearly so, as it is only one piece of circumstantial evidence relevant in the quest to determine whether the defendants had subjective knowledge of the overall risk, which is an element of Whitson's Eighth Amendment claim. If Whitson *had* complained about Leach prior to the transport, that evidence would obviously be relevant to the inquiry regarding the officers' state of mind. That she had *not*, however, is not conclusive of the issue. Merely relying on the fact that these officials could not have guessed beforehand that Leach might attack Whitson does not warrant a summary judgment ruling in their favor.

* * *

In the end, the basis for the district court's ruling has been rejected by the Supreme Court and this record does not clearly establish the defendants' entitlement to judgment as a matter of law on the issue of their subjective knowledge. We do not resolve the ultimate issue of whether Whitson can prevail on her § 1983 claims. We are remanding so that the district court can apply the proper test. We simply hold that, assuming the truth of plaintiff's substantiated assertions, she has sufficiently *alleged* a deliberate indifference claim, and the defendants' lack of knowledge that the particular attack would occur does not extinguish the legal existence of her claim. Because the disposition of this case was fundamentally flawed, remand is the proper course. Hand in hand with this conclusion, we likewise reverse the district court's grant of qualified immunity as it was premised on the court's ruling that there was no constitutional violation.

* * *

NOTES AND QUESTIONS

1. *De novo* review is reserved for questions of law. Precisely what question of law did the district court rule on?

2. Why is it appropriate for the Eighth Circuit Court of Appeals to review the district court's ruling without deference? Which characteristics of appellate courts make them well-suited for answering questions of law?

B.   Abuse of Discretion

The abuse of discretion standard is deferential to the trial court. It ordinarily applies to a trial judge's decision about the course of proceedings, for example, the timetable for discovery, whether to grant a continuance, or how to instruct the jury. It also applies to a trial judge's admission or exclusion of evidence. "Judicial discretion at the trial court level exists both because the judge is the only decision-maker present to evaluate the situation, and because there can be no precise rule for every situation." John J. Brunetti, *Searching for Methods of Trial Court Fact-Finding and Decision-Making*, 49 HASTINGS L.J. 1491, 1497 (1998).

This standard of review purports to uphold the trial court's decision as long as the trial court did not abuse its discretion. But what are the parameters of the trial court's discretion? And what constitutes an abuse? The answers are complex and have evolved over time. As a matter of statistics, however, appellate courts are more likely than not to conclude that the trial court acted within its discretion. Why do you think that is so?

Below are two examples of appellate courts applying the abuse of discretion standard to jury selection. Notice how the courts articulate the standard. Why do the courts reach contrary results?

HERRINGTON v. FORD MOTOR CO., INC.
— S.W.3d —, 2010 Ark. App. 407

JOHN MAUZY PITTMAN, JUDGE.

[Nine passengers were injured or killed when a van rolled over on an interstate highway. Appellants sued the Ford Motor Company unsuccessfully for tort and contract claims. Then, on appeal, they challenged the trial court's selection of several jurors.]

* * *

II. *Jury selection*

Following the exercise of peremptory strikes, the court seated a jury that included Jean Wyant, Russell Hulse, Cheryl Fiser, and Matt Foggiano. Appellants argue that these jurors should have been stricken for cause because they expressed a predisposition to hold appellants to a higher burden of proof. They cite Ark.Code Ann. § 16-31-102(b) (Supp.2009) for the proposition that no person shall serve as a juror who has formed or expressed an opinion concerning the matter in controversy that may influence his judgment, or who is biased or prejudiced for or against any party.

Persons comprising the venire are presumed to be unbiased and qualified to serve, and the burden is on the party challenging a juror to prove actual bias. The issue of a juror's qualifications lies within the sound discretion of the trial court and we will not reverse absent an abuse of discretion.

During voir dire, appellants' attorney asked the potential jurors as a group, "Is there anybody on our jury panel that believes there ought to be caps on damages of some kind, limits on damages?" Venireman Gerald Baxter responded, "You can't put a price on humans," and expressed his disagreement with large damage awards in cases where accidents occurred through "nobody's fault." Mr. Baxter concluded that "there's a lot of lawyers, and they've got to make a living, and that's my theory." Appellants' attorney asked Mr. Baxter if his feelings were so strong that appellants "would have a bit of a burden to overcome those feelings in getting you to award large damages in a death case?" Baxter responded, "Yes."

The following then occurred:

COUNSEL: [S]o I have a greater burden with you than I might a person that didn't have those feelings. Is that a fair statement?

BAXTER: Yes.

COUNSEL: Okay. Who agrees with that statement?

            (Several venirepersons raise their hands.)

COUNSEL: Here's what I need you to do. Those of you who raised your hand[s] and agree and feel as strongly as he does about it, tell me your names please.

            (Fifteen venirepersons, including Wyant, Hulse, Fiser, and Foggiano, give their names.)

COUNSEL: Of those of you who've expressed that belief as a strong belief, how many of you would put a greater burden on me in this case to get damages as a result? Could I see a show of hands?

            (Two venirepersons, Clark Bailey and Joe DeSoto, respond and give their names.)

COUNSEL: What I'm saying is, if this is the scale, and I'm going to ask you to award what I believe a life is worth, which is very large money, [how many of you] would tilt the scale toward Ford as you sit here today. Anybody have that feeling?

            (No hands are raised.)

Thereafter, appellants' attorney again questioned Mr. Baxter, who eventually stated that he would not place a higher burden on appellants because their lawsuit was "not frivolous." Counsel also made individual inquiries to more than a dozen other venirepersons regarding subjects that included damage caps, tort reform, and frivolous lawsuits. An incamera hearing followed, in which counsel challenged "those three jurors" who said that they would "put a greater burden on me in a large personal injury case." Another of appellants' attorneys provided the judge with the names of all fifteen venirepersons who had raised their hands during the initial questioning of Mr. Baxter. However, the court remembered that "there were only two or three that said they would hold you to a higher burden." The court denied the challenge for cause at that point but stated that it would speak to the venire.

Proceedings resumed in open court and the trial judge told the potential jurors that he would instruct the jury on the burden of proof. The court reminded them that two lives had been lost and that the plaintiffs were seeking "significant damages." The court specifically asked Mr. Baxter if he was "convinced and confident" that he could follow the court's instructions on burden of proof. Mr. Baxter said that he could. The court then addressed those on the venire who had "raised their hands about a higher burden." The court asked if they could follow the court's instructions and not hold the plaintiffs to a higher burden of proof, specifically stating, "I need to know if there is anybody that can't follow those instructions?" No one responded. Appellants' counsel then thanked the court and continued to question venirepersons both individually and as a group.

When the jury was selected, it did not include Baxter, Bailey, and DeSoto — the three men who clearly expressed the possibility of holding appellants to a higher burden. The jury did include Fiser, Wyant, Hulse, and Foggiano, who raised their hands in response to appellants' initial inquiry about a higher burden but otherwise remained silent. Appellants now argue that Fiser, Wyant, Hulse, and Foggiano were predisposed to place a greater burden on them than required by law and should have been stricken for cause.

Appellants have not demonstrated that Fiser, Wyant, Hulse, and Foggiano should have been stricken for cause. While these jurors raised their hands to indicate that they felt as strongly as Mr. Baxter about a higher burden of proof, when appellants' counsel asked them directly "how many of you would put a greater burden on me in this case to get damages," the four jurors did not raise their hands as did other venirepersons. Nor did they raise their hands when asked if they would "tilt the scale" toward Ford. Given the jurors' lack of response to counsel's questions and their implicit indication that they would not impose a greater burden of proof on appellants, we cannot say that the circuit court abused its discretion in refusing to strike the jurors for cause based on bias.

Furthermore, any potential bias was cured by the circuit court's inquiries and instructions. When a juror states that he or she can lay aside preconceived opinions and follow the law, a trial court may find the juror acceptable. In particular, a juror who holds a mistaken view of the law as to a defense, a particular principle of law, *the burden of proof*, the presumption of innocence, or the weight or effect of the evidence but is willing to abide by the law as explained or stated by the court and not by his own ideas, is not disqualified for cause. Here, the court was careful to assure that the potential jurors could follow the law regarding burden of proof.

Appellants argue, however, that the circuit court's attempt to cure the jurors' bias was insufficient and that the court should have allowed appellants to question each person individually who had raised a hand during the initial voir dire. However, the record does not reveal an explicit request by appellants to pose individual questions to those persons nor an express objection to the court's addressing the venire as a group. Further, the record shows that appellants' counsel had the opportunity to examine several venirepersons individually during voir dire but did not make inquiries of those jurors now challenged on appeal. For these reasons, and in light of the circuit court's discretion in controlling the scope and extent of voir dire, we find no basis for reversal.

* * *

HAM v. STATE
692 S.E.2d 828 (Ga. Ct. App. 2010)

PHIPPS, JUDGE.

[Paul Ham, III was convicted of armed robbery, kidnapping, burglary, aggravated assault, and possession of a firearm during the commission of a felony. He argued on appeal that the trial court erred when it refused to strike certain jurors for cause.]

* * *

Ham claims that the trial court abused its discretion in refusing to remove [Juror No. 21] for cause.

During individual questioning, Juror No. 21 expressed his belief that defendants had too many rights, stated that he would be upset if defense counsel attacked the credibility of prosecution witnesses if their accounts were consistent, and stated that he honestly believed that a person charged with a crime must be guilty of something. When asked if he would retain that belief if the judge told him that all defendants are presumed innocent, he responded, "At this point I don't think I'm presuming that — I don't think I have a presumption of innocence." When the trial court allowed counsel to further question Juror No. 21 the following day, he stated that he did not know what reasonable doubt meant, and the trial court declined to define it for him. He did state that he would listen to the trial court's definition of that term at trial. Juror No. 21 expressed his belief that the grand jury's indictment indicated that there was enough evidence to go to trial and that he had already formed an opinion that because the defendants were indicted something must have happened. When asked if he could find the defendants not guilty if the state could not prove they were criminals, he responded that he could do so because "those guys aren't criminals yet." Nonetheless, when presented with a football analogy where the state must prove guilt beyond a reasonable doubt to get into the end zone, he acknowledged he had already formed an opinion that because of the grand jury indictment, the prosecution was starting at about mid-field instead of the one-yard line.

In denying Ham's motion to excuse Juror No. 21 for cause, the trial court concluded that the prospective juror was conservative and had some opinions, but stated, "I haven't heard that he's leaning one way or the other." The defendants subsequently used a peremptory strike to remove prospective Juror No. 21 from the panel.

Only upon a finding of manifest abuse of discretion may a trial judge's decision concerning juror qualification be reversed. But even given this latitude, the potential impact of juror bias must not be underestimated. Running through the entire fabric of our Georgia decisions is a thread which plainly indicates that the broad general principle intended to be applied in every case is that each juror shall be so free from either prejudice or bias as to guarantee the inviolability of an impartial trial.

In this situation, Juror No. 21 was clearly biased against the defendants and gave no indication that he intended to be impartial during the trial. Here, the trial court never questioned Juror No. 21 and the questioning by counsel for the parties "failed to elicit the necessary response that [he] would be able to lay aside [his] prejudices and personal experiences and fairly and impartially decide the case on the evidence presented at trial." Accordingly, we conclude that the trial court abused its discretion in failing to remove Juror No. 21 for cause. For this reason, Ham's convictions must be reversed.

* * *

NOTES AND QUESTIONS

1.   An appellate opinion that employs the abuse of discretion standard should, at a minimum, state the standard of review and whether it has been met. Ending the analysis there, however, will not satisfy litigants who seek an explanation for the court's conclusion. In *Herrington* and *Ham*, the courts provide explanations. Why does the court not find an abuse of discretion in *Herrington*? And why does the court find an abuse of discretion in *Ham*?

2.   Slippery as the abuse of discretion standard can be, there are two ways to reason through it. First, an appellate court may delve into the record, examine closely the court's action, and discuss the reasonableness of the action. Second, the appellate court may compare the facts of the subject case to precedent, thereby plotting the subject case on a spectrum of relevant authority. Which methods did the courts employ in *Herrington* and *Ham*?

3.   Imagine that the same court decided *Herrington* and *Ham*, and you were drafting an opinion that discussed them. How would you distinguish the cases?

C.   Clearly Erroneous

The clearly erroneous standard of review applies to factual findings made by a trial judge. Ordinarily, these findings emerge from hearings or bench trials. The standard is strictly deferential to the trial judge, and, accordingly, it presents an imposing hurdle for appellants to jump. A finding is clearly erroneous if the appellate court "is left with a 'definite and firm conviction that a mistake has been committed.'" *Hernandez v. Tanninen*, 604 F.3d 1095, 1100 (9th Cir. 2010). Likewise, Federal Rule of Civil Procedure 52(a)(6) states that "[f]indings of fact, whether based on oral or other evidence, must not be set aside unless clearly erroneous, and the reviewing court must give due regard to the trial court's opportunity to judge the witnesses' credibility." For further discussion of what constitutes a finding of fact, refer to Chapter Eight.

A jury's findings of fact are afforded great deference too, arguably even more deference than that afforded the factual findings of a trial judge. The rationale for this deference leads directly back to the Sixth and Seventh Amendments to the U.S. Constitution. The Sixth Amendment guarantees a criminal defendant a "public trial" with "an impartial jury." And the Seventh Amendment provides that "no fact tried by a jury shall be otherwise re-examined in any Court of the United States, than according to the rules of common law."

Why do appellate courts afford great deference to fact-finders? What would happen if the appellate courts applied a less-deferential standard?

KNIGHT v. KNIGHT
— So. 3d —, 2010 WL 1837780 (Ala. Civ. App. 2010)

THOMPSON, PRESIDING JUDGE.

Kevin J. Knight ("the father") and Sarah J. Knight ("the mother") were divorced by an August 29, 2008, judgment of the trial court. The divorce judgment incorporated an agreement reached by the parties. Pursuant to the divorce judgment, the parties shared joint legal and physical custody of their minor child.

On February 19, 2009, the mother filed a petition seeking to modify custody of the child, requesting permission to relocate to California with the child and seeking a modification of child support. The father filed an answer in which he objected to the proposed relocation and asserted counterclaims seeking an award of custody of the child and an award of child support.

The trial court conducted a hearing over the course of two days. On September 9, 2009, the trial court entered a judgment in which it awarded primary physical custody of the child to the mother, authorized the mother to relocate with the child to California, and modified the father's child-support obligation. The father filed a postjudgment motion, and the trial court denied that motion. The father timely appealed.

The record indicates that the parties moved to Alabama some time before the birth of their child in October 2006. The parties' testimony established that they each grew up in or near Santa Ynez, California, that they went to school there, and that they moved from the Santa Ynez area to Alabama in order for the father to work with his uncle in constructing houses in Alabama. The father's testimony indicates that the initial plans to work with or for his uncle did not work out and that, thereafter, the father created his own construction business. The father and his business partner construct and remodel homes to sell to others.

The mother owned a clothing store until January 2009. The mother testified that she traveled to California monthly to purchase merchandise for her store and that she often took the child with her on those buying trips. The mother explained that she had a great deal of extended family in the Santa Ynez area and that the mother and the child visited family and friends when they went on buying trips.

The parties divorced in August 2008. The custody agreement incorporated into the parties' divorce judgment provided that the mother have custody of the child for 7 of 11 days and for the father to have the child for the remaining 4 days of the 11-day period. The mother explained that the parties anticipated that the father would have the child for two consecutive four-day periods when she traveled to California for her business. However, the mother testified that, after the divorce, the father did not exercise all the custodial periods available to him and that, on at least one occasion after the parties' divorce, she had taken the child with her when she traveled to California. The mother submitted into evidence an exhibit documenting the dates on which she had had custody of the child, the dates on which the father had had custody of the child, and custodial days available to the father that he had not exercised. The mother testified that, after she filed her February 2009 complaint seeking authorization to relocate to California with the child, the father fully exercised his custodial time.

The father disputed that he had not fully exercised his custodial periods. The father stated that he had rescheduled some of the days he was to have the child but that he believed he had not missed any opportunity to have custody of the child.

After the parties moved to Alabama from California, the mother's sister and parents, who had lived in the Santa Ynez area, also relocated to Alabama to be closer to the parties. The mother explained that her parents are attending college in Alabama in order to obtain their teaching certificates. The mother testified that her sister and the sister's family had spent a great deal of time traveling between California and Alabama but that her sister and her sister's family had recently returned to live in California.

The mother testified that she wanted to relocate with the child to California for several reasons. The mother testified that her business had been unprofitable and that she had sold the business. The mother stated that she had attempted to locate employment in Alabama but that her efforts had been unsuccessful. At the time of the hearing in this matter, the mother and the child were living in government-subsidized housing.

The mother testified that she had received an offer for a job in California with a salary of $48,000, plus commissions; the mother stated that she believed her annual income could be as much as $60,000 in that job. According to the mother, the job offer was a position in event sales for a winery. The mother explained that, in addition to the salary, the job was attractive because she would be required to work away from her house for only two days each week; the mother stated that she could work from home for the remainder of the time, which would enable her to spend more time with the child. The mother testified that she could rent a home in Santa Ynez for $500 per month from the parents of a long-term male friend.

The mother presented evidence regarding a Montessori preschool she planned for the child to attend on the days she worked away from her home. The mother stated that, although she had been satisfied initially with the church preschool the child has been attending, she believed that it was in the nature of a "day care." The mother testified that she believed the child needed more educational opportunities, such as those available at the preschool in California. The mother had also identified a local charter school as a possible elementary school for the child when he reached school age.

The mother also testified regarding the great number of aunts, uncles, cousins, and friends she and the child had in the Santa Ynez area. The mother stated that the extended-family members could provide support if she needed help with the child.

The mother also testified that she has facilitated, and will continue to facilitate, the relationship between the child and the father. It is undisputed that the child speaks on the telephone daily with the parent who does not then have custody of him. The mother testified that she had proposed a custodial arrangement to allow the father visitation with the child if she were allowed to relocate with the child. Pursuant to that proposed agreement, the mother would have the child for four consecutive weeks and the father would have the child for two consecutive weeks. The mother explained that that arrangement would result in the father having only six fewer days per year with the child than he is afforded under the custody arrangement specified in the divorce judgment. The mother also stated that the father often visits California to see friends and family and that he could exercise additional visitation with the child during those times. In addition, the mother proposed that the father use the Internet to have video-telephone conversations with the child.

The parties presented evidence regarding the cost of flying from Alabama to California, and they agreed that an adult would have to fly with the child, who was two years old at the time of the hearing, when he traveled to and from California, thereby increasing the transportation costs. The mother stated that the child enjoyed flying on an airplane. The mother testified that the trip normally took five to six hours, including time for a layover. The mother stated that a direct flight from Alabama to California took only four hours, but she stated that she had never taken a direct flight with the child. The mother explained that she believed the child would do better if he were able to leave the plane during a layover for exercise and a meal.

The father conceded that the mother was a good mother and that she has been the child's primary caretaker. The father testified that he did not want the child to be removed from Alabama; the father stated that he intended to make Alabama his permanent home and that he wanted the child to be raised in Alabama. In addition, the parties agreed that the father and the child have a close relationship.

The father stated that, because he was self-employed, his schedule was flexible and he could meet the child's needs. The father presented evidence indicating that the child had been attending a church day care or preschool while in Alabama and that the child could continue to do so until he reached school age. The father presented evidence concerning a private school he wanted the child to attend when the child reached school age.

The father also stated that, when necessary, he could leave the child in the care of the father's mother, who lived nearby. The father admitted that the mother was concerned about leaving the child with the paternal grandmother, who has a felony drug conviction. However, the father stated that he would not leave the child with the paternal grandmother if he had any concerns about her ability to properly care for the child. The father also testified that the child was close to the father's nine-year-old brother.

In addition, the father testified that the mother's parents would be willing to help him with the child if necessary. The mother's father testified, however, that he anticipated that he and the child's maternal grandmother would return to

California if the mother was allowed to relocate; he explained that the mother's sister had already returned to California and that he and his wife wanted to be near their children and grandchildren.

The father testified that he believed that the mother lived an extravagant lifestyle that was beyond her financial means. The mother alleged that the father had been controlling during their marriage and that she believed he was continuing to attempt to control her after their divorce. The father disputed that the mother could not find employment in Alabama, and he questioned whether she had truly attempted to do so. The father presented evidence indicating that one of the mother's former employers had job openings for positions with salaries in the range of $25,000 to $40,000 per year. The operator of that business acknowledged that the mother had earned only $22,000 per year when she was employed with his business, and he stated that he was not offering the mother a $40,000 per year job.

The father indicated that he had traveled to the Santa Ynez area twice in the year since the parties' divorce. We note that, on one of those trips, the father was accompanied by his girlfriend and that, during that trip, the mother and the child were also in California. The father conceded that he did not attempt to see the child in the five days he was in California during that trip. Rather, the father admitted that he spent much of that time following the mother, surveilling the home of the man with whom he suspects the mother is involved, and asking questions of the mother's prospective employer.

At the close of the hearing in this matter, the trial court noted, with regard to the issues of custody and the proposed relocation:

> "I will say this to both of you. This is one of those cases that judges hate. Two good people. Two good parents, and no good solutions, so whatever I decide is going to be tough. I will do my best, but there is not a good guy and a bad guy. . . ."

* * *

As stated earlier, the record supports a conclusion that the mother has been the primary caretaker for the child. The mother also presented evidence indicating that she had encouraged and assisted the child in maintaining his relationship with the father, and she testified that she would continue to do so. The mother testified that she wanted to move because of the job opportunity and to be close to her extended family in California. Both parties have ties to California, and the child has a great deal of extended family there. The mother presented evidence indicating that she had a good job opportunity that would allow her flexibility to spend a great deal of time with the child.

The mother proposed a visitation schedule that would allow the father only six fewer days per year with the child in Alabama. The mother also testified that she would work with the father to allow him additional visitation during the times he visits California.

The father testified that he wanted to be able to take part in the child's daily activities, which he could not do if the child lived in California with the mother. The father stated that he enjoyed a close relationship with the child, and he disputed the mother's allegation that he had not exercised his full custodial rights before the mother initiated this action. However, the father admitted that he had spent five days in California following the mother and had not taken advantage of the mother's offer to allow him to visit the child during that time. Thus, the trial court could have questioned the credibility of the father's statements that he had fully exercised his custodial time with the child before the mother initiated this action and his denial that he was attempting to exercise control over the mother.

This case, like *Sankey v. Sankey* and *Nichols v. Nichols*, involves the application of the ore tenus rule. In both of those cases, this court, citing the ore tenus rule, affirmed the trial courts' judgments. The father insists that the evidence does not support the trial court's judgment in this case. However, our supreme court has recently reiterated the limited nature of an appellate court's review of a judgment reached by the trial court after the trial court received ore tenus evidence:

* * *

The trial court is in the best position to make a custody determination — it hears the evidence and observes the witnesses. Appellate courts do not sit in judgment of disputed evidence that was presented ore tenus before the trial court in a custody hearing.

Our standard of review is very limited in cases where the evidence is presented ore tenus. A custody determination of the trial court entered upon oral testimony is accorded a presumption of correctness on appeal, and we will not reverse unless the evidence so fails to support the determination that it is plainly and palpably wrong, or unless an abuse of the trial court's discretion is shown. To substitute our judgment for that of the trial court would be to reweigh the evidence. This Alabama law does not allow

The trial court is in the better position to consider all of the evidence, as well as the many inferences that may be drawn from that evidence, and to decide the issue of custody. Thus, appellate review of a judgment modifying custody when the evidence was presented ore tenus is limited to determining whether there was *sufficient evidence to support the trial court's judgment.* Under the ore tenus rule, where the conclusion of the trial court is so opposed to the weight of the evidence that the variable factors of a witness's demeanor and credibility and the inferences that can be drawn from the evidence, even after considering those factors, *could not reasonably substantiate it*, then the conclusion is clearly erroneous and must be reversed.

As the trial court noted at the close of the evidence, this is a close case. It is clear that both parties are good parents and that they each love the child. The trial court, after considering the ore tenus evidence, found that awarding custody to the mother and allowing the proposed change of principal residence was in the child's best interests. Given our standard of review and the record on appeal, we cannot say that the father has demonstrated that there is no evidence to "reasonably substantiate" the trial court's custody determination. Accordingly, we affirm that part of the trial court's judgment awarding the mother primary physical custody of the child.

* * *

NOTES AND QUESTIONS

1. "Ore Tenus" refers to oral testimony. The appellate court defers to the trial court's decision about which oral testimony to accept. The trial court, after all, observes and hears witnesses as they testify. Similarly, in a jury trial, the jury decides who to believe (credibility) and the importance of each piece of evidence (the weight of the evidence). The self-conscious appellate court will not interfere with these jury findings.

2. An appellate law clerk reads many pages of trial transcript in reviewing a case on appeal, but the evidence gleaned from those pages is not always included in an appellate opinion. The court in *Knight v. Knight*, however, detailed the evidence presented at trial. Did that help you understand why the trial court's ruling withstood review? Would you have accepted the same conclusion with a brief, say one-page, summary of the evidence?

3. Take note of how the court articulated the standard of review. What evidence could the father have presented to satisfy the standard of review and warrant reversal of the custody determination?

4. What is the purpose of a written opinion when the appellate court merely affirms the trial court's decision? Imagine if the appellate court in *Knight v. Knight* had affirmed the trial court without discussion. Would there be any harm in that?

5. What happens when the trial court's decision is subject to a deferential standard of review, but it is not clear how the trial court reached its decision? In *Woodington v. Shokoohi*, 792 N.W.2d 63, 74–75(Mich. Ct. App. 2010), for example, the appellate court noted that it could not "discern the trial court's general plan

in dividing assets" following a divorce. The court explained:

> The trial court's failure to make findings in support of its uneven property division raises questions regarding why it ordered a property division in near compliance with a prenuptial agreement it found to be inapplicable. Furthermore, it appears that the trial court's decision may have been based on the unstated premise that defendant was the primary contributor to the marital estate. Although plaintiff's financial contributions to the marital estate are negligible, it is well established that a non-earning spouse can make substantial contributions to the marital estate by running the household and caring for the parties' children. Plaintiff, a lawyer, quit her law practice and suspended her legal career to stay at home with the parties' children. She also testified that she devoted substantial energy and time to serving the needs of defendant and his family. The trial court's failure to make relevant findings on this matter precludes meaningful review of whether the trial court's findings were clearly erroneous, and on whether its division of property constituted an abuse of discretion.

The appellate court remanded the case for "adequate findings of fact." Appellate review requires a developed trial record, even when the standard of review is deferential.

EXERCISE

Research and answer the following questions, citing to cases, statutes, or rules to support your answers. For some of the questions, more than one standard of review may apply.

1. You are a law clerk for the Alaska Court of Appeals. What standard applies when you review a trial court's grant of summary judgment?

2. You are a law clerk for the New York Court of Appeals. The question before you is whether the trial court properly admitted into evidence the criminal defendant's hearsay statements. What standard of review applies?

3. You are a law clerk for the Rhode Island Supreme Court. What standard applies when appellant challenges the revocation of his driver's license by the Department of Motor Vehicles?

4. You are a law clerk for the Virginia Supreme Court. The issue on appeal is whether a trial court properly awarded $10,000 in attorney's fees to the defendant in a civil trial because the performance of plaintiff's counsel was "substandard." The trial court noted in it its ruling that plaintiff's counsel submitted documents to the court that contained typos and citation errors. What standard of review applies?

5. You are a law clerk for the Colorado Court of Appeals, working on a custody dispute. The trial court granted full custody of three children to their father. It found that the mother left them home alone on three occasions in unsafe circumstances. The mother states on appeal, as she did in the trial court, that these allegations are false. What standard of review applies?

III. PRESERVATION DOCTRINE

Beyond selecting a standard of review, another way that appellate courts define the scope of their review is with adherence to the preservation doctrine. The preservation doctrine requires litigants to raise — preserve — their claim of error at an earlier point in time before presenting it to the appellate court. It seeks to prevent a claim of error from being raised and decided for the first time on appeal. Why? What is the danger in having claims presented for the first time on appeal?

In *Dilliplaine v. Lehigh Valley Trust Co.*, 322 A.2d 114, 116 (Pa. 1974), the Supreme Court of Pennsylvania answered as follows:

> Appellate court consideration of issues not raised in the trial court results in the trial becoming merely a dress rehearsal. This process removes the professional necessity for trial counsel to be prepared to litigate the case fully at trial and to create a record adequate for appellate review. The ill-prepared advocate's hope is that an appellate court will come to his aid after the fact and afford him relief despite his failure at trial to object to an alleged error. The diligent and prepared trial lawyer — and his client — are penalized when an entire case is retried because an appellate court reverses on the basis of an error opposing counsel failed to call to the trial court's attention. Failure to interpose a timely objection at trial denies the trial court the chance to hear argument on the issue and an opportunity to correct error. It also tends to postpone unnecessarily disposition of other cases not yet tried for the first time.

> The notion of basic and fundamental error not only erodes the finality of the trial court holdings, but also encourages unnecessary appeals and thereby further burdens the decisional capacity of our appellate courts. Trial counsel, though he may not have claimed error at trial, is inspired after trial and an adverse verdict by the thought that an appellate court may seize upon a previously unclaimed error and afford relief on a ground not called to the trial court's attention.

Preservation operates at two levels. First, it means that a party must raise an issue in the trial court before presenting it to the appellate court. A party typically raises the issue with an objection in open court or by a written motion. Sometimes the parties dispute whether an objection lodged in the trial court adequately corresponds to an issue raised on appeal. Leniency generally prevails, so that even an inarticulate or incomplete objection at trial will satisfy the requirement of preservation. But when an objection is entirely lacking, the appellate claim is usually lost.

The second level of the preservation doctrine concerns the appeal itself. To preserve a claim of error on appeal, litigants must explain the point of error in the brief, indicate where the error occurred in the record, and provide legal authority for their position. Also, counsel may argue at oral argument only what they included in their appellate briefs. What is the purpose of these rules?

At times, judges are uncomfortable adhering to the preservation doctrine. Imagine ignoring a claim of error that is unpreserved, but meritorious on its face. An exception to the preservation doctrine has developed that allows appellate courts to address an unpreserved claim if there is "plain error" or if "justice requires it." Federal Rule of Criminal Procedure 52(b), for example, states that "[a] plain error that affects substantial rights may be considered even though it was not brought to the court's attention." This requires that: "(1) there is an 'error;' (2) the error is 'clear or obvious, rather than subject to reasonable dispute;' (3) the error 'affected the appellant's substantial rights, which in the ordinary case means' it 'affected the outcome of the district court proceedings;' and (4) 'the error seriously affect[s] the fairness, integrity or public reputation of judicial proceedings.' " *United States v. Marcus*, 130 S. Ct. 2159 (2010).

For weaker claims, appellate courts may invoke the preservation doctrine, and then give cursory review of the claim and a brief explanation of why the claim would not warrant reversal even if it had been preserved. The following excerpt from *Bagheri v. State*, 2010 WL 1904265 (Tex. App. 2010) illustrates this approach:

> Turning to Bagheri's issue complaining of the denial of his challenge for cause to venire member no. 13, Candace Martinez, it appears Bagheri failed to preserve the issue. To preserve error on the denial of his challenge for cause, Bagheri must show on the record that: (1) he asserted a clear and specific challenge for cause to that venire member; (2) he used a peremptory challenge on the complained-of venire member; (3) he exhausted all his peremptory challenges; (4) his request for additional peremptory strikes was denied; and (5) an objectionable juror sat on the jury. The record shows Bagheri did not use a peremptory strike on Martinez, and she ended up sitting on the jury. Bagheri therefore cannot show he was harmed by being forced to use a peremptory strike to remove Martinez and then suffering a detriment from the loss of the strike. Even if the issue was preserved, the record does not show the trial court abused its discretion in denying the defense challenge for cause on Martinez. Although Martinez initially stated she would automatically assume someone who was arrested for D.W.I. was

guilty, she was rehabilitated during individual voir dire when the State explained there are different standards for an arrest and a conviction. After hearing the explanation of the law, Martinez stated she would require the State to meet the higher burden of proof beyond a reasonable doubt in order to find Bagheri guilty, and if it failed to meet that higher burden she could then find Bagheri not guilty. Martinez indicated she understood the law, and stated she could follow it; therefore, the trial court did not abuse its discretion in denying Bagheri's challenge for cause to Martinez.

IV. THE SELF-CONSCIOUS APPELLATE COURT: A CASE STUDY

The next case demonstrates how the three most common standards of review may intersect in a single case. It also exemplifies principles of the preservation doctrine. If you read the opinion closely, you will note six instances where the court explicitly shows its self-conscious tendencies by commenting on the scope of its review.

OESBY v. STATE
788 A.2d 662 (Md. Ct. Spec. App. 2002)

CHARLES E. MOYLAN, JR., JUDGE, RETIRED, SPECIALLY ASSIGNED.

During the month of February 2001, the appellant, Antonio Donnell Oesby, was convicted in three separate trials by three separate Prince George's County juries, all presided over by Judge E. Allen Shepherd, of a variety of assaults on women.

On February 1, 2001, he was convicted of 1) a third degree sexual offense, 2) second degree assault, and 3) carrying a deadly weapon openly with intent to injure (No. 0445). The victim of those crimes, committed on November 3, 1999, was Teresa Hicks. On February 5, he was convicted of 1) attempted armed robbery, 2) second degree assault, and 3) carrying a deadly weapon openly with intent to injure (No. 0447). The victim of those crimes, committed on November 4, 1999, was Madinah Rasheed. On February 14, he was convicted of 1) a third degree sexual offense, 2) armed robbery, and 3) carrying a deadly weapon openly with intent to injure (No. 0448). The victim of those crimes, committed on October 27, 1999, was Martha Yates.

Two of the appellant's four contentions challenge pretrial rulings made at a single pretrial hearing that applied to all three trials. The appellant complains:

1. that Judge Shepherd erroneously failed to suppress physical evidence seized pursuant to an allegedly defective search warrant; and

2. that Judge Shepherd, in ruling on a motion in limine, erroneously agreed to admit "other crimes evidence" at each of the three trials.

The third contention concerns a proposed jury instruction that was requested and denied in two of the three cases. The appellant complains:

3. that Judge Shepherd erroneously failed to give his requested instruction concerning the specific intent element of the crime of carrying a weapon openly with intent to injure; with respect to the third trial, the appellant claims, pursuant to the notion of "plain error," that Judge Shepherd erroneously failed to give the instruction spontaneously even though he was never requested to do so.

The fourth and final contention arose out of the sentencing hearing that was common to all three trials. In that regard, the appellant complains:

4. that Judge Shepherd erroneously failed to merge lesser included second degree assault convictions into other convictions for greater inclusive offenses.

Because of the commonality of the issues, it is meet that we consolidate these three appeals into a single appeal.

The Search Warrant

The first contention concerns the pretrial denial of the appellant's suppression motion. Pursuant to a search warrant issued by District of Columbia Superior Court Judge Peter Wolf to Detective Karen Moss, D.C. police searched the appellant's residence at 625 L Street, Northeast, in the District. Recovered in that search and later received in evidence were 1) a black knit hat and 2) a black leather jacket, both identified by both victims as having been worn by the assailant in the assaults committed on Hicks and Rasheed.

The appellant does not challenge the probable cause to believe that he was the assailant. Indeed, all three victims (plus a fourth not directly involved with this appeal) had selected a photograph of him from photographic arrays. The basis of the appellant's challenge was that the warrant application failed to establish an adequate nexus between the appellant and 625 L Street, Northeast. The application and its supporting affidavit sought a warrant:

FOR THE PREMISES OF 625 "L" STREET, NORTHEAST, WASHINGTON, D.C. THE PREMISES IS A THREE STORY, PINK AND WHITE BRICK ROWHOUSE. . . .

On October 31, 1999, an adult complainant reported to the member of the Prince George's County Police Department that she had been the victim of a sexual assault.

The complainant explained that she was approached by the defendant while unloading groceries from her vehicle. . . . The defendant displayed a knife. . . . [After committing forced sexual acts on the complainant], the defendant took one hundred and forty dollars in U.S. Currency and a business card with the complainant's name printed on it.

Members of the Prince George's County Police Department became aware of an arrest made by the affiant with similar circumstances. A photograph of the defendant was obtained from the affiant and utilized in a photo array by members of the Prince George's County Police Department. The defendant was positively identified as the person who sexually assaulted her.

All other identifiable information of the defendant was submitted to Prince George's County Police Department from the affiant.

Based on the aforementioned facts, the affiant has probable cause to believe that ANTONIO DONNELL OESBY, did commit the Sexual Assault which occurred in Prince George's County Maryland and that *evidence of this crime may be located inside of 625 "L" Street, Northeast, Washington, D.C.* Specifically, a business card, clothing worn and the weapon used during the offense. It is therefore respectfully requested that a District of Columbia Superior Court Judge issue a Search Warrant, directing a search of the premises described herein, authorizing the seizure of any evidence connected to the case.

A. Inadequacy of the Nexus

We agree with the appellant that the application for the search warrant failed to establish an adequate nexus between the person of the appellant and the Washington, D.C. residence that was searched. Dispositive on this issue is Judge Hollander's definitive opinion for this Court in *Braxton*. The issue there was indistinguishable from the issue here:

> *Appellant posits that the warrant* was not based on probable cause because the supporting affidavit *failed to specify that the targeted apartment actually was appellant's residence.* Even if the affidavit implied that the subject premises was appellant's place of abode, Braxton contends that the affidavit was defective because it lacked any factual foundation to substantiate that assertion. Specifically, *Braxton complains that the affidavit was devoid of facts particularizing the basis for the affiant's belief that the targeted premises was actually appellant's residence.*

The warrant application in that case actually represented more of a predicate than we have here for an inference of the required connection, as it at least linked the name of the suspect with the street address of the place to be searched:

Persons/Premises to be Searched:

Arnold Braxton, Jr. M/B/10-31-75 BPI# 440-492, *4310 Seminole Ave. Apt.* A three story brick apartment building with the numbers 4310 affixed. Apt. 203 has a white door the numbers 203 on the same.

In our case, there is no such juxtaposition of the person and the place.

* * *

The requirement placed on the police in this regard is not onerous, but it is something that cannot be ignored. Again, Judge Hollander explained:

> Given the urgency that is often associated with matters such as this one, we acknowledge that a police officer cannot always prepare the kind of detailed statement that would serve as a textbook example of a model affidavit. But *the quantum of facts needed to show the connection between the suspect and the purported place of occupancy is hardly daunting.* Typically, an affidavit includes an averment tying the suspect to the targeted location on the basis of surveillance, a check of utility records, verification with a landlord, an address from the phone book, or the like.

B. The "Good Faith" Exception

On the ultimate issue of suppression, however, the appellant wins the battle but loses the war. In foretelling this contrapuntal swing of the pendulum, *Braxton v. State* is again the soothsayer. Although the drawing of the inference in this case, as we have been discussing, may not have been legally sustainable, the failure to spell out a more detailed nexus was by no means so egregious a flaw that the officers could be held to have acted in "bad faith" in submitting the warrant application and in relying on the warrant. As one of the detectives testified at the suppression hearing, the police believed that the appellant was living with his aunt, Kim Powell, at the Washington address recited in the warrant application.

The police inadvertently neglected to set forth some easily ascertainable facts and then to connect the dots. It was a fault, but hardly a grievous one. Although more than a hypertechnicality, to be sure, the establishment of the nexus is understandably a peripheral aspect of the police focus as attention concentrates on the core issue of underlying criminality. The officers were fully entitled to the "good faith" exception to the Exclusionary Rule established by *Massachusetts v. Sheppard* and *United States v. Leon.*

At the outset, our entitlement to consider the applicability of the "good faith" exception for the first time on appeal, notwithstanding that the issue was not addressed by Judge Shepherd, is not to be doubted. *McDonald v. State; Connelly v. State* ("As the application of the good faith exception to the allegations of the affidavit presents an objectively ascertainable question, it is for the appellate court to decide whether the affidavit was sufficient to support the requisite belief that the warrant was valid.").

* * *

We affirm the ruling of Judge Shepherd that the physical evidence should not have been suppressed.

The "Other Crimes" Evidence

Within a nine-day period, four lone women, living in close proximity to each other in Prince George's County, were approached in the common areas of their garden style apartment complexes in an ostensibly friendly and unthreatening manner and, when their guards were then relaxed, were attacked. The crimes against three of the women are the subject of this consolidated appeal. The crimes against the fourth woman also constitutes part of the "other crimes" evidence. The multitudinous similarities in the crimes were carefully detailed by Judge Shepherd. [The court then reviewed the factual similarities between the assaults.]

* * *

A. Stage One of the Analysis: The "Right or Wrong" Standard of Appellate Review

Before evidence of "other crimes" may be admitted against a defendant, a three-step analysis must be undertaken by the trial judge. The first determination is an exclusively legal one, with respect to which the trial judge will be found to have been either right or wrong. In *State v. Faulkner*, Judge Adkins described that first step:

> When a trial court is faced with the need to decide whether to admit evidence of another crime — that is, evidence that relates to an offense separate from that for which the defendant is presently on trial — it first determines whether the evidence fits within one or more of the *Ross v. State* exceptions. *This is a legal determination and does not involve any exercise of discretion.*

In *Moore v. State*, Judge Wilner further explained this first step of the analysis:

> *For the evidence even to qualify for admission, it must fall within one of the exceptions that the court has recognized or would be willing to recognize as having an independent relevance* and, although, because

this is largely a factual question, it will ultimately depend on how the last appellate court to review the case happens to view the matter, *it is not a discretionary ruling. The element of discretion arises only when the evidence does fall within a permissible exception and is thus prima facie admissible.* It is then that the court must balance the independent relevance against the danger of undue prejudice and decide whether to exclude the evidence notwithstanding its facial admissibility. *That* is the discretionary decision — to *ex* clude otherwise admissible evidence, not to *in* clude otherwise inadmissible evidence.

* * *

C. The Special or Heightened Relevance in This Case

In this case, we hold that at each of the respective trials involving the crimes against Madinah Rasheed and Martha Yates,[1] the evidence of the other three sets of crimes was properly admitted. In terms of the classic or more generic categories of exceptions, the special relevance of the "other crimes" evidence could take its label from the fact that it helped to establish the "identity" of the appellant as the assailant. As an academic or philosophic matter, however, it might as readily be maintained that the evidence tended to establish the "absence of mistake" when the direct victim of the crimes on trial identified the appellant as her assailant. In the circumstances of this case, that second categorization is simply a corollary of the first.

One could also, moreover, categorize the evidence as establishing a "signature" *modus operandi*. That, of course, is just one particular way of proving "identity." The label does not really matter when the labels are frequently but different ways of saying the same thing. "A rose by any other name. . . ." What matters is that the evidence of the "other crimes," however it might be categorized or labeled, enjoyed a special or heightened relevance in helping to establish the identity of the appellant as the perpetrator of the crimes on trial.

---

[1] We decline to examine the "other crimes" evidence in the trial of the crimes against Teresa Hicks (No. 0445). After the appellant's motion *in limine* was denied, he neglected, inexplicably, to renew his objection to the "other crimes" evidence at the trial of that particular case. Such a renewal is required in order to preserve the issue for appellate review.

Although it is inconceivable that our resolution of this issue would not have been the same as were our resolutions of the indistinguishable issues in the two companion cases, we steadfastly refuse to compromise the preservation requirement.

* * *

D. Stage Two of the Analysis: The "Clearly Erroneous" Standard of Appellate Review

The second stage of the analysis that must be undertaken, as well as the appropriate standard of appellate review for such second-stage decisions, was well described by *Solomon v. State*:

> The second procedural step calls for preliminary fact finding by the trial judge. The allusion to some other crime allegedly committed by the defendant may be no more than a bald and unsubstantiated assertion by the witness. The alleged crime may never have led to an arrest, let alone a conviction. Indeed, it may never have been investigated or even discovered. *It is for that reason that the trial judge needs to be persuaded,* by the clear and convincing standard, *that the alleged crime did, indeed, take place before he allows evidence of it to come into evidence.* Judge Adkins explained:

>> If one or more of the exceptions applies, the next step is to decide whether the accused's involvement in the other crimes is established by clear and convincing evidence. We will review this decision to determine whether the evidence was sufficient to support the trial judge's finding.

>> *Because the weight to be given the preliminary evidence as to the existence of the other crime is of necessity for the trial judge in his ancillary fact-finding capacity, the reviewing court, under the clearly erroneous standard, is limited to determining the existence of a prima facie case in that regard.*

At that stage of the analysis, it is the trial judge who must be persuaded, not the appellate court. The only appellate concern is whether there was some basis from which a rational fact-finding trial judge could have concluded that the "other crimes," in fact, took place.

In this case, Judge Shepherd made the appropriate finding:

> "The court is persuaded that the defendant's involvement in the other crimes evidence has been established by clear and convincing evidence."

That finding by Judge Shepherd was unassailable. *A fortiori*, it was not clearly erroneous.

E. Stage Three of the Analysis: The "Abuse of Discretion" Standard of Appellate Review

The third stage of the analysis requires a balancing by the trial judge between the probative value of the "other crimes" evidence and its possibly unfair prejudicial effect. *Solomon v. State* described this analytic stage:

> The third step for the trial judge is discretionary. Even when the first two hurdles have been cleared, the judge must still weigh the necessity for and probative value of "other crimes" evidence against any undue prejudice that it may cause the defendant:
>
> > If this requirement is met, the trial court proceeds to the final step. The necessity for and probative value of the "other crimes" evidence is to be carefully weighed against any undue prejudice likely to result from its admission. This segment of the analysis implicates the exercise of the trial court's discretion.

F. What Do We Weigh? All Prejudice Or Only Unfair Prejudice?

The ill effect that militates against admissibility is not prejudice generally, but only *unfair* prejudice. In a larger sense, all competent and trustworthy evidence offered against a defendant is prejudicial. If it were not, there would be no purpose in offering it. The special relevance that gives "other crimes" evidence its probative value *ipso facto* makes it prejudicial in that it is, by definition, strong but legitimate proof that the defendant is guilty.

Such self-evident prejudice in the larger sense, however, is not the "unfair" prejudice that should enter into the balancing process. To measure probative value against legitimate prejudice would be to measure probative value against itself. In such an exercise in futility, the scales could never tilt in favor of probative value. That obviously is not what the balancing test is designed to do. The "unfair" component of the prejudice is not the tendency of the evidence to prove the identity of the defendant as the perpetrator of the crimes. What is "unfair" is only the incremental tendency of the evidence to prove that the defendant was a "bad man." As we balance, therefore, the emphasis must be not on the noun "prejudice" but on the qualifying, and limiting, adjective "unfair."

It is the failure to appreciate this distinction that leads many analyses astray. There is frequently a tendency to conclude that if the State's case is otherwise a strong one, the probative value of "other crimes" evidence is proportionately diminished. That is not the case. Probative value does not depend on necessity. When we are talking only about the legitimate prejudice that inevitably results from competent evidence enjoying a special or heightened relevance, there is no downside to making a strong case even stronger.

The probative value must, of course, be measured against the "unfair" component of the prejudicial evidence. When that is the subject of the balancing, necessity is a factor. We balance 1) the need for the evidence against 2) the tendency of the evidence to prejudice the defendant unfairly. In terms of legitimate prejudice, on the other hand, the State is not constrained to forego relevant evidence and to risk going to the fact finder with a watered down version of its case. Were it not for the incremental ill effect, "other crimes" evidence of identity would be no more challengeable than a fingerprint or an identification by the victim. There is nothing inherently suspect about it as a modality of proof. We are wary only about its peripheral effect, not about its core function.

The first two stages of the "other crimes" analysis having been satisfied, Judge Shepherd engaged in the final balancing procedure in this case:

> "The court is persuaded that due to the unique circumstances of this case, the evidence of other crimes has special or heightened relevance, and due to the special or heightened relevance of the evidence, *it is more probative than unfairly prejudicial* to the defendant. . . ."

Astutely, Judge Shepherd did not rule that the evidence was "more probative than prejudicial." That, as we have explained, would be mathematically impossible, because probative value is directly proportionate to legitimate prejudice and could never, therefore outweigh it. The two are flip sides of the same coin. Inculpatory evidence is, by definition, prejudicial to the defendant's case, but prejudice in that sense gives us no pause. Judge Shepherd ruled, rather, that the evidence was "more probative than *unfairly* prejudicial." That, and that alone, is the thing that should have been measured.

This final balancing between probative value and unfair prejudice is something that is entrusted to the wide discretion of the trial judge. The appellate standard of review, therefore, is the highly deferential abuse-of-discretion standard. The fact that we might have struck the balance otherwise is beside the point. We know of no case where a trial judge was ever held to have abused his discretion in this final weighing process. As a practical matter, that will almost never be held to have occurred. A properly disciplined appellate court will not reverse an exercise of discretion because it thinks the trial judge's decision was wrong. That would be substituting its judgment for that of the trial court, which is inappropriate if not forbidden. Reversal should be reserved for those rare and bizarre exercises of discretion that are, in the judgment of the appellate court, not only wrong but flagrantly and outrageously so. In this case, we see no faint or distant glimmer of even arguable abuse.

G. The Admissibility of the "Other Crimes" Evidence

We hold that Judge Shepherd 1) was not legally incorrect in determining that the "other crimes" evidence in this case had special or heightened relevance; 2) was not clearly erroneous in being persuaded that the other crimes had, in fact, occurred; and 3) did not abuse his discretion in ruling that the probative value of the evidence outweighed the unfair prejudice that might result from it. We affirm his decision to admit the evidence.

Jury Instruction:

". . . With the Intent or Purpose of Injuring"

In each of the three cases against him, the appellant was convicted, *inter alia,* of having violated Art. 27, Sect. 36(a), which provides in pertinent part:

> Every person who shall . . . carry any . . . knife . . . openly *with the intent or purpose of injuring any person* in any unlawful manner shall be guilty of a misdemeanor. . . .

In two of his trials, those involving the offenses committed against Madinah Rasheed and Martha Yates, the appellant expressly requested a jury instruction on the mental element of specific intent. The pertinent part of that requested instruction was:

> *The offense* of openly carrying a dangerous and deadly weapon with the intent to injure *requires proof of the specific intent to cause injury.* If the State fails to prove beyond a reasonable doubt that the Defendant had *the specific intent to injure* [the victim] you must find him not guilty of this charge.

In effect, Judge Shepherd instructed the jury in just such a fashion. His instruction tracked, essentially verbatim, Maryland Pattern Jury Instruction--Criminal (MPJI-Cr) 4:35, which in pertinent part provides:

> The defendant is charged with the crime of carrying a dangerous weapon openly *with the intent to injure another person.* In order to convict the defendant, the State must prove:
>
> (1) that the defendant wore or carried a dangerous weapon; and
>
> (2) that it was carried openly *with the intent to injure another person.*

Omitting only the words "the crime of," Judge Shepherd advised the jury:

> [T]he Defendant is charged with carrying a dangerous weapon openly *with the intent to injure.* In order to convict the Defendant, the State must prove, first, that the Defendant wore or carried a dangerous weapon, and second, that it was carried openly *with the intent to injure another person.*

We agree with the appellant that the crime that was the subject of this instruction is a specific intent crime. The jury in this case was so instructed. The only specific intent of any pertinence to this case was fully and precisely explained to the jury. The appellant's chagrin, however, appears to be that the term of art "specific intent" was never expressly employed.

* * *

Article 27, Sect. 36(a)'s specific "intent or purpose of injuring any person" is simply a particular instance of that generic category. Where there is such an additional mental element, a defendant is fully entitled to have the jury instructed as to the necessity that it find such an element in order to convict. In this case the jury was so instructed. It was instructed with respect to the additional mental element in the detailed and particularized language pertinent to the case at hand rather than in more abstract and generalized terms. When Judge Shepherd twice told the jury that, in order to convict, it would have to find that the appellant carried a dangerous weapon openly "with the intent to injure another person," he defined precisely the only specific intent that was before the jury for its consideration. He did not ignore the mental element of specific intent. He spelled it out — twice.

Having done everything that was required in the particular, there was no requirement that he, in the course of doing so, use the generic adjective "specific." There is no talismanic magic in the incantation of the phrase "specific intent." It is an academic term of art, not a mantra. What matters is that the definition of the required intent **BE SPECIFIC**, not that it necessarily **DE-SCRIBE ITSELF AS BEING "SPECIFIC."** We are concerned with what the definition actually **DOES**, not with what it **SAYS IT DOES.**

The Comment to MPJI Cr-3:31.1 catalogues 45 Maryland crimes requiring proof of a specific intent. In each of the 45 pattern jury instructions spelling out what must be found in those respective cases, the individual specific intent involved is described in the particularized language appropriate to that particular intent. Not once over the course of those 45 pattern instructions is the generic adjective "specific" ever employed. The utility of such an adjective is obviated by an instruction that is, in its very articulation, *specific.* A precise description of the species eliminates any need to designate the genus. There was no error in the jury instruction in this case. The definition, in fact, was specific whether it ever used the word "specific" or not.

With respect to the trial of the offenses committed against Teresa Hicks (No. 0445), Judge Shepherd also gave the jury MPJI-Cr 4:35. In that trial, however, the appellant made no objection to the instruction as given nor had he requested any special instruction. With respect to that set of convictions, therefore, there is nothing properly before us for review. Were the issue before us, it is inconceivable that our resolution of it would be different than is our resolution of the same issue as we review the other two sets of convictions. No matter how easy it would be to do so, however, we once again steadfastly refuse to compromise the integrity of the preservation requirement. Whatever we may intimate about the merits, we hold nothing.

The Merger of the Second-Degree Assaults

In his final contention, the appellant claims that his convictions in each case for the lesser included offense of second degree assault should have merged into his respective convictions for the greater inclusive offenses of 1) the third degree sexual offense against Teresa Hicks (No. 0445), 2) the attempted armed robbery of Madinah Rasheed (No. 0447), and 3) the armed robbery of Martha Yates (No. 0448).

As a matter of fact, the merger of the second degree assault conviction in Case No. 0448 (the crimes against Martha Yates) did take place. At the time of sentencing, Judge Shepherd ruled that the assault conviction was merged into that for armed robbery.

With respect to the other two cases, the appellant is right. The assault was an integral part of the third degree sexual offense in Case No. 0445, just as it was an integral part of the attempted armed robbery in Case No. 0447. Commendably, the State agrees that these mergers were mandatory.

* * *

NOTES AND QUESTIONS

1.   What standard of review did the court employ when it reviewed the adequacy of the nexus between appellant and the searched address? How about when it reviewed the propriety of the jury instruction or the request for merger of convictions?

2.   Return to the three points in the opinion where the court comments on preservation. What did you learn from these comments?

V.   SUGGESTED FURTHER READING

RUGGERO J. ALDISERT, OPINION WRITING 83-102 (AuthorHouse 2d ed., 2010).

Bryan L. Adamson, *Federal Rule of Civil Procedure 52(a) as an Ideological Weapon*, 34 FLA. ST. U. L. REV. 1025 (2007).

Theodore Eisenberg & Michael Heise, *Plaintiphobia in State Court? An Empirical Study of State Court Trials in Appeal*, 38 J. LEGAL STUD. 121 (2009).

Chad M. Oldfather, *Error Correction*, 85 Ind. L. Rev 49 (2010).

Chad M. Oldfather, *Universal De Novo Review*, 77 GEO. WASH. L. REV. 308 (2009).

Timothy J. Storm, *The Standard of Review Does Matter: Evidence of Judicial Self-Restraint in the Illinois Appellate Court*, 34 S. ILL. U. L.J. 73 (2009).

Chapter 4

UNRAVELING THE THREADS OF *STARE DECISIS*

I. INTRODUCTION

To follow *stare decisis* is to adhere to controlling precedent. As you well know from your law school studies, *stare decisis* is a fundamental principle of our judicial system. Without it, judges might resolve disputes without regard to what other judges had decided in similar circumstances. But with the rule of *stare decisis*, judges must consider precedent, and they are compelled to explain themselves when they deviate from it.

Naturally, to adhere to controlling precedent, you must first understand it. As an appellate law clerk, one of your primary responsibilities is to understand the precedent for the cases assigned to you. It is as if each case represents a haphazard heap of threads. Your job is to unravel the threads, separate them into piles, and then weave them, if you can, into a harmonious and congruent pattern.

The process begins with unraveling the threads of law presented in the parties' brief. This requires research and careful reading of the precedent. The process continues towards distilment of the controlling law, so you may organize the law in your mind. This is an active pursuit; get physical! As you read cases, keep good notes and diagram the relationship between ideas. From here, you move towards synthesis, weaving together all the separate strands of law that you found in your research. Now you can explain the parameters of the precedent, identifying the logic and policy that underlies it.

II. *STARE DECISIS* IN ACTION

We may learn the most about *stare decisis* when courts decline to follow it, that is, when the exception proves the rule. Are you satisfied with the U.S. Supreme Court's explanation for overruling precedent in the following case?

CITIZENS UNITED v. FED. ELEC. COMM'N
— U.S. —, 130 S. Ct. 876 (2010)

Justice Kennedy delivered the opinion of the Court.

Federal law prohibits corporations and unions from using their general treasury funds to make independent expenditures for speech defined as an "electioneering communication" or for speech expressly advocating the election or defeat of a candidate. Limits on electioneering communications were upheld in *McConnell v. Federal Election Comm'n*. The holding of *McConnell* rested to a large extent on an earlier case, *Austin v. Michigan Chamber of Commerce*. *Austin* had held that political speech may be banned based on the speaker's corporate identity.

In this case we are asked to reconsider *Austin* and, in effect, *McConnell*. It has been noted that "*Austin* was a significant departure from ancient First Amendment principles." We agree with that conclusion and hold that *stare decisis* does not compel the continued acceptance of *Austin*. The Government may regulate corporate political speech through disclaimer and disclosure requirements, but it may not suppress that speech altogether. We turn to the case now before us.

I

A

Citizens United is a nonprofit corporation. It brought this action in the United States District Court for the District of Columbia. A three-judge court later convened to hear the cause. The resulting judgment gives rise to this appeal.

Citizens United has an annual budget of about $12 million. Most of its funds are from donations by individuals; but, in addition, it accepts a small portion of its funds from for-profit corporations.

In January 2008, Citizens United released a film entitled *Hillary: The Movie*. We refer to the film as *Hillary*. It is a 90-minute documentary about then-Senator Hillary Clinton, who was a candidate in the Democratic Party's 2008 Presidential primary elections. *Hillary* mentions Senator Clinton by name and depicts interviews with political commentators and other persons, most of them quite critical of Senator Clinton. *Hillary* was released in theaters and on DVD, but Citizens United wanted to increase distribution by making it available through video-on-demand.

Video-on-demand allows digital cable subscribers to select programming from various menus, including movies, television shows, sports, news, and music. The viewer can watch the program at any time and can elect to rewind or pause the program. In December 2007, a cable company offered, for a payment of $1.2 million, to make *Hillary* available on a video-on-demand channel called "Elections '08." Some video-on-demand services require viewers to pay a small fee to view a selected program, but here the proposal was to make *Hillary* available to viewers free of charge.

To implement the proposal, Citizens United was prepared to pay for the video-on-demand; and to promote the film, it produced two 10-second ads and one 30-second ad for *Hillary*. Each ad includes a short (and, in our view, pejorative) statement about Senator Clinton, followed by the name of the movie and the movie's Website address. Citizens United desired to promote the video-on-demand offering by running advertisements on broadcast and cable television.

B

Before the Bipartisan Campaign Reform Act of 2002 (BCRA), federal law prohibited — and still does prohibit — corporations and unions from using general treasury funds to make direct contributions to candidates or independent expenditures that expressly advocate the election or defeat of a candidate, through any form of media, in connection with certain qualified federal elections. BCRA § 203 amended § 441b to prohibit any "electioneering communication" as well. An electioneering communication is defined as "any broadcast, cable, or satellite communication" that "refers to a clearly identified candidate for Federal office" and is made within 30 days of a primary or 60 days of a general election. The Federal Election Commission's (FEC) regulations further define an electioneering communication as a communication that is "publicly distributed." "In the case of a candidate for nomination for President . . . *publicly distributed* means" that the communication "[c]an be received by 50,000 or more persons in a State where a primary election . . . is being held within 30 days." Corporations and unions are barred from using their general treasury funds for express advocacy or electioneering communications. They may establish, however, a "separate segregated fund" (known as a political action committee, or PAC) for these purposes. The moneys received by the segregated fund are limited to donations from stockholders and employees of the corporation or, in the case of unions, members of the union.

C

Citizens United wanted to make *Hillary* available through video-on-demand within 30 days of the 2008 primary elections. It feared, however, that both the film and the ads would be covered by § 441b's ban on corporate-funded independent expenditures, thus subjecting the corporation to civil and criminal penalties under § 437g. In December 2007, Citizens United sought declaratory and injunctive relief against the FEC. It argued that (1) § 441b is unconstitutional as applied to *Hillary;* and (2) BCRA's disclaimer and disclosure requirements, BCRA §§ 201 and 311, are unconstitutional as applied to *Hillary* and to the three ads for the movie.

The District Court denied Citizens United's motion for a preliminary injunction and then granted the FEC's motion for summary judgment. The court held that § 441b was facially constitutional under *McConnell*, and that § 441b was constitutional as applied to *Hillary* because it was "susceptible of no other interpretation than to inform the electorate that Senator Clinton is unfit for office, that the United States would be a dangerous place in a President Hillary Clinton world, and that viewers should vote against her."

We noted probable jurisdiction. The case was reargued in this Court after the Court asked the parties to file supplemental briefs addressing whether we should overrule either or both *Austin* and the part of *McConnell* which addresses the facial validity of 2 U.S.C. § 441b.

* * *

III

The First Amendment provides that "Congress shall make no law . . . abridging the freedom of speech." Laws enacted to control or suppress speech may operate at different points in the speech process. The following are just a few examples of restrictions that have been attempted at different stages of the speech process — all laws found to be invalid: restrictions requiring a permit at the outset; imposing a burden by impounding proceeds on receipts or royalties; seeking to exact a cost after the speech occurs; and subjecting the speaker to criminal penalties.

The law before us is an outright ban, backed by criminal sanctions. Section 441b makes it a felony for all corporations — including nonprofit advocacy corporations — either to expressly advocate the election or defeat of candidates or to broadcast electioneering communications within 30 days of a primary election and 60 days of a general election. Thus, the following acts would all be felonies under § 441b: The Sierra Club runs an ad, within the crucial phase of 60 days before the general election, that exhorts the public to disapprove of a Congressman who favors logging in national forests; the National Rifle Association publishes a book urging the public to vote for the challenger because the incumbent U.S. Senator supports a handgun ban; and the American Civil Liberties Union creates a Web site telling the public to vote for a Presidential candidate in light of that candidate's defense of free speech. These prohibitions are classic examples of censorship.

Section 441b is a ban on corporate speech notwithstanding the fact that a PAC created by a corporation can still speak. A PAC is a separate association from the corporation. So the PAC exemption from § 441b's expenditure ban, § 441b(b)(2), does not allow corporations to speak. Even if a PAC could somehow allow a corporation to speak — and it does not — the option to form PACs does not alleviate the First Amendment problems with § 441b. PACs are burdensome alternatives; they are expensive to administer and subject to extensive regulations. For example, every PAC must appoint a treasurer, forward donations to the treasurer promptly, keep detailed records of the identities of the persons making donations, preserve receipts for three years, and file an organization statement and report changes to this information within 10 days.

* * *

Section 441b's prohibition on corporate independent expenditures is thus a ban on speech. As a "restriction on the amount of money a person or group can spend on political communication during a campaign," that statute "necessarily reduces the quantity of expression by restricting the number of issues discussed, the depth of their exploration, and the size of the audience reached." Were the Court to uphold these restrictions, the Government could repress speech by silencing certain voices at any of the various points in the speech process. If § 441b applied to individuals, no one would believe that it is merely a time, place, or manner restriction on speech. Its purpose and effect are to silence entities whose voices the Government deems to be suspect.

Speech is an essential mechanism of democracy, for it is the means to hold officials accountable to the people. The right of citizens to inquire, to hear, to speak, and to use information to reach consensus is a precondition to enlightened self-government and a necessary means to protect it. The First Amendment " 'has its fullest and most urgent application' to speech uttered during a campaign for political office."

For these reasons, political speech must prevail against laws that would suppress it, whether by design or inadvertence. Laws that burden political speech are "subject to strict scrutiny," which requires the Government to prove that the restriction "furthers a compelling interest and is narrowly tailored to achieve that interest." While it might be maintained that political speech simply cannot be banned or restricted as a categorical matter, the quoted language from *WRTL* provides a sufficient framework for protecting the relevant First Amendment interests in this case. We shall employ it here.

Premised on mistrust of governmental power, the First Amendment stands against attempts to disfavor certain subjects or viewpoints. Prohibited, too, are restrictions distinguishing among different speakers, allowing speech by some but not others. As instruments to censor, these categories are interrelated:

Speech restrictions based on the identity of the speaker are all too often simply a means to control content.

Quite apart from the purpose or effect of regulating content, moreover, the Government may commit a constitutional wrong when by law it identifies certain preferred speakers. By taking the right to speak from some and giving it to others, the Government deprives the disadvantaged person or class of the right to use speech to strive to establish worth, standing, and respect for the speaker's voice. The Government may not by these means deprive the public of the right and privilege to determine for itself what speech and speakers are worthy of consideration. The First Amendment protects speech and speaker, and the ideas that flow from each.

The Court has upheld a narrow class of speech restrictions that operate to the disadvantage of certain persons, but these rulings were based on an interest in allowing governmental entities to perform their functions. The corporate independent expenditures at issue in this case, however, would not interfere with governmental functions, so these cases are inapposite. These precedents stand only for the proposition that there are certain governmental functions that cannot operate without some restrictions on particular kinds of speech. By contrast, it is inherent in the nature of the political process that voters must be free to obtain information from diverse sources in order to determine how to cast their votes. At least before *Austin*, the Court had not allowed the exclusion of a class of speakers from the general public dialogue.

We find no basis for the proposition that, in the context of political speech, the Government may impose restrictions on certain disfavored speakers. Both history and logic lead us to this conclusion.

A

1

The Court has recognized that First Amendment protection extends to corporations. *Bellotti* (citing *Linmark Associates, Inc. v. Willingboro*; *Time, Inc. v. Firestone*; *Doran v. Salem Inn, Inc.*; *Southeastern Promotions, Ltd. v. Conrad*; *Cox Broadcasting Corp. v. Cohn*; *Miami Herald Publishing Co. v. Tornillo*; *New York Times Co. v. United States*; *Time, Inc. v. Hill*; *New York Times Co. v. Sullivan*; *Kingsley Int'l Pictures Corp. v. Regents of Univ. of N. Y.*; *Joseph Burstyn, Inc. v. Wilson*); see, e.g., *Turner Broadcasting System, Inc. v. FCC*; *Denver Area Ed. Telecommunications Consortium, Inc. v. FCC*; *Turner*; *Simon & Schuster*; *Sable Communications of Cal., Inc. v. FCC*; *Florida Star v. B.J. F.*; *Philadelphia Newspapers, Inc. v. Hepps*; *Landmark Communications, Inc. v. Virginia*; *Young v. American Mini Theatres, Inc.*; *Gertz v. Robert Welch, Inc.*; *Greenbelt Cooperative Publishing Assn., Inc. v. Bresler*.

This protection has been extended by explicit holdings to the context of political speech. Under the rationale of these precedents, political speech does not lose First Amendment protection "simply because its source is a corporation." The Court has thus rejected the argument that political speech of corporations or other associations should be treated differently under the First Amendment simply because such associations are not "natural persons."

At least since the latter part of the 19th century, the laws of some States and of the United States imposed a ban on corporate direct contributions to candidates. Yet not until 1947 did Congress first prohibit independent expenditures by corporations and labor unions in § 304 of the Labor Management Relations Act. In passing this Act Congress overrode the veto of President Truman, who warned that the expenditure ban was a "dangerous intrusion on free speech."

For almost three decades thereafter, the Court did not reach the question whether restrictions on corporate and union expenditures are constitutional. The question was in the background of *United States v. CIO.* There, a labor union endorsed a congressional candidate in its weekly periodical. The Court stated that "the gravest doubt would arise in our minds as to [the federal expenditure prohibition's] constitutionality" if it were construed to suppress that writing. The Court engaged in statutory interpretation and found the statute did not cover the publication. Four Justices, however, said they would reach the constitutional question and invalidate the Labor Management Relations Act's expenditure ban. The concurrence explained that any " 'undue influence' " generated by a speaker's "large expenditures" was outweighed "by the loss for democratic processes resulting from the restrictions upon free and full public discussion."

In *United States v. Automobile Workers*, the Court again encountered the independent expenditure ban, which had been recodified at 18 U.S.C. § 610 (1952 ed.). After holding only that a union television broadcast that endorsed candidates was covered by the statute, the Court "[r]efus[ed] to anticipate constitutional questions" and remanded for the trial to proceed. Three Justices dissented, arguing that the Court should have reached the constitutional question and that the ban on independent expenditures was unconstitutional:

> "Under our Constitution it is We The People who are sovereign. The people have the final say. The legislators are their spokesmen. The people determine through their votes the destiny of the nation. It is therefore important — vitally important — that all channels of communications be open to them during every election, that no point of view be restrained or barred, and that the people have access to the views of every group in the community."

The dissent concluded that deeming a particular group "too powerful" was not a "justificatio[n] for withholding First Amendment rights from any group —

labor or corporate." The Court did not get another opportunity to consider the constitutional question in that case; for after a remand, a jury found the defendants not guilty.

Later, in *Pipefitters v. United States*, the Court reversed a conviction for expenditure of union funds for political speech — again without reaching the constitutional question. The Court would not resolve that question for another four years.

2

In *Buckley*, the Court addressed various challenges to the Federal Election Campaign Act of 1971 (FECA) as amended in 1974. These amendments created 18 U.S.C. § 608(e), an independent expenditure ban separate from § 610 that applied to individuals as well as corporations and labor unions.

Before addressing the constitutionality of § 608(e)'s independent expenditure ban, *Buckley* first upheld § 608(b), FECA's limits on direct contributions to candidates. The *Buckley* Court recognized a "sufficiently important" governmental interest in "the prevention of corruption and the appearance of corruption." This followed from the Court's concern that large contributions could be given "to secure a political *quid pro quo*."

The *Buckley* Court explained that the potential for *quid pro quo* corruption distinguished direct contributions to candidates from independent expenditures. The Court emphasized that "the independent expenditure ceiling . . . fails to serve any substantial governmental interest in stemming the reality or appearance of corruption in the electoral process," because "[t]he absence of prearrangement and coordination . . . alleviates the danger that expenditures will be given as a *quid pro quo* for improper commitments from the candidate." *Buckley* invalidated § 608(e)'s restrictions on independent expenditures, with only one Justice dissenting.

Buckley did not consider § 610's separate ban on corporate and union independent expenditures, the prohibition that had also been in the background in *CIO*, *Automobile Workers*, and *Pipefitters*. Had § 610 been challenged in the wake of *Buckley*, however, it could not have been squared with the reasoning and analysis of that precedent. The expenditure ban invalidated in *Buckley*, § 608(e), applied to corporations and unions; and some of the prevailing plaintiffs in *Buckley* were corporations. The *Buckley* Court did not invoke the First Amendment's overbreadth doctrine to suggest that § 608(e)'s expenditure ban would have been constitutional if it had applied only to corporations and not to individuals. *Buckley* cited with approval the *Automobile Workers* dissent, which argued that § 610 was unconstitutional.

Notwithstanding this precedent, Congress recodified § 610's corporate and union expenditure ban at 2 U.S.C. § 441b four months after *Buckley* was decided.

Section 441b is the independent expenditure restriction challenged here.

Less than two years after *Buckley*, *Bellotti* reaffirmed the First Amendment principle that the Government cannot restrict political speech based on the speaker's corporate identity. *Bellotti* could not have been clearer when it struck down a state-law prohibition on corporate independent expenditures related to referenda issues:

> We thus find no support in the First . . . Amendment, or in the decisions of this Court, for the proposition that speech that otherwise would be within the protection of the First Amendment loses that protection simply because its source is a corporation that cannot prove, to the satisfaction of a court, a material effect on its business or property. . . . [That proposition] amounts to an impermissible legislative prohibition of speech based on the identity of the interests that spokesmen may represent in public debate over controversial issues and a requirement that the speaker have a sufficiently great interest in the subject to justify communication.

* * *

> In the realm of protected speech, the legislature is constitutionally disqualified from dictating the subjects about which persons may speak and the speakers who may address a public issue.

It is important to note that the reasoning and holding of *Bellotti* did not rest on the existence of a viewpoint-discriminatory statute. It rested on the principle that the Government lacks the power to ban corporations from speaking.

Bellotti did not address the constitutionality of the State's ban on corporate independent expenditures to support candidates. In our view, however, that restriction would have been unconstitutional under *Bellotti* 's central principle: that the First Amendment does not allow political speech restrictions based on a speaker's corporate identity.

3

Thus the law stood until *Austin*. *Austin* "uph[eld] a direct restriction on the independent expenditure of funds for political speech for the first time in [this Court's] history." There, the Michigan Chamber of Commerce sought to use general treasury funds to run a newspaper ad supporting a specific candidate. Michigan law, however, prohibited corporate independent expenditures that supported or opposed any candidate for state office. A violation of the law was punishable as a felony. The Court sustained the speech prohibition.

To bypass *Buckley* and *Bellotti*, the *Austin* Court identified a new governmental interest in limiting political speech: an antidistortion interest. *Austin* found a compelling governmental interest in preventing "the corrosive and distorting effects of immense aggregations of wealth that are accumulated with the help of the corporate form and that have little or no correlation to the public's support for the corporation's political ideas."

B

The Court is thus confronted with conflicting lines of precedent: a pre-*Austin* line that forbids restrictions on political speech based on the speaker's corporate identity and a post-*Austin* line that permits them. No case before *Austin* had held that Congress could prohibit independent expenditures for political speech based on the speaker's corporate identity. Before *Austin* Congress had enacted legislation for this purpose, and the Government urged the same proposition before this Court.

In its defense of the corporate-speech restrictions in § 441b, the Government notes the antidistortion rationale on which *Austin* and its progeny rest in part, yet it all but abandons reliance upon it. It argues instead that two other compelling interests support *Austin*'s holding that corporate expenditure restrictions are constitutional: an anticorruption interest, and a shareholder-protection interest. We consider the three points in turn.

1

As for *Austin*'s antidistortion rationale, the Government does little to defend it. And with good reason, for the rationale cannot support § 441b.

If the First Amendment has any force, it prohibits Congress from fining or jailing citizens, or associations of citizens, for simply engaging in political speech. If the antidistortion rationale were to be accepted, however, it would permit Government to ban political speech simply because the speaker is an association that has taken on the corporate form. The Government contends that *Austin* permits it to ban corporate expenditures for almost all forms of communication stemming from a corporation. If *Austin* were correct, the Government could prohibit a corporation from expressing political views in media beyond those presented here, such as by printing books. The Government responds "that the FEC has never applied this statute to a book," and if it did, "there would be quite [a] good as-applied challenge." This troubling assertion of brooding governmental power cannot be reconciled with the confidence and stability in civic discourse that the First Amendment must secure.

Political speech is "indispensable to decisionmaking in a democracy, and this is no less true because the speech comes from a corporation rather than an individual." This protection for speech is inconsistent with *Austin* 's antidistortion rationale. *Austin* sought to defend the antidistortion rationale as a means to prevent corporations from obtaining " 'an unfair advantage in the political marketplace' " by using " 'resources amassed in the economic marketplace.' " But *Buckley* rejected the premise that the Government has an interest "in equalizing the relative ability of individuals and groups to influence the outcome of elections." *Buckley* was specific in stating that "the skyrocketing cost of political campaigns" could not sustain the governmental prohibition. The First Amendment's protections do not depend on the speaker's "financial ability to engage in public discussion."

* * *

Austin interferes with the "open marketplace" of ideas protected by the First Amendment. It permits the Government to ban the political speech of millions of associations of citizens. Most of these are small corporations without large amounts of wealth. This fact belies the Government's argument that the statute is justified on the ground that it prevents the "distorting effects of immense aggregations of wealth." It is not even aimed at amassed wealth.

The censorship we now confront is vast in its reach. The Government has "muffle[d] the voices that best represent the most significant segments of the economy." And "the electorate [has been] deprived of information, knowledge and opinion vital to its function." By suppressing the speech of manifold corporations, both for-profit and nonprofit, the Government prevents their voices and viewpoints from reaching the public and advising voters on which persons or entities are hostile to their interests. Factions will necessarily form in our Republic, but the remedy of "destroying the liberty" of some factions is "worse than the disease." Factions should be checked by permitting them all to speak, and by entrusting the people to judge what is true and what is false.

The purpose and effect of this law is to prevent corporations, including small and nonprofit corporations, from presenting both facts and opinions to the public. This makes *Austin*'s antidistortion rationale all the more an aberration. "[T]he First Amendment protects the right of corporations to petition legislative and administrative bodies." Corporate executives and employees counsel Members of Congress and Presidential administrations on many issues, as a matter of routine and often in private. An *amici* brief filed on behalf of Montana and 25 other States notes that lobbying and corporate communications with elected officials occur on a regular basis. When that phenomenon is coupled with § 441b, the result is that smaller or nonprofit corporations cannot raise a voice to object when other corporations, including those with vast wealth, are cooperating with the Government. That cooperation may sometimes be voluntary, or it may be at the demand of a Government official who uses his or her authority, influence, and power to threaten corporations to support the Government's policies. Those kinds of interactions are often unknown and unseen. The speech that § 441b forbids, though, is public, and all can judge its content and purpose. References to massive corporate treasuries should not mask the real operation of this law. Rhetoric ought not obscure reality.

Even if § 441b's expenditure ban were constitutional, wealthy corporations could still lobby elected officials, although smaller corporations may not have the resources to do so. And wealthy individuals and unincorporated associations can spend unlimited amounts on independent expenditures. Yet certain disfavored associations of citizens — those that have taken on the corporate form — are penalized for engaging in the same political speech.

When Government seeks to use its full power, including the criminal law, to command where a person may get his or her information or what distrusted source he or she may not hear, it uses censorship to control thought. This is unlawful. The First Amendment confirms the freedom to think for ourselves.

2

What we have said also shows the invalidity of other arguments made by the Government. For the most part relinquishing the antidistortion rationale, the Government falls back on the argument that corporate political speech can be banned in order to prevent corruption or its appearance. In *Buckley*, the Court found this interest "sufficiently important" to allow limits on contributions but did not extend that reasoning to expenditure limits. When *Buckley* examined an expenditure ban, it found "that the governmental interest in preventing corruption and the appearance of corruption [was] inadequate to justify [the ban] on independent expenditures."

* * *

When *Buckley* identified a sufficiently important governmental interest in preventing corruption or the appearance of corruption, that interest was limited to *quid pro quo* corruption. The fact that speakers may have influence over or access to elected officials does not mean that these officials are corrupt:

> "Favoritism and influence are not . . . avoidable in representative politics. It is in the nature of an elected representative to favor certain policies, and, by necessary corollary, to favor the voters and contributors who support those policies. It is well understood that a substantial and legitimate reason, if not the only reason, to cast a vote for, or to make a contribution to, one candidate over another is that the candidate will respond by producing those political outcomes the supporter favors. Democracy is premised on responsiveness."

Reliance on a "generic favoritism or influence theory . . . is at odds with standard First Amendment analyses because it is unbounded and susceptible to no limiting principle."

The appearance of influence or access, furthermore, will not cause the electorate to lose faith in our democracy. By definition, an independent expenditure is political speech presented to the electorate that is not coordinated with a candidate. The fact that a corporation, or any other speaker, is willing to spend money to try to persuade voters presupposes that the people have the ultimate influence over elected officials. This is inconsistent with any suggestion that the electorate will refuse " 'to take part in democratic governance' " because of additional political speech made by a corporation or any other speaker.

* * *

3

The Government contends further that corporate independent expenditures can be limited because of its interest in protecting dissenting shareholders from being compelled to fund corporate political speech. This asserted interest, like *Austin*'s antidistortion rationale, would allow the Government to ban the political speech even of media corporations. Assume, for example, that a shareholder of a corporation that owns a newspaper disagrees with the political views the newspaper expresses. Under the Government's view, that potential disagreement could give the Government the authority to restrict the media corporation's political speech. The First Amendment does not allow that power. There is, furthermore, little evidence of abuse that cannot be corrected by shareholders "through the procedures of corporate democracy."

Those reasons are sufficient to reject this shareholder-protection interest; and, moreover, the statute is both underinclusive and overinclusive. As to the first, if Congress had been seeking to protect dissenting shareholders, it would not have banned corporate speech in only certain media within 30 or 60 days before an election. A dissenting shareholder's interests would be implicated by speech in any media at any time. As to the second, the statute is overinclusive because it covers all corporations, including nonprofit corporations and for-profit corporations with only single shareholders. As to other corporations, the remedy is not to restrict speech but to consider and explore other regulatory mechanisms. The regulatory mechanism here, based on speech, contravenes the First Amendment.

* * *

C

Our precedent is to be respected unless the most convincing of reasons demonstrates that adherence to it puts us on a course that is sure error. "Beyond workability, the relevant factors in deciding whether to adhere to the principle of *stare decisis* include the antiquity of the precedent, the reliance interests at stake, and of course whether the decision was well reasoned."

These considerations counsel in favor of rejecting *Austin*, which itself contravened this Court's earlier precedents in *Buckley* and *Bellotti*. "This Court has not hesitated to overrule decisions offensive to the First Amendment." "*[S]tare decisis* is a principle of policy and not a mechanical formula of adherence to the latest decision."

For the reasons above, it must be concluded that *Austin* was not well reasoned. The Government defends *Austin*, relying almost entirely on "the quid pro quo interest, the corruption interest or the shareholder interest," and not *Austin*'s expressed antidistortion rationale. When neither party defends the reasoning of a precedent, the principle of adhering to that precedent through *stare decisis* is diminished. *Austin* abandoned First Amendment principles, furthermore, by relying on language in some of our precedents that traces back to the *Automobile Workers* Court's flawed historical account of campaign finance laws.

Austin is undermined by experience since its announcement. Political speech is so ingrained in our culture that speakers find ways to circumvent campaign finance laws. Our Nation's speech dynamic is changing, and informative voices should not have to circumvent onerous restrictions to exercise their First Amendment rights. Speakers have become adept at presenting citizens with sound bites, talking points, and scripted messages that dominate the 24-hour news cycle. Corporations, like individuals, do not have monolithic views. On certain topics corporations may possess valuable expertise, leaving them the best equipped to point out errors or fallacies in speech of all sorts, including the speech of candidates and elected officials.

Rapid changes in technology — and the creative dynamic inherent in the concept of free expression — counsel against upholding a law that restricts political speech in certain media or by certain speakers. Today, 30-second television ads may be the most effective way to convey a political message. Soon, however, it may be that Internet sources, such as blogs and social networking Web sites, will provide citizens with significant information about political candidates and issues. Yet, § 441b would seem to ban a blog post expressly advocating the election or defeat of a candidate if that blog were created with corporate funds. The First Amendment does not permit Congress to make these categorical distinctions based on the corporate identity of the speaker and the content of the political speech.

No serious reliance interests are at stake. As the Court stated in *Payne v. Tennessee*, reliance interests are important considerations in property and contract cases, where parties may have acted in conformance with existing legal rules in order to conduct transactions. Here, though, parties have been prevented from acting — corporations have been banned from making independent expenditures. Legislatures may have enacted bans on corporate expenditures believing that those bans were constitutional. This is not a compelling interest for *stare decisis*. If it were, legislative acts could prevent us from overruling our own precedents, thereby interfering with our duty "to say what the law is."

Due consideration leads to this conclusion: *Austin* should be and now is overruled. We return to the principle established in *Buckley* and *Bellotti* that the Government may not suppress political speech on the basis of the speaker's corporate identity. No sufficient governmental interest justifies limits on the political speech of nonprofit or for-profit corporations.

D

Austin is overruled, so it provides no basis for allowing the Government to limit corporate independent expenditures. As the Government appears to concede, overruling *Austin* "effectively invalidate[s] not only BCRA Section 203, but also 2 U.S.C. 441b's prohibition on the use of corporate treasury funds for express advocacy." Section 441b's restrictions on corporate independent expenditures are therefore invalid and cannot be applied to *Hillary*.

Given our conclusion we are further required to overrule the part of *McConnell* that upheld BCRA § 203's extension of § 441b's restrictions on corporate independent expenditures. The *McConnell* Court relied on the antidistortion interest recognized in *Austin* to uphold a greater restriction on speech than the restriction upheld in *Austin*, and we have found this interest unconvincing and insufficient. This part of *McConnell* is now overruled.

Chief Justice ROBERTS, with whom Justice ALITO joins, concurring.

* * *

This is the first case in which we have been asked to overrule *Austin*, and thus it is also the first in which we have had reason to consider how much weight to give *stare decisis* in assessing its continued validity. The dissent erroneously declares that the Court "reaffirmed" *Austin*'s holding in subsequent cases — namely, *Federal Election Comm'n v. Beaumon*; *McConnell*; and *WRTL*. Not so. Not a single party in any of those cases asked us to overrule *Austin*, and as the dissent points out, the Court generally does not consider constitutional arguments that have not properly been raised. *Austin*'s validity was therefore not directly at issue in the cases the dissent cites. The Court's unwillingness to overturn *Austin* in those cases cannot be understood as a *reaffirmation* of that decision.

A

Fidelity to precedent — the policy of *stare decisis* — is vital to the proper exercise of the judicial function. "*Stare decisis* is the preferred course because it promotes the evenhanded, predictable, and consistent development of legal principles, fosters reliance on judicial decisions, and contributes to the actual and perceived integrity of the judicial process." For these reasons, we have long recognized that departures from precedent are inappropriate in the absence of a "special justification."

At the same time, *stare decisis* is neither an "inexorable command," nor "a mechanical formula of adherence to the latest decision," especially in constitutional cases. If it were, segregation would be legal, minimum wage laws would be unconstitutional, and the Government could wiretap ordinary criminal suspects without first obtaining warrants. As the dissent properly notes, none of us has viewed *stare decisis* in such absolute terms.

Stare decisis is instead a "principle of policy." When considering whether to reexamine a prior erroneous holding, we must balance the importance of having constitutional questions *decided* against the importance of having them *decided right*. As Justice Jackson explained, this requires a "sober appraisal of the disadvantages of the innovation as well as those of the questioned case, a weighing of practical effects of one against the other."

In conducting this balancing, we must keep in mind that *stare decisis* is not an end in itself. It is instead "the means by which we ensure that the law will not merely change erratically, but will develop in a principled and intelligible fashion." Its greatest purpose is to serve a constitutional ideal — the rule of law. It follows that in the unusual circumstance when fidelity to any particular precedent does more to damage this constitutional ideal than to advance it, we must be more willing to depart from that precedent.

Thus, for example, if the precedent under consideration itself departed from the Court's jurisprudence, returning to the " 'intrinsically sounder' doctrine established in prior cases" may "better serv[e] the values of *stare decisis* than would following [the] more recently decided case inconsistent with the decisions that came before it." Abrogating the errant precedent, rather than reaffirming or extending it, might better preserve the law's coherence and curtail the precedent's disruptive effects.

Likewise, if adherence to a precedent actually impedes the stable and orderly adjudication of future cases, its *stare decisis* effect is also diminished. This can happen in a number of circumstances, such as when the precedent's validity is so hotly contested that it cannot reliably function as a basis for decision in future cases, when its rationale threatens to upend our settled jurisprudence in related areas of law, and when the precedent's underlying reasoning has become so discredited that the Court cannot keep the precedent alive without jury-rigging new and different justifications to shore up the original mistake.

Justice STEVENS, with whom Justice GINSBURG, Justice BREYER, and Justice SOTOMAYOR join, concurring in part and dissenting in part.

* * *

The final principle of judicial process that the majority violates is the most transparent: *stare decisis*. I am not an absolutist when it comes to *stare decisis*, in the campaign finance area or in any other. No one is. But if this principle is to do any meaningful work in supporting the rule of law, it must at least demand a significant justification, beyond the preferences of five Justices, for overturning settled doctrine. "[A] decision to overrule should rest on some special reason over and above the belief that a prior case was wrongly decided." No such justification exists in this case, and to the contrary there are powerful prudential reasons to keep faith with our precedents.

The Court's central argument for why *stare decisis* ought to be trumped is that it does not like *Austin*. The opinion "was not well reasoned," our colleagues assert, and it conflicts with First Amendment principles. This, of course, is the Court's merits argument, the many defects in which we will soon consider. I am perfectly willing to concede that if one of our precedents were dead wrong in its reasoning or irreconcilable with the rest of our doctrine, there would be a compelling basis for revisiting it. But neither is true of *Austin*, and restating a merits argument with additional vigor does not give it extra weight in the *stare decisis* calculus.

Perhaps in recognition of this point, the Court supplements its merits case with a smattering of assertions. The Court proclaims that "*Austin* is undermined by experience since its announcement." This is a curious claim to make in a case that lacks a developed record. The majority has no empirical evidence with which to substantiate the claim; we just have its *ipse dixit* that the real world has not been kind to *Austin*. Nor does the majority bother to specify in what sense *Austin* has been "undermined." Instead it treats the reader to a string of non sequiturs: "Our Nation's speech dynamic is changing;" "[s]peakers have become adept at presenting citizens with sound bites, talking points, and scripted messages;" "[c]orporations . . . do not have monolithic views." How any of these ruminations weakens the force of *stare decisis*, escapes my comprehension.[18]

---

[18] THE CHIEF JUSTICE suggests that *Austin* has been undermined by subsequent dissenting opinions. Under this view, it appears that the more times the Court stands by a precedent in the face of requests to overrule it, the weaker that precedent becomes. THE CHIEF JUSTICE further suggests that *Austin* "is uniquely destabilizing because it threatens to subvert our Court's decisions even outside" its particular facts, as when we applied its reasoning in *McConnell*. Once again, the theory seems to be that the more we utilize a precedent, the more we call it into question. For those who believe *Austin* was correctly decided — as the Federal Government and the States have long

The majority also contends that the Government's hesitation to rely on *Austin*'s antidistortion rationale "diminishe[s]" "the principle of adhering to that precedent." Why it diminishes the value of *stare decisis* is left unexplained. We have never thought fit to overrule a precedent because a litigant has taken any particular tack. Nor should we. Our decisions can often be defended on multiple grounds, and a litigant may have strategic or case-specific reasons for emphasizing only a subset of them. Members of the public, moreover, often rely on our bottom-line holdings far more than our precise legal arguments; surely this is true for the legislatures that have been regulating corporate electioneering since *Austin*. The task of evaluating the continued viability of precedents falls to this Court, not to the parties.

Although the majority opinion spends several pages making these surprising arguments, it says almost nothing about the standard considerations we have used to determine *stare decisis* value, such as the antiquity of the precedent, the workability of its legal rule, and the reliance interests at stake. It is also conspicuously silent about *McConnell*, even though the *McConnell* Court's decision to uphold BCRA § 203 relied not only on the antidistortion logic of *Austin* but also on the statute's historical pedigree, and the need to preserve the integrity of federal campaigns.

We have recognized that "[s]tare decisis has special force when legislators or citizens 'have acted in reliance on a previous decision, for in this instance overruling the decision would dislodge settled rights and expectations or require an extensive legislative response.' " *Stare decisis* protects not only personal rights involving property or contract but also the ability of the elected branches to shape their laws in an effective and coherent fashion. Today's decision takes away a power that we have long permitted these branches to exercise. State legislatures have relied on their authority to regulate corporate electioneering, confirmed in *Austin*, for more than a century. The Federal Congress has relied on this authority for a comparable stretch of time, and it specifically relied on *Austin* throughout the years it spent developing and debating BCRA. The total record it compiled was *100,000 pages* long. Pulling out the rug beneath Congress after affirming the constitutionality of § 203 six years ago shows great disrespect for a coequal branch.

By removing one of its central components, today's ruling makes a hash out of BCRA's "delicate and interconnected regulatory scheme." Consider just one example of the distortions that will follow: Political parties are barred under BCRA from soliciting or spending "soft money," funds that are not subject to the statute's disclosure requirements or its source and amount limitations. Going

---

believed, as the majority of Justices to have served on the Court since *Austin* have believed, and as we continue to believe — there is nothing "destabilizing" about the prospect of its continued application. It is gutting campaign finance laws across the country, as the Court does today, that will be destabilizing.

forward, corporations and unions will be free to spend as much general treasury money as they wish on ads that support or attack specific candidates, whereas national parties will not be able to spend a dime of soft money on ads of any kind. The Court's ruling thus dramatically enhances the role of corporations and unions — and the narrow interests they represent — vis-à-vis the role of political parties — and the broad coalitions they represent — in determining who will hold public office.

Beyond the reliance interests at stake, the other *stare decisis* factors also cut against the Court. Considerations of antiquity are significant for similar reasons. *McConnell* is only six years old, but *Austin* has been on the books for two decades, and many of the statutes called into question by today's opinion have been on the books for a half-century or more. The Court points to no intervening change in circumstances that warrants revisiting *Austin*. Certainly nothing relevant has changed since we decided *WRTL* two Terms ago. And the Court gives no reason to think that *Austin* and *McConnell* are unworkable.

In fact, no one has argued to us that *Austin*'s rule has proved impracticable, and not a single for-profit corporation, union, or State has asked us to overrule it. Quite to the contrary, leading groups representing the business community, organized labor, and the nonprofit sector, together with more than half of the States, urge that we preserve *Austin*. As for *McConnell*, the portions of BCRA it upheld may be prolix, but all three branches of Government have worked to make § 203 as user-friendly as possible. For instance, Congress established a special mechanism for expedited review of constitutional challenges; the FEC has established a standardized process, with clearly defined safe harbors, for corporations to claim that a particular electioneering communication is permissible under *WRTL*; and, as noted above, THE CHIEF JUSTICE crafted his controlling opinion in *WRTL* with the express goal of maximizing clarity and administrability. The case for *stare decisis* may be bolstered, we have said, when subsequent rulings "have reduced the impact" of a precedent "while reaffirming the decision's core ruling."

In the end, the Court's rejection of *Austin* and *McConnell* comes down to nothing more than its disagreement with their results. Virtually every one of its arguments was made and rejected in those cases, and the majority opinion is essentially an amalgamation of resuscitated dissents. The only relevant thing that has changed since *Austin* and *McConnell* is the composition of this Court. Today's ruling thus strikes at the vitals of *stare decisis*, "the means by which we ensure that the law will not merely change erratically, but will develop in a principled and intelligible fashion" that "permits society to presume that bedrock principles are founded in the law rather than in the proclivities of individuals."

* * *

NOTES AND QUESTIONS

1. What is the structure of the majority's analysis in Part III of the opinion? What information does it provide before treating *Austin*, the case it is overruling?

2. For the populace, *stare decisis* ensures consistent and predictable application of the law. But what does the doctrine mean for the exercise of judicial power? Consider the U.S. Supreme Court's explanation in *Planned Parenthood v. Casey*, 505 U.S. 833, 865-68 (1992):

> The root of American governmental power is revealed most clearly in the instance of the power conferred by the Constitution upon the Judiciary of the United States and specifically upon this Court. As Americans of each succeeding generation are rightly told, the Court cannot buy support for its decisions by spending money and, except to a minor degree, it cannot independently coerce obedience to its decrees. The Court's power lies, rather, in its legitimacy, a product of substance and perception that shows itself in the people's acceptance of the Judiciary as fit to determine what the Nation's law means and to declare what it demands.

> The underlying substance of this legitimacy is of course the warrant for the Court's decisions in the Constitution and the lesser sources of legal principle on which the Court draws. That substance is expressed in the Court's opinions, and our contemporary understanding is such that a decision without principled justification would be no judicial act at all. But even when justification is furnished by apposite legal principle, something more is required. Because not every conscientious claim of principled justification will be accepted as such, the justification claimed must be beyond dispute. The Court must take care to speak and act in ways that allow people to accept its decisions on the terms the Court claims for them, as grounded truly in principle, not as compromises with social and political pressures having, as such, no bearing on the principled choices that the Court is obliged to make. Thus, the Court's legitimacy depends on making legally principled decisions under circumstances in which their principled character is sufficiently plausible to be accepted by the Nation.

> The need for principled action to be perceived as such is implicated to some degree whenever this, or any other appellate court, overrules a prior case. This is not to say, of course, that this Court cannot give a perfectly satisfactory explanation in most cases. People understand that some of the Constitution's language is hard to fathom and that the

Court's Justices are sometimes able to perceive significant facts or to understand principles of law that eluded their predecessors and that justify departures from existing decisions. However upsetting it may be to those most directly affected when one judicially derived rule replaces another, the country can accept some correction of error without necessarily questioning the legitimacy of the Court.

* * *

It is true that diminished legitimacy may be restored, but only slowly. Unlike the political branches, a Court thus weakened could not seek to regain its position with a new mandate from the voters, and even if the Court could somehow go to the polls, the loss of its principled character could not be retrieved by the casting of so many votes. Like the character of an individual, the legitimacy of the Court must be earned over time. So, indeed, must be the character of a Nation of people who aspire to live according to the rule of law. Their belief in themselves as such a people is not readily separable from their understanding of the Court invested with the authority to decide their constitutional cases and speak before all others for their constitutional ideals. If the Court's legitimacy should be undermined, then, so would the country be in its very ability to see itself through its constitutional ideals. The Court's concern with legitimacy is not for the sake of the Court, but for the sake of the Nation to which it is responsible.

3.   In *Planned Parenthood v. Casey*, 505 U.S. 833, 854 (1992), the Court explained:

> [W]hen this Court reexamines a prior holding, its judgment is customarily informed by a series of prudential and pragmatic considerations designed to test the consistency of overruling a prior decision with the ideal of the rule of law, and to gauge the respective costs of reaffirming and overruling a prior case. Thus, for example, we may ask whether the rule has proven to be intolerable simply in defying practical workability; whether the rule is subject to a kind of reliance that would lend a special hardship to the consequences of overruling and add inequity to the cost of repudiation; whether related principles of law have so far developed as to have left the old rule no more than a remnant of abandoned doctrine; or whether facts have so changed, or come to be seen so differently, as to have robbed the old rule of significant application or justification.

Three years later, the Court explained that when the precedent under scrutiny was recently decided, these considerations do not apply. *See Adarand Constructors, Inc. v. Pena*, 515 U.S. 200, 233-34 (1995). Why does the age of the precedent under scrutiny matter? How should a court determine if precedent is long-established and worthy of the jurisprudential concerns expressed in *Casey*?

4. Should individual judges feel bound by their votes in earlier cases? In other words, do you expect judges to adhere to a personal measure of *stare decisis*?

EXERCISE

Read *Adarand Constructors, Inc. v. Pena*, 515 U.S. 200 (1995). "Get physical" with the affirmative action precedent detailed in that case. For example, you might create a chart that lists the affirmative action cases discussed in *Adarand* and identifies the kind of action challenged (federal or state) and the level of scrutiny the Court applied (strict or intermediate), as follows:

Case Name	Challenged Action	Level of Scrutiny
Bakke		
Fullilove		
Wygant		
Croson		
Metro Broadcasting		
Adarand		

Having diagramed this precedent, are you satisfied with the Court's explanation for overruling *Metro Broadcasting*?

III. SUGGESTED FURTHER READING

Michael Gentithes, *In Defense of Stare Decisis*, 45 WILLAMETTE L. REV. 799 (2009).

Goutam U. Jois, *Stare Decisis Is Cognitive Error*, 75 BROOK. L. REV. 63 (2009).

Randy J. Kozel, *Stare Decisis As Judicial Doctrine*, 67 WASH. & LEE L. REV. 411 (2010).

Chapter 5

SCIENCE AND ART: DRAFTING APPELLATE OPINIONS

I. INTRODUCTION

You have already read countless appellate opinions. Until now, you likely read them to learn black letter law or to enhance your analytical skills. As you begin drafting appellate opinions for a judge's review, however, your attention will shift to the structure of the opinions you read. You will notice how judges begin their opinions, where they discuss the facts of the case, how they organize the analysis, and when they state the holding.

This chapter begins with a sample opinion and continues with strategies for drafting the four elements of an opinion. The chapter also includes often-asked questions and answers about the drafting process, as well as suggestions for improved writing. By the end of this chapter, you should understand that drafting an opinion is a deliberate act, built upon incremental choices about how to organize and express ideas. There is more than one "right way" to draft an opinion, and you will begin to identify your personal preferences for structure and style. Indeed, you probably recall opinions that you liked reading and those you did not. Use these examples to guide your own drafting.

Judge Ruggero Aldisert of the U.S. Court of Appeals, Third Circuit, has written widely about how judges should write opinions. Below is a sample opinion by Judge Aldisert. As you read it, focus on the organization of the ideas, rather than the substance of the ideas themselves. The bracketed questions throughout the opinion should help you do so.

JOHNSON v. TENNIS
549 F.3d 296 (3d. Cir. 2008)

ALDISERT, CIRCUIT JUDGE.

This appeal by Gary Johnson from the denial of his petition for habeas corpus by the District Court of the Eastern District of Pennsylvania requires us to decide an issue of first impression in this Circuit: Do the teachings of *Bruton v. United States*, 391 U.S. 123 (1968), apply to a bench trial in a criminal proceeding? *Bruton* and its progeny established that in a joint criminal trial before a jury, a defendant's Sixth Amendment right of confrontation is violated by admitting a confession of a non-testifying codefendant that implicates the defendant, regardless of any limiting instruction given to the jury. We hold that the *Bruton* rule is inapplicable to the incriminating confession of a non-testifying codefendant in a joint bench trial. By its own terms, *Bruton* applies to jury trials only. In so deciding we agree with every United States Court of Appeals that has considered the question. Because of this threshold determination, we easily dispose of Johnson's claims that he was denied the effective assistance of counsel under *Strickland v. Washington.*

[What information did you learn in the first paragraph?]

Our review is limited to those issues approved by this Court in issuing a Certificate of Appealability: (1) whether Johnson was denied the right to effective assistance of trial and appellate counsel where trial counsel failed to litigate a motion for severance under *Bruton* and appellate counsel failed to raise the severance issue on appeal; (2) whether Johnson was denied the right to effective assistance of trial counsel where trial counsel failed to move the trial judge to recuse himself; and (3) whether the Superior Court's determination of these issues was contrary to, or an unreasonable application of, United States Supreme Court precedent.

The merits of this habeas appeal are further circumscribed by the Antiterrorism and Effective Death Penalty Act of 1996 ("AEDPA"). When, as here, the legal claims of a petitioner in custody pursuant to a state court judgment have been adjudicated on the merits in state court proceedings, the "only question that matters" is whether the adjudication of the claims "resulted in a decision that was contrary to, or involved an unreasonable application of, clearly established federal law, as determined by the Supreme Court of the United States."

[What is the purpose of the preceding two paragraphs?]

I.

Because this appeal raises only questions of law, we set forth a brief description of the facts in the margin.[3] Appellant Gary Johnson and co-

---

[3] Appellant Gary Johnson and co-conspirator Shawn Davis arrived at the IPI Club, an after-hours nightclub, sometime around 2:00 a.m. on January 21, 1991. At approximately the same time, Alphonso Broadnax (the victim) and Antoine DeLoach also arrived at the club. Shortly thereafter, Johnson and DeLoach bumped into each other on the dance floor and exchanged words. Both Broadnax and Davis approached the altercation, but matters seemed to diffuse and the parties parted ways.

conspirator Shawn Davis were found guilty of second degree murder and criminal conspiracy after a bench trial in the Common Pleas Court of Philadelphia. Each gave conflicting statements to the police implicating the other. Davis sought to suppress his statement but the state trial judge, Judge Latrone, denied his motion. At the behest of Johnson's defense counsel, Judge Latrone did, however, order that the statement be redacted prior to presentation to the court by substituting an "X" in place of Johnson's name.

At the joint non-jury trial of both Johnson and Davis, also held before Judge Latrone, the statement was only admitted against Davis, not Johnson. The trial judge found Johnson guilty of murder in the second degree and of conspiracy. At trial, Johnson was represented by Bernard Turner. After attorney Turner withdrew his appearance, attorney Louis Savino entered his appearance and filed post-trial motions. These motions were denied and Johnson was sentenced on February 9, 1995, to life imprisonment for murder in the second degree and a concurrent term of one to two years for criminal conspiracy.

Following Johnson's conviction, Judge Latrone wrote an extensive opinion in which he addressed the *Bruton* issue raised by Johnson in post-trial motions, stating: "The primary reasoning behind the *Bruton* Court's decision was that there was a tremendous risk due to the practical and human limitations of a jury that it would or could not follow instructions to disregard the prejudicial statements of a codefedant at a joint trial." Judge Latrone explained that the teachings of *Bruton* could not be applied to Johnson's case because "this Court presided over a trial without a jury" and that "the risks inherent in the jury system of which the *Bruton* Court was so concerned would seemingly not exist when a judge is sitting as a trier of fact."

On appeal, the Superior Court of Pennsylvania in a memorandum disposition adopted the trial court's opinion "in its entirety and affirm[ed] on the basis of the opinion of the trial court." Similarly, on a subsequent appeal from the Common Pleas Court denying Johnson's petition for post-conviction relief, the Superior Court in a memorandum disposition adopted in full several pages of the post-conviction judge's opinion explaining that the teachings of *Bruton* could not apply because the stated rationale of the United States Supreme Court limited its application only to jury trials in criminal cases.

DeLoach and Broadnax subsequently decided to leave the club fearing trouble between the parties upon witnessing a separate altercation between Davis and another man. DeLoach stopped at the restroom as Broadnax headed towards DeLoach's vehicle, parked across the street from the IPI Club. At approximately the same time, witnesses Desiree Feaster, Sharon Johnson, Michele Green and Vernell Washington were entering Feaster's car, parked by the IPI Club. The witnesses observed Johnson and Davis in the same area. Washington additionally overheard a conversation between Johnson and Davis about wanting to get "the guy with the money."

As Johnson and Davis passed Feaster's vehicle, the witnesses observed Davis holding a gun as he headed in the direction of Broadnax, who was then about to enter DeLoach's vehicle. Davis shot the victim, Broadnax, five times.

[How are the facts organized? What is the topic of each paragraph in the fact section?]

II.

The *Bruton* rule is inapplicable to the incriminating confession of a non-testifying codefendant in a joint bench trial because *Bruton* applies solely to jury trials. In so deciding, we join the myriad Courts of Appeals that have recognized that the rule and rationale of *Bruton* do not apply to bench trials. *See, e.g., Castro* ("A jury may have difficulty in disregarding extrajudicial statements implicating a defendant. We will not presume that a judge suffers from the same disability. Indeed, the presumption is to the contrary."); *Cardenas* ("Nothing in *Bruton*, or in later Supreme Court cases discussing *Bruton*, suggests that in a bench trial a judge is incapable of disregarding inadmissible extrajudicial statements implicating a defendant."); *Rogers* ("To apply *Bruton* to bench trials would be to conclude that judges, like jurors, may well be incapable of separating evidence properly admitted against one defendant from evidence admitted against another."); *Faulisi* (*Bruton* "is simply inapplicable in the case of a bench trial."); *Cockrell* ("The *Bruton* rule does not apply to [petitioner] because she was tried by the court and not by a jury. Nothing in *Bruton* suggests that a judge is incapable of applying the law of limited admissibility which he has himself announced.").

We also join the *Cardenas* and *Rogers* courts in rejecting the notion that *Lee v. Illinois* expanded the *Bruton* doctrine to encompass bench trials. *Lee* dealt with whether a state trial judge's reliance upon a codefendant's incriminating pre-trial confession in a bench trial violates the right to confrontation, not, as in *Bruton*, whether the mere admission of such a confession is a violation. The Court accordingly observed that Lee was "not strictly speaking a *Bruton* case." *Bruton*, the Court explained, was based "on the fact that a confession that incriminates an accomplice is so . . . 'devastating' that the ordinarily sound assumption that a jury will be able to follow faithfully its instructions could not be applied." In contrast, in *Lee* the question was not whether the judge had been able to disregard the evidence, but whether the judge's actual use of the incriminating confession was permissible; the Court concluded that it was not.

The holding of *Lee* is thus distinguishable from, and does not expand the reach of, *Bruton*. "[A]bsent an *express* reliance by a trial judge on a non-testifying defendant's pre-trial confession — which facially implicates a co-defendant — in determining that co-defendant's guilt, we do not see how a Sixth Amendment confrontation issue can arise in a bench trial. No such express reliance exists in the instant case."

[What is the topic of section II? What is the topic of each paragraph in section II? How do the second and third paragraphs refine the first paragraph?]

III.

Because *Bruton* does not apply to a bench trial, Johnson cannot have been deprived of any constitutional right based on *Bruton*. Accordingly, trial counsel was not ineffective for failing to make a pretrial motion for severance after the redacted statement of Johnson's non-testifying codefendant was admitted into evidence, and the Pennsylvania Superior Court's adjudication of this issue was not contrary to, or an unreasonable determination of, Supreme Court precedent.

The Superior Court reasonably and correctly rejected the application of *Bruton* to Johnson's joint bench trial, therefore eliminating any argument that trial counsel should have moved for severance to avoid constitutional problems under *Bruton*. The Superior Court adopted in full the trial court opinion by Judge Latrone, which stated that "the risk of prejudice that comes with the admission of a non-testifying codefendant's confession at a joint trial is greatly reduced, if not eliminated, when the case is tried before a judge sitting without a jury." Judge Latrone explained that he disregarded the codefendant's statement in determining petitioner's guilt, and that the trial court "predicated its decision solely on the properly admitted statement of Johnson and the other directly relevant evidence presented by the Commonwealth" and "was unaffected by the statement of the codefendant which it knew was inadmissable against him."

We dismiss Johnson's contentions that severance would have eliminated the complaint that Davis's confession was not properly redacted and that the Superior Court acted contrary to established federal law by failing to address *Gray v. Maryland* in its affirmation of conviction. The Supreme Court in *Gray*, in a decision decided six months prior to the Superior Court's affirmation of Johnson's conviction, established that redactions in a *Bruton* case that replace a proper name with a symbol, or similarly signify to the jury the fact of redaction, are similar enough to unredacted confessions to violate the Confrontation Clause. The inapplicability of *Bruton* to bench trials, however, renders the question of whether Davis's statement was properly redacted under *Bruton* and *Gray* a nonissue.

It further is highly unlikely that the trial court would have granted a severance at petitioner's trial given the strong interest courts have in maintaining joint trials. Public interest in judicial economy favors joint trials where, as in Johnson's case, the same evidence would otherwise be presented at separate trials of defendants charged with a single conspiracy. Johnson nevertheless contends that "[i]f [his] trial attorney had requested a severance, and if the severance had been granted, there was a 'reasonable probability' the

Commonwealth would have dropped the charges against Johnson for lack of evidence. Otherwise, there was a 'reasonable probability' of an acquittal because the evidence against Johnson was practically nonexistent." This argument not only borders on, but is truly ridiculous. The Superior Court reasonably found that the evidence against Johnson was substantial, and the Superior Court's rejection of an ineffective assistance claim based on failure to move for severance pursuant to *Bruton* was reasonable under, and not contrary to, established federal law.

[What is the topic of section III? What is the topic of each paragraph in section III?]

IV.

It follows that Johnson's derivative claim of ineffective assistance of appellate counsel also fails. The Superior Court's adjudication of Johnson's claim that appellate counsel was ineffective for failing to contend on appeal that trial counsel was ineffective for failing to move for severance, cannot be considered contrary to, or an unreasonable determination of, Supreme Court precedent. The Supreme Court has repeatedly admonished that appellate counsel need not, and should not, raise every non-frivolous claim, but rather may select from them in order to maximize the likelihood of success on appeal. Indeed, an appellate lawyer's exercise of professional judgment in omitting weaker claims is obviously of benefit to the client: the more claims an appellate brief contains, the more difficult for an appellate judge to avoid suspecting that "there is no merit to any of them."

Here, there was minimal likelihood of success on an ineffective assistance claim based on trial counsel's failure to move for severance. It is far-fetched to contend that on direct appeal the state courts would have found that trial counsel was constitutionally ineffective for failing to move for severance under *Bruton*, a constitutional rule inapplicable to bench trials. Furthermore, the Superior Court determined on direct appeal that Johnson was not prejudiced by the trial judge's non-recusal (see *infra* Part V). As the Superior Court concluded on Johnson's post-conviction appeal, this determination is flatly inconsistent with Johnson's contention that, in the same appeal, the Superior Court would have held that Johnson was prejudiced by trial counsel's failure to seek severance as a result of the trial judges's same pre-trial exposure to Davis's statement. Given the weakness of Johnson's ineffective assistance of trial counsel claim, it would be difficult to consider appellate counsel unreasonably deficient for failing to raise it.

[What is the topic of section IV? What is the topic of each paragraph in section IV? What does the second paragraph add to this section?]

V.

Finally, Johnson was not denied the right to effective assistance of trial counsel where trial counsel failed to move the trial judge to recuse himself, and the Superior Court's determination of this claim was not contrary to, or an unreasonable application of, clearly established federal law.

Johnson's contention is based on the trial judge's participation in a suppression hearing prior to the joint bench trial. Prior to trial, Judge Latrone acknowledged before the parties and their counsel that he had been exposed to some evidence in Johnson's codefendant's pre-trial motion to suppress, but he indicated he did not remember exactly what that evidence was. After codefendant Davis's counsel reminded him that it was Davis's statement to the police that had been presented for suppression, Judge Latrone, in the presence of Johnson, provided Davis with a thorough explanation of his right to request the judge to recuse himself. Judge Latrone then received Davis's waiver of recusal. Then the judge stated directly to Johnson that in Johnson's case there should be no problem because he had been the pre-trial judge in Davis's case but not Johnson's case.

Given that Johnson heard the trial judge explain a defendant's right to request recusal and Johnson did not thereafter express concern to the trial court about proceeding to trial with the same judge who presided over that motion to suppress, it was reasonable for his counsel not to ask for recusal of the trial judge. Indeed, in an evidentiary hearing on Johnson's post-trial motions, his trial counsel stated that he strategically chose not to request recusal because he "felt that [Johnson's] best opportunity for a fair trial would have been with this judge who heard the evidence and was experienced to sift [through it] and give my client a fair trial." We grant great deference to counsel's choice of trial strategy.

Furthermore, even if a recusal motion had been made and granted, recusal of Judge Latrone would not have removed the evidence from the case: the same redacted statement would have been presented to any presiding judge. It thus would have been fruitless to make a motion for recusal in the hope that the new judge would somehow not hear the redacted statement that previously had been ruled admissible. Counsel cannot be found ineffective for failing to bring meritless motions.

For the foregoing reasons, the order of the United States District Court for the Eastern District of Pennsylvania denying Johnson's petition for writ of habeas corpus will be affirmed.

[What is the topic of section V? What is the topic of each paragraph in section V?]

NOTES AND QUESTIONS

1. According to Judge Aldisert, "[t]he purpose of a judicial opinion is to tell the participants in the lawsuit why the court acted the way it did." RUGGERO J. ALDISERT, OPINION WRITING 27 (AuthorHouse 2d ed. 2010). Did *Johnson v. Tennis* meet this purpose?

2. What is the holding of *Johnson*? What part of the opinion states the holding?

3. Other than the parties to an appeal, who else reads judicial opinions? What are those readers looking for in the opinions?

4. "Those who apply the rule to particular cases, must of necessity expound and interpret that rule." *Marbury v. Madison*, 5 U.S. 137, 177 (1803). Can appellate judges "expound and interpret" without issuing written opinions? Nearly all of the circuits in the federal system allow their appellate courts to issue opinions affirming a judgment without explanation, if certain conditions are met. The Eighth Circuit, for example, provides:

> A judgment or order appealed may be affirmed or enforced without opinion if the court determines an opinion would have no precedential value and any of the following circumstances disposes of the matter submitted to the court for decision:
>
> (1) a judgment of the district court is based on findings of fact that are not clearly erroneous;
>
> (2) the evidence in support of a jury verdict is not insufficient;
>
> (3) the order of an administrative agency is supported by substantial evidence on the record as a whole; or
>
> (4) no error of law appears.

8th Cir. R. 47B. Is summary disposition at the appellate level a good idea? Why do courts employ it?

5. What purpose does the written opinion serve for the judge who issues it? Would appellate judges reach different conclusions if they did not routinely read and write opinions?

II.   ELEMENTS OF AN APPELLATE OPINION

There are four elements to an appellate opinion. Because judges render decisions by applying law to fact, the two obvious elements are a *review of the facts* and a *legal analysis*. Moreover, it has become customary to include an *introductory paragraph* at the start of the opinion that previews what is to follow. And an appellate opinion ordinarily ends with a *mandate*, which states simply the outcome of the appeal. Each of these elements is discussed below.

A.   Introductory Paragraph

An introductory paragraph summarizes the essence of the appeal. It is most helpful for a reader who is not familiar with the case, but, even for the parties, it serves the noteworthy function of announcing up front who has prevailed on the appeal. Moreover, a well-conceived introductory paragraph signifies "that you will give your readers practical help without wasting their time." Stephen V. Armstrong & Timothy P. Terrell, Thinking Like a Writer: A Lawyer's Guide to Effective Writing and Editing 130 (2d ed., Practicing Law Institute 2003).

An introductory paragraph should articulate the legal issue(s) before the court and state the court's holding(s). It may also introduce the parties, briefly summarize the facts, or explain the order(s) or judgment(s) of lower courts that have weighed in on the controversy. Sometimes a summary of the appeal requires more than one paragraph. There is no harm in that, of course, as the point is to adequately introduce the case with clear language.

EXERCISE

Which of the elements described above are included in the following introductory paragraphs?

1.   *Holland v. Florida,* — U.S. —, 130 S. Ct. 2549 (2010).

We here decide that the timeliness provision in the federal habeas corpus statute is subject to equitable tolling. We also consider its application in this case. In the Court of Appeals' view, when a petitioner seeks to excuse a late filing on the basis of his attorney's unprofessional conduct, that conduct, even if it is "negligent" or "grossly negligent," cannot "rise to the level of egregious attorney misconduct" that would warrant equitable tolling unless the petitioner offers "proof of bad faith, dishonesty, divided loyalty, mental impairment or so forth." In our view, this standard is too rigid. We therefore reverse the judgment of the Court of Appeals and remand for further proceedings.

2.   *Carter v. Senate Masonry,* 846 A.2d 50 (Md. Ct. Spec. App. 2004).

This appeal concerns the legal doctrine of "last clear chance." Preston Carter accused an employee of Senate Masonry, Incorporated of negligently harming him at a construction site. A jury in the Circuit Court for Prince George's County accepted that accusation, but found Carter negligent as well. Nonetheless, it awarded Carter damages, with the apparent belief that the Senate employee had the last clear chance to avoid the injury, and his failure to do so warranted compensation for Carter. The trial court disagreed and granted Senate's post-trial motion for judgment notwithstanding the jury's verdict ("JNOV"). We disagree with the trial court and reinstate the jury's verdict.

3. *People v. Dreyden*, 931 N.E.2d 526 (N.Y. 2010).

On the evening of June 2, 2007, a police officer stopped a van on a street corner in Brooklyn for a traffic violation. The officer recovered a knife and a ziplock bag containing marihuana from defendant James Dreyden, who was a passenger in the vehicle. Defendant was charged in a misdemeanor complaint with unlawful possession of marihuana and criminal possession of a weapon in the fourth degree. He waived his right to prosecution by information and pleaded guilty to the weapon charge, in full satisfaction of the accusatory instrument, in exchange for a sentence of time served.

Defendant then appealed his conviction, arguing that the accusatory instrument was jurisdictionally defective. Defendant pointed out that the misdemeanor complaint included no non-conclusory allegations establishing the basis of the arresting officer's belief that defendant's knife was a gravity knife as defined in the statute — only a conclusory statement that the police officer had observed defendant in possession of a gravity knife and recovered one from him. The Appellate Term affirmed the judgment of conviction and sentence, holding that an accusatory instrument need not contain the statutory criteria for a gravity knife or state that the knife was operational, in order to satisfy jurisdictional requirements.

B.   Review of the Facts

The fact section is vital to an opinion. For litigants in the case, it reveals the court's intellectual focus on appeal. For readers of the opinion who are not the litigants, the fact section gives identity and meaning to the case. It summarizes the controversy for strangers and allows them to compare the case to other cases, thereby developing the common law. Indeed, attorneys could not analogize to precedent without knowing facts. The saying that "facts drive the law" captures this truth.

A review of the facts should include details of historical fact and procedural fact. Historical facts are the who, what, where, when, and how of the controversy. Strive for an interesting, even compelling, rendition of the historical facts. After all, you are composing a fresh piece of writing, rather than filling out an incident report. As with drafting an appellate brief, you should include all the material facts, though you may also want to include some facts that are not material, to make the review interesting. Procedural facts tell how the case made its way to the appellate bench. They include all the courts that have judged the controversy. Ordinarily, it is helpful to explain the lower court's decisions, as exemplified above, in *Johnson v. Tennis*. But sometimes, a discussion of the lower court's action is reserved for the analysis section, particularly if you intend to show why the reasoning of a lower court was or was not convincing.

Most often, appellate opinions include a complete review of the historical and procedural facts before tackling the legal issue(s) on appeal. *Johnson v. Tennis* follows this model. If, however, the case on appeal includes various, unrelated points of error, the author of the opinion may choose to discuss the facts and procedural history for each point of error separately, as each issue arises. The opinion of *Oesby v. State* in Chapter Three exemplifies this approach.

You gather the historical and procedural facts from the briefs and record. And you decide which of them to include based on the legal question at issue. Above, in *Johnson v. Tennis*, for example, the historical facts of the murder were not necessary to the question on appeal. The appellate court included those facts in a footnote and focused instead on the procedural history of the case. On the other hand, in *Knight v. Knight* in Chapter Three, the appellate court judged whether the trial court abused its discretion in fashioning a custody arrangement. This task required knowledge of the historical facts upon which the trial court exercised its discretion. Accordingly, the appellate court included many details of historical fact in its opinion. Knowing which factual details to include is a talent that develops with practice, as your research and analytical skills evolve.

A plea for sensitivity as you begin drafting factual reviews: Avoid gratuitous embarrassment of the litigants. Imagine, for example, that the case on appeal involves a conviction for sexual abuse. The better opinion would include only those details of the abuse that would be necessary to understand and make use of the opinion. A lesser opinion would reflexively include all details of the sexual abuse, simply because they were included in the briefs. Doing so would sensationalize the abuse and could cause unnecessary embarrassment to the real people in the case.

Writing a review of the facts for an appellate opinion is a creative process. It allows you to sift through multiple sources and craft a narrative that complements the legal discussion to follow. It is also a deliberate act that requires you to choose facts for inclusion, based on what the parties have presented in their briefs and what you have read in the record. No two people will draft the fact section the same way. Flex your story-telling muscle, but if your way differs from your judge's way, respect the judge's wishes.

NOTES AND QUESTIONS

1.   Imagine that the issue on appeal is whether the trial court had personal jurisdiction for a claim of age discrimination. Specifically, the employee lives in Scottsdale, Arizona, but tele-commuted to his job in San Francisco, California. He filed his claim of discrimination in Arizona. The employer argues that California, not Arizona, has personal jurisdiction. Would you expect the appellate court to include facts about where the alleged discrimination occurred and where the effects of the discrimination were felt? Should the court include details of the discrimination itself, even though the merits of the claim are not before it?

2.   Read the factual review of *Knight v. Knight* in Chapter Three. Do you agree with the way the court organized the historical facts? Would you have drafted the review differently?

3.   Consider the following quotation:

> Action with words is after all a form of action, in relation both to a cultural inheritance and to other people, and it is charged with ethical and political significance. The excellence of the opinion is not one of "mere style," but an excellence of thought, represented and enacted in language in such a way as to live in the minds of others.

James Boyd White, *What's an Opinion For?*, 62 U. CHI. L. REV. 1363, 1367 (1995).

C.   Legal Analysis

In professional kitchens, before cooks prepare a dish, they arrange all the ingredients and utensils in a *mise en place* ("everything in place"). This way, they can focus on the dish without scurrying to chop herbs or find the bowl for the food processor. You too, should prepare a *mise en place* before you begin drafting an analysis. Your *mise en place* will include the two objectives of a legal analysis, accuracy and clarity. Accuracy in research and thinking, like quality ingredients for a recipe, will produce a fine product. Similarly, clarity in your writing, like good kitchen tools, will convey your meaning fruitfully.

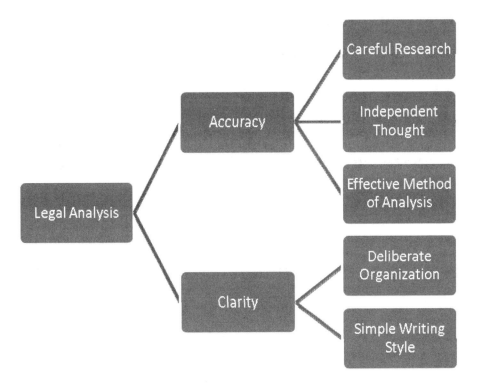

1.   Accuracy

The only way to reach accuracy in the analysis section is to research carefully and think independently. If you miss an important case in your research, accuracy is lost. It is also lost if you recite the legal analysis of the trial court without independent consideration. Chapter Three on the scope of appellate review and Chapter four on stare decisis discuss the process for thinking through a case. Another aspect of accuracy in analytical writing is choosing an effective means to prove your point. Legal arguments rely on at least one of the following methods of analysis: (1) applying a rule to a set of facts; (2) analogizing; (3) developing a rule from many sets of facts; and (4) espousing a sound policy or philosophy to support your conclusion. Consider the following examples of each method:

(1) *Applying a rule to a set of facts:* Imagine, for example, that the appeal concerns whether a federal district court issued a satisfactory scheduling order. You would likely begin your research with Federal Rule of Civil Procedure 16 (b)(3)(A), which provides that a scheduling order "must limit the time to join other parties, amend the pleadings, complete discovery, and file motions." You would then consider whether the scheduling order at issue met these requirements.

(2) *Analogizing:* Analogy involves a comparison of one set of facts to another set of facts. For example, in determining whether a ceramic knife constituted a "deadly weapon," you might compare its properties to the metallic pizza cutter that was the subject of an earlier appeal.

(3) *Developing a rule from many sets of facts:* Imagine, for instance, that you are working on a case of intentional infliction of emotional distress. Researching the precedent, you discern that courts consistently, though only implicitly, consider the relationship between plaintiff and defendant in determining how egregious the defendant's conduct was. Using inductive reasoning, you might state explicitly in your draft analysis that "relationship" is a factor for consideration. That opinion, once filed, would establish a rule that the relationship between plaintiff and defendant is a factor for consideration.

(4) *Espousing a sound policy or philosophy to support your conclusion:* Suppose a trial court sentenced a defendant to two terms of imprisonment for two separate crimes. The defendant argues on appeal that the sentences are ambiguous because the court did not state whether they should be served concurrently (at the same time) or consecutively (one after the other). In drafting the analysis, you might reference the rule of lenity, which is a policy that requires strict construction of criminal statutes to the benefit of the accused. This policy could lead to a conclusion that the sentences should be served concurrently.

You will find examples of these four methods in all the opinions you read, including the opinions in this book, and no doubt, you have been using these methods of analysis without recognizing it. As you begin drafting appellate opinions, however, attend to the methods that you use to prove your point, and, as you revise your drafts, consider whether a different method would be more effective. In other words, once again, flex your muscles of deliberation and discernment.

2.   Clarity

Clarity, the second objective in drafting an analysis, is achieved with a simple writing style. Appellate clerkships tend to attract people who like to write, because they offer so many opportunities to develop and perfect a writing style. Even if you clerk for a judge who writes all of his or her own opinions, you will be asked to compose other kinds of writing, such as bench memoranda. The judge will expect clean writing in all of these documents.

Good organization is likewise critical. Notice how the analysis in *Johnson v. Tennis* is divided; each Roman numeral corresponds to a specific topic. If your analysis is longer than two pages, consider adding subdivisions, either Roman numerals, as exemplified in *Johnson v. Tennis*, or topic headings, as exemplified in *Oesby v. State* in Chapter Three. Keep in mind, however that full-sentence sub-headings may hinder rather than help the opinion. Readers may ascribe too much meaning to the sub-heading, neglecting the text of the opinion that follows it.

As for the content of your analysis, there is more than one right way to organize your thoughts. Judges, after all, are not robots and their reasoning will not abide a scripted form. Nonetheless, at the start of your analysis, it has become customary to state the standard of review for the issue on appeal and then proceed to a logical discussion of the governing law. Notice how the courts accomplish this in *Whitson v. Stone County Jail*, *Ham v. State*, and *Oesby v. State* in chapter three. You may have noticed that in *Johnson v. Tennis*, the standard of review is not stated explicitly. What standard of review did the court apply implicitly?

The enduring precept for good organization is deliberation. After reading your draft, a judge should be able to outline your analysis, and identify the topic of each paragraph. You will likely find that you spend just as much time arranging your thoughts as actually writing them.

Of course, the mechanics of writing, including punctuation, sentence structure, and word choice, is fundamental to a well-drafted opinion. So is proper citation format. Chapter seven reinforces the importance of these elements. A draft riddled with typos will not hold a judge's attention for long, even if the analysis is dazzling.

NOTES AND QUESTIONS

1.   Which of the four methods of analysis did the court use in *Johnson v. Tennis*? Was there another method the court could have used?

2.   Psychologists Carl Bereiter and Marlene Scardamalia have identified two models for writing, "knowledge telling" and "knowledge transforming." *See* CARL BEREITER & MARLENE SCARDAMALIA, THE PSYCHOLOGY OF WRITTEN COMPOSITION 1987. For knowledge telling, the writer's goal is to transfer blocks of information from the writer to the reader. Knowledge transforming, on the other hand, allows the writer to "reprocess," or transform, the information that the writer conveys to the reader. For knowledge transforming, the writer asks "whether the text they have written says what they want it to say and whether they themselves believe what the text says." *Id.* at 11. Which model of writing do judges and law clerks use in the analysis section of an opinion? What would be the shortcoming of a draft opinion that evinced knowledge telling, but not knowledge transforming?

3.   Judge Patricia Wald described dicta as "excursions into the implications of a decision one way or the other, predictions on the nature and course of future cases, and even personal observations of the author." Patricia M. Wald, *Rhetoric and Results*, 62 U. CHI. L. REV. 1371, 1408 (1995). She suggested that "the more

'extras' an opinion contains, the more there is to take issue with and explain away in future opinions." *Id.* Do you agree?

4. Suppose the judge directed you to draft an opinion to affirm the trial court's judgment, but as you research and write the draft, you come to believe that reversal is in order. What would you do next?

5. Is humor acceptable in an appellate opinion? How about references to literature, sports, or other aspects of cultural life? Consider the opinion of *Denny v. Radar Indus., Inc.*, 184 N.W.2d 289 (Mich. Ct. App. 1970), which consists of three sentences:

> The appellant has attempted to distinguish the factual situation in this case from that in *Renfroe v. Higgins Rack Coating and Manufacturing Co., Inc.* (1969). He didn't. We couldn't.
>
> Affirmed. Costs to appellee.

Also, consider the introductory paragraph of *Gray v. State*, 456 A.2d 1290, 1291 (Md. Ct. Spec. App. 1983), as follows:

> In Paris at the height of the Reign of Terror, Sidney Carton visited a friend at the Bastille, where Charles Darnay awaited execution. Following a quick switch of clothing, Darnay was spirited from the Bastille, posing as the visiting Sidney Carton. In Baltimore on August 19, 1981, the appellant, Edward Gray, visited a friend at the Maryland Penitentiary, where Steven Lloyd Everett was serving a lengthy sentence. Following a quick switch into similar clothing, Everett walked out of the Maryland Penitentiary, posing as the visiting Edward Gray. For his role in the Paris escape, Sidney Carton received immortality at the hands of Charles Dickens. For his role in the Baltimore escape, Edward Gray received a five-year sentence at the hands of Judge Paul Dorf. Heroically, Sidney Carton accepted his fate with the words, "It is a far, far better thing I do than I have ever done." Less heroically, the appellant Gray has taken the present appeal.

D.   Mandate

The mandate is the final section of an appellate opinion. The first part of the mandate states in certain terms the judgment, or outcome of the appeal. Most of the time, appellate courts either affirm or reverse the lower court's judgment. An appellate court will remand if it wants the trial court to do something more, for example, to make specific findings of fact. It will vacate the judgment if it wants the trial court to try the case anew. Indeed, vacating is akin to erasing the judgment to create a clean slate.

The second part of a mandate is the assignment of costs, and ordinarily, the losing party will pay the costs of an appeal. The exact language of mandates differs among jurisdictions, as does the discretion provided appellate courts in assigning costs. Nonetheless, here are three examples of mandates:

1. Judgment affirmed; petitioner to pay costs.

2. Judgment vacated and remanded for further proceedings consistent with this opinion. Appellee to pay costs.

3. Judgment reversed with costs.

III.   NITTY-GRITTY QUESTIONS AND ANSWERS

Now that you have reviewed a sample structure for an opinion and considered the elements of an opinion generally, it is time to draft an appellate opinion of your own. Naturally, you will have many questions. Below are the answers to some of the more common questions that first-time opinion drafters often ask. These answers may differ from the rules or customs that have developed in your chambers. At the very least, though, the answers provide you with one perspective that you can discuss with the judge.

A.   *How should I refer to the parties in an appellate opinion?*

Provide each party's full name the first time you use it. Thereafter, refer to the party by last name. If it would be confusing to use the last name, for example, if the parties share a last name, you may use the parties' first names. But explain why you are using first names in a footnote. If a party's name is long, write it fully the first time you use it and indicate in parenthesis how you will refer to the party throughout the opinion, as follows:

> New York State United Teachers ("NYSUT") appeals the judgment of the New York City Supreme Court. NYSUT argues that the trial court erred in admitting hearsay testimony.

Avoid referring to the parties as appellant, appellee, petitioner, respondent, or other procedural designations because they detract from a flowing narrative. Also, sometimes it is difficult to remember to whom these designations correspond. Two pages into the opinion, for example, you do not want the reader asking if petitioner is the wife or the husband, or if appellant is the employer or the employee.

B.   *How should I refer to courts in an appellate opinion?*

When you are referring to a court that has rendered a decision in the case, for example, a trial court whose judgment is on appeal, give the full, proper name of the court the first time you mention it. After that, you may refer to the court simply as "the trial court" or "the lower court." When you are referring to precedent, you do not need to provide the proper name of the deciding court, although you may, if the court's identity is particularly important. For example, if you were discussing a case that the U.S. Supreme Court decided, you might write, "The Court held" or "The U.S. Supreme Court held"

Whether to capitalize the "c" in court is largely a matter of custom. Ordinarily, you should capitalize the letter whenever you are referring to your own court and any court in your jurisdiction that is of higher authority. Imagine, for example, that you are a law clerk for the Appellate Division of the Superior Court, which is the intermediate appellate court in New Jersey. In drafting an opinion, you would capitalize the "c" in court if you were referring to the Appellate Division of the Superior Court, the Supreme Court of New Jersey, and the U.S. Supreme Court. You would not capitalize the "c," however, if you were referring to one of the trial courts in New Jersey, a court in a sister state, or even a U.S. district or circuit court.

C.   Must I include all the facts provided in the briefs and the trial court's order?

The short answer is no. As this chapter has emphasized, drafting an appellate opinion is a deliberative act. Your purpose in drafting the opinion differs from what the litigants hoped to achieve in submitting their briefs. Naturally, the final appellate opinion will reflect these differences.

You should include the facts that are necessary to decide the appeal and those that help to tell the story of the case. You may also include some facts that are simply interesting. You may decide to organize the facts as the parties have done or to quote some of the content that they included in their briefs. You might also decide to organize the material differently or to briefly summarize content to which they devoted a lot of space. Let logic and the art of storytelling guide your decisions.

D.   Should I include citations in the fact section?

Ordinarily, the final version of an appellate opinion does not include citations in the review of the facts, although you might see a citation if the court quotes directly from a party's brief. When you are preparing a draft opinion, however, you should include citations to the record for the facts you include. This will assist the judge and your co-clerks in evaluating your draft. In many chambers, these citations will remain in the draft opinion until the opinion has been clerked and is ready for circulation among the other judges.

E.   *What verb tense should I use in the draft opinion?*

Ordinarily, historical and procedural facts are written in the past tense. This applies to contracts, wills, or other documents that are at issue, as well as any lower court orders or judgments. For example, you would write, "The contract provided" and "The trial court reasoned." When, however, you describe the parties' arguments on appeal, you may choose to use the past tense, "In her brief, appellant argued" or present tense, "Appellant argues on appeal." But as you move into the analysis section, use the past tense to explain the facts or holding of precedent, so for example, you would write, "The court held" not "The court holds."

F.   *Must I answer all the questions presented in the briefs?*

Appellate courts have the prerogative to resolve appeals as they deem appropriate, so they may not answer all of the questions presented in the parties' briefs. Sometimes, this is a matter of logic, as the resolution of one question may moot the other questions presented. For example, if an appellate court concluded that evidence at trial did not support a criminal conviction, it would not need to address whether the trial court also erred in admitting particular testimony; reversal of the conviction would moot the evidentiary concerns. At other times, the appellate court chooses to recast the questions presented or consolidate them. Intermediate appellate courts are less likely than the highest appellate courts to modify the questions presented.

Many judges maintain a custom of including appellant's questions presented verbatim, either as part of the introductory paragraph or at the beginning of the legal analysis. Other judges paraphrase the questions presented, but quote the actual questions in a footnote. And still other judges simply state the issue on appeal, without quoting from appellant's brief.

G.   *Should I address all the arguments that the parties raise?*

Here too, you have discretion. There is no requirement that you respond to every argument that the parties raise. Similarly, you need not address every case cited in the parties' briefs. Indeed, if you did so, reflexively, you would likely end up with a dull and unconvincing opinion. Instead, think through the issues independently and draft an opinion that satisfies the analytical needs of the issues on appeal. At the same time, the best way to tackle a complicated appeal is to break it down into bite-size parts. Usually, the parties will have done this for you by organizing their arguments in a certain way. Go ahead and follow their structure, if it is sensible.

H.   *What should I draft first, the factual review or the legal analysis?*

Begin with the task that is easier for you. Most people prefer to draft the factual review first, to focus their attention on the determinative facts. However, if the facts are complicated, but the governing law is straightforward, it will be easier to begin with a neat review of the governing rules. And no matter which section you draft first, the symbiotic relationship between fact and law will have you shuffling between the factual review and the legal analysis many times before the draft is complete.

IV.   THREE TECHNIQUES FOR IMPROVED WRITING

A.   Topic Sentences

As you begin writing the analysis, strive to include topic sentences for each paragraph. They are the hallmarks of a well-organized and compelling analysis. Below is an excerpt from Justice Brenan's dissent in *Deshaney v. Winnebago County Department of Social Services*, 489 U.S. 189, 208-10 (1989). Notice the topic sentences that begin each of his paragraphs: How would the analysis change if the topic sentences were not there?

> Wisconsin has established a child-welfare system specifically designed to help children like Joshua. Wisconsin law places upon the local departments of social services such as respondent (DSS or Department) a duty to investigate reported instances of child abuse. While other governmental bodies and private persons are largely responsible for the reporting of possible cases of child abuse, Wisconsin law channels all such reports to the local departments of social services for evaluation and, if necessary, further action. Even when it is the sheriff's office or police department that receives a report of suspected child abuse, that report is referred to local social services departments for action; the only exception to this occurs when the reporter fears for the child's *immediate* safety. In this way, Wisconsin law invites — indeed, directs — citizens and other governmental entities to depend on local departments of social services such as respondent to protect children from abuse.
>
> The specific facts before us bear out this view of Wisconsin's system of protecting children. Each time someone voiced a suspicion that Joshua was being abused, that information was relayed to the Department for investigation and possible action. When Randy DeShaney's second wife told the police that he had " 'hit the boy causing marks and [was] a prime case for child abuse,' " the police referred her complaint to DSS. When, on three separate occasions, emergency room personnel noticed suspicious injuries on Joshua's body, they went to DSS with this

information. When neighbors informed the police that they had seen or heard Joshua's father or his father's lover beating or otherwise abusing Joshua, the police brought these reports to the attention of DSS. And when respondent Kemmeter, through these reports and through her own observations in the course of nearly 20 visits to the DeShaney home, compiled growing evidence that Joshua was being abused, that information stayed within the Department — chronicled by the social worker in detail that seems almost eerie in light of her failure to act upon it. (As to the extent of the social worker's involvement in, and knowledge of, Joshua's predicament, her reaction to the news of Joshua's last and most devastating injuries is illuminating: " 'I just knew the phone would ring some day and Joshua would be dead.' "

Even more telling than these examples is the Department's control over the decision whether to take steps to protect a particular child from suspected abuse. While many different people contributed information and advice to this decision, it was up to the people at DSS to make the ultimate decision (subject to the approval of the local government's Corporation Counsel) whether to disturb the family's current arrangements. When Joshua first appeared at a local hospital with injuries signaling physical abuse, for example, it was DSS that made the decision to take him into temporary custody for the purpose of studying his situation — and it was DSS, acting in conjunction with the corporation counsel, that returned him to his father. Unfortunately for Joshua DeShaney, the buck effectively stopped with the Department.

In these circumstances, a private citizen, or even a person working in a government agency other than DSS, would doubtless feel that her job was done as soon as she had reported her suspicions of child abuse to DSS. Through its child-welfare program, in other words, the State of Wisconsin has relieved ordinary citizens and governmental bodies other than the Department of any sense of obligation to do anything more than report their suspicions of child abuse to DSS. If DSS ignores or dismisses these suspicions, no one will step in to fill the gap. Wisconsin's child-protection program thus effectively confined Joshua DeShaney within the walls of Randy DeShaney's violent home until such time as DSS took action to remove him. Conceivably, then, children like Joshua are made worse off by the existence of this program when the persons and entities charged with carrying it out fail to do their jobs.

B.   Transitional Phrases

Another technique to improve your writing is to employ transitional phrases to string together the sentences of your paragraphs and to weave one paragraph to another. Transitional phrases include words such as "also," "however," and "therefore." They show the relationship between ideas and will help the reader absorb your writing. Transitional phrases are also used to connect one paragraph to the next. For instance, return to *Johnson v. Tennis* again and note the way the court employed transitional phrases to connect ideas, particularly from one paragraph to the next.

C.   Effective Use of Quotations

As you review the record for an appeal, fragments of testimony or documentary language may resonate in your mind because they capture the emotion underlying the dispute. Quote these phrases directly in your draft opinion. But, as you have likely been cautioned already, beware of block-quoting because readers tend to only skim this material. Also, block-quoting often reflects a writer's unease with the quoted material; it may signal to the reader that the writer has not independently absorbed the quoted material. If you choose to include a long block-quote, at least add a sentence before or after it explaining why it is significant.

Consider the effective use of quotations in the following excerpt from *State v. Mendola*, 8 A.3d 127 (N.H. 2010).

> The defendant, Katherine Mendola, was convicted by a jury of criminal solicitation to commit murder, On appeal, she argues that the Superior Court erred when it failed to instruct the jury on entrapment, excluded evidence that her sometimes boyfriend had abused her, and admitted evidence that she wanted two additional people to be killed. We affirm.
>
> The jury could have found the following facts. The woman the defendant sought to have killed was the wife of her workers' compensation lawyer. She first hired this attorney in late 2004 or early 2005. Over time, she developed romantic feelings for him, which she expressed by calling him repeatedly and by saying inappropriate things to him, such as referring to her cleavage, describing herself as "young," "hot," and "sexy," and telling him that she would make "the best wife in the whole wide world." Between September 1 and November 1, 2007, the defendant called her attorney 458 times. In one of her many visits to his office, the defendant embraced him and told him that she wanted to have a romantic relationship with him. Although he demurred, the defendant told others that they had kissed.
>
> The defendant talked about her attorney to her friends "all the time," telling them that she loved him and wanted to marry him. She said that her attorney yearned to be with her, but that he did not want to disrupt his marriage. The defendant then sought to break up her attorney's marriage. At first, she tried magic spells that she ordered from

witchcraft websites. When these did not work, she sought to hire someone to kill her attorney's wife.

She first asked T. Thomas Austin, who lived at the same campground as the defendant. In the summer of 2007, she twice asked Austin to "eliminate" her attorney's wife because she was in love with her attorney and wanted to marry him. Austin declined. She then asked Daniel Cloutier, with whom she sometimes lived, if he knew of someone who could do the job. Although Cloutier initially did not take the defendant seriously, he became concerned that she might be capable of hurting someone when she threatened him with a knife because he left a mess in the bathroom.

Cloutier contacted agents from the drug task force for the New Hampshire Attorney General in October 2007. Ten years earlier, he had been an informant for the task force for approximately one year. Cloutier told two task force agents that he had a roommate who wanted to hire an assassin to kill the wife of a man with whom she was having an affair. The agents spoke with the state police, and, as a result, State Trooper Christopher Huse was assigned to pose as a hit man. Huse first met with Cloutier, who told him that the defendant was his roommate and that she wanted a hit man to kill her attorney's wife. Huse told Cloutier to tell the defendant that he knew someone who would contact her about the job. The defendant seemed "overjoyed" when Cloutier told her this.

On November 16, 2007, Huse called the defendant, posing as a hit man, and asked if she were still interested in his services, to which she said, "Yes, I am." When the defendant told Huse that she'd rather talk in person, he told her that they would meet in New Hampshire and that he would call her when he was "ready." Huse told the defendant that "business is gonna be taken care of," to which she said, "I appreciate that," and laughed.

Huse called the defendant again on November 19, 2007. The defendant told him that nobody knew "about this" except Cloutier and that when she and Huse met she was planning to wear "a hood and sunglasses so [she wouldn't] be recognizable." She told Huse that where they were going for the hit was within a twenty-minute ride from Manchester, but was "out in the middle of nowhere so nobody is gonna see nothing." She told Huse not to worry because she had "directions to where we're going" and that she had "thought, like, ten steps ahead here." Huse asked the defendant if she still "want[ed] to do this," to which she replied, "I'm very serious about this." They agreed to meet that afternoon in Manchester.

Later that day, Huse and the defendant met in the parking lot of a Wendy's restaurant in Manchester. The defendant told Huse that she thought this was "funny" because "[t]he name of [the wife] is Wendy." The defendant told Huse that she'd "been waiting for this for five years." When Huse asked why she had not hired him earlier, she said: "I just found out about you. . . . If I had known about you a year ago, . . . I would have jumped on this sooner." She explained that she had been asking Cloutier for a month to "get this done."

The defendant further explained that she "kn[e]w what [she was] doing" because she had talked to a well-known psychic who had told her: "You need to get rid of this woman. I'm not going to tell you specifically how. You know how. You need to get rid of her." When Huse again asked the defendant if this was what she wanted to do, she said that she was a "hundred and million percent" sure that it was.

* * *

V. SUGGESTED FURTHER READING

Douglas E. Abrams, *Judges and their Editors*, 3 ALB. GOV'T L. REV. 392 (2010).

RUGGERO J. ALDISERT, OPINION WRITING (AuthorHouse 2d ed. 2010).

IAN GALLACHER, A FORM AND STYLE MANUAL FOR LAWYERS (2007).

JOYCE J. GEORGE, JUDICIAL OPINION WRITING HANDBOOK (5th ed. 2007).

Hon. Gerald Lebovits & Lucero Ramirez Hidalgo, *Advice to Law Clerks: How to Draft Your First Judicial Opinion*, 36 WESTCHESTER B.J. 29 (2009).

Richard A. Posner, *Judges' Writing Styles (And Do They Matter?)*, 62 U. CHI. L. REV. 1421 (1995).

Jennifer Sheppard, *The "Write" Way: A Judicial Clerk's Guide to Writing for the Court*, 38 U. BALT. L. REV. 73 (2008).

WILLIAM STRUNK JR. & E.B. WHITE, THE ELEMENTS OF STYLE (4th ed. 2000).

Patricia M. Wald, *The Rhetoric of Results and the Results of Rhetoric: Judicial Writings*, 62 U. CHI. L. REV. 1371 (1995).

Patricia M. Wald, *A Reply to Judge Posner*, 62 U. CHI. L. REV. 1451 (1995).

James Boyd White, *What's an Opinion for?*, 62 U. CHI. L. REV. 1363 (1995).

Charles R. Wilson, *How Opinions Are Developed in the United States Court of Appeals for the Eleventh Circuit*, 32 STETSON L. REV. 247 (2003).

Ryan Benjamin Witte, *The Judge As Author /The Author As Judge*, 40 GOLDEN GATE U. L. REV. 37 (2009).

Chapter 6

A DIVIDED BENCH: DISSENTS AND CONCURRENCES

I. INTRODUCTION

Judges write dissents when they disagree with the outcome of the majority's opinion. They write concurrences when they agree with the outcome, but not the reasoning leading up to it. In other words, the concurring judge indicates that the majority reached the correct result for the wrong reasons. A concurrence also might identify an alternative ground for the outcome in the case.

Most of the time, judges issue written dissents and concurrences only when they believe strongly in the points they want to express. If a judge disagrees with only a few phrases in the majority's decision, or even with a particular strain of argument, he or she is more likely to seek revision of these portions of the majority decision than write a separate opinion. Why? As Judge Patricia Wald explained, "[a] dissent makes no new law; it highlights one's difference from a majority of colleagues, and it means extra, self-assigned work." Patricia M. Wald, *Rhetoric and Results*, 62 U. Chi. L. Rev. 1371, 1412 (1995). Concurrences, too, do not carry the force of law and they create extra work for the judge, although compared to dissents, they are less likely to impair collegiality among the judges.

Nonetheless, when judges choose to dissent or concur, they may break from habitual modes of legal analysis and traditional writing styles. Strict application of precedent, for example, may give way to a discussion of philosophy or psychology. And dissenters may linger on only those portions of the appeal that they want to discuss, having no obligation to address fully the parties' contentions. Moreover, the formal "we" and "this Court" of a majority decision becomes a personal "I" in a dissent or concurrence. Minority opinions demonstrate a judge's individuality of thought and style in ways that majority opinions never could. Accordingly, judges often, but not always, draft dissents and concurrences themselves, relying on law clerks mostly for research and editing.

II. CASE STUDY

The following case includes a majority opinion, a concurrence, and a dissent. What do the minority opinions add to your understanding of the case? You might also compare the majority and minority opinions in *Citizens United v. Federal Election Commission*, 130 S. Ct. 876 (2010), included in Chapter Four.

PINKNEY v. STATE
827 A.2d 124 (Md. Ct. Spec. App. 2003)

JAMES R. EYLER, J.

Appellant, Walter Pinkney, challenges his first degree murder and child abuse convictions for the brutal killing of his step-grandson, six-month-old Ta'mar Hamilton. Following a four-day trial on the merits, the jury returned verdicts of guilty on the first degree murder and felony child abuse counts, and appellant was subsequently sentenced to a term of life imprisonment for the first degree murder conviction and 30 years imprisonment for the child abuse conviction, to be served consecutively.

On appeal, appellant alleges three errors. First, he argues that the evidence was legally insufficient to sustain a conviction of first degree murder, *i.e.*, that the court erred in failing to grant his motion for judgment of acquittal. Next, he contends that the trial court erred in admitting the prior statements of Renita Pinkney, Ta'mar's paternal grandmother, who was appellant's girlfriend at the time and who is now appellant's wife. Finally, appellant claims that the court erred in precluding the defense from pursuing relevant testimony about the actions and behavior of Larry Hamilton, Jr., Ta'mar's father. Perceiving no error in the trial court's evidentiary rulings and finding that there was sufficient evidence to sustain the first degree murder conviction, we affirm appellant's convictions.

Factual Background

On the evening of November 27, 1999, officers of the Baltimore City Police Department went to The Johns Hopkins Hospital in response to a call of suspected child abuse of six-month-old Ta'mar Hamilton. David Peckoo, one of the investigating officers, interviewed Renita Pinkney and appellant, who, he had been told, were responsible for the care and custody of Ta'mar, before Ta'mar was rushed to the hospital earlier that day.

Ta'mar died from his injuries on December 1, 1999. On December 3, 1999, after an autopsy had been performed on Ta'mar, police investigators again interviewed Ms. Pinkney and appellant. On December 14, 1999, appellant was arrested and charged with first degree murder and child abuse.

The evidence at trial portrayed the following chronology of events surrounding Ta'mar's death. On Thursday, November 25, 1999, Thanksgiving, arrangements were made for Larry Hamilton, Sr., Ta'mar's paternal grandfather, and appellant to pick up Ta'mar and his brother, Davon Hamilton, then 15 months old, from their mother, Shawntel Rice, and take them to the home of Ms. Pinkney and appellant to stay for the remainder of the Thanksgiving weekend. The men arrived at the home of Ms. Rice and placed both children in their car seats. During the car ride to Ms. Pinkney's and appellant's house, Ta'mar was cranky and cried for most of the trip.

Upon their arrival, Larry Hamilton, Sr. instructed his son, Larry Hamilton, Jr., the boys' father, to remove the children from the car and bring them into the house. There is conflicting testimony about Hamilton, Jr.'s actions following his father's demand, suggesting varying levels of harshness with which Hamilton, Jr. physically brought the children into the home. According to Ms. Pinkney, Hamilton, Jr. removed the children from the car and, while they still were strapped into their car seats, threw them up several steps into the vestibule of the house. Hamilton, Jr. testified that he retrieved one child at a time and handed the first car seat off to someone before retrieving the second. Finally, another witness described Hamilton, Jr.'s dropping the car seats into the vestibule, after carrying them up the stairs, because his pants were falling down. There was undisputed testimony that the car seats were padded, and that they landed upright.

Once the children were inside the house, Hamilton, Jr. and other visitors remained for one to two hours. They then departed, leaving Ms. Pinkney and appellant alone with Ta'mar and Davon. Ta'mar continued to cry and was generally cranky. Before putting the children to bed, appellant gave Ta'mar a bath. Ta'mar slept only a few hours on Thursday night. He awoke at 3 a.m. on Friday morning and required feeding and changing. He did not fall back to sleep until 6 a.m.

On Friday afternoon, after observing Ta'mar's continued crankiness, Ms. Pinkney took Ta'mar to a clinic. Davon remained in the care and custody of appellant. Ms. Pinkney waited several hours only to be told that the clinic would not treat Ta'mar because he was not covered by insurance. She returned home with Ta'mar late Friday afternoon. When she tried to feed him, Ta'mar would not eat or drink.

Ms. Pinkney and appellant fell asleep on the couch for a few hours with both children. They then took the children upstairs to bed, keeping Davon in the room with them, and putting Ta'mar to sleep in another room. During that night, Ta'mar cried constantly, and Ms. Pinkney and appellant took turns patting his back, walking him around the room, and trying to calm him. Ta'mar briefly slept between the hours of 3 and 6 a.m. Thereafter, he slept only for short periods of time.

At approximately 10 a.m., Ms. Pinkney went to the store for diapers, leaving the children in appellant's care. She checked and saw that Ta'mar was asleep before she left. According to appellant, while Ms. Pinkney was away, Ta'mar awoke and began crying, so he went into the room where Ta'mar was and picked him up to try to calm him. He tried to feed Ta'mar from a bottle, but Ta'mar only drank a small amount, approximately 3 and a half ounces. Appellant testified that he was changing Ta'mar's diaper following a suspected bowel movement when Ta'mar gasped for breath and stopped breathing. Immediately, he called 911 and began giving Ta'mar CPR. He was still trying to resuscitate Ta'mar when Ms. Pinkney returned home. An ambulance then arrived and transported Ta'mar to The Johns Hopkins Hospital ("Hopkins").

Ta'mar was admitted to the Pediatric Emergency Department. Dr. Allen Walker, Director of that Department, was contacted to evaluate Ta'mar. Dr. Walker diagnosed Ta'mar as having sustained a severe brain injury. Dr. Walker interviewed Ms. Pinkney and appellant, trying to ascertain what had happened before Ta'mar was brought into the hospital. During the interview, appellant described Ta'mar's constant crankiness, refusal to eat, how Ta'mar had stopped breathing while he was changing his diaper, how he had immediately contacted 911, and his attempts at CPR. Thereafter, Dr. Walker spoke with the police.

Officer Brian Rice arrived at the hospital and interviewed Ms. Pinkney and appellant. During the interview, appellant again explained that Ta'mar had been cranky and crying all weekend and that he had stopped breathing on Saturday morning.

Devoark Maddox, a clinical social worker at Hopkins, testified regarding her completion of a child maltreatment form, based on her interview with appellant and Ms. Pinkney at the hospital. During the interview, appellant described the events, including his telephone call to 911 and his attempt to resuscitate Ta'mar. Ms. Maddox described appellant as calm and forthcoming during their interview.

Detective David Peckoo also interviewed appellant and Ms. Pinkney at the hospital that day. The interview revealed much of the same information discussed above.

The autopsy revealed that the cause of Ta'mar's death was blunt force trauma as a result of four injuries to his head. After receiving the autopsy results, Detective Peckoo asked Ms. Pinkney and appellant to come to the police station for a second interview. They did so voluntarily on December 3, 1999, and he took recorded statements from them both. During this second interview, appellant indicated that he might have hit Ta'mar's head on the bed rail while trying to get him to respond after he stopped breathing. He also admitted that he had shaken Ta'mar a few times.

As part of the investigation, Detective Peckoo removed the bed rail from Ms.

Pinkney's home and tested it for blood, semen, and hair. The test results were negative for those substances and did not reveal any evidence of human contact. On December 14, 1999, appellant was arrested and charged with first degree murder and child abuse of Ta'mar Hamilton.

Following selection of a jury and an unsuccessful pre-trial suppression hearing, a trial on the merits began on September 19, 2000. The State presented the testimony of eight witnesses in the following order: Officer Brian Rice, Devoark Maddox, Dr. Allen Walker, Shawntel Rice, Renita Pinkney, Detective David Peckoo, Larry Hamilton, Jr., and Dr. Joseph Pestaner. The defense offered the testimony of Larry Hamilton, Sr., Sheena Watkins, and appellant. These witnesses testified to the following additional information.

Dr. Walker testified in great detail about the extent and cause of Ta'mar's fatal injuries, explaining that (1) severe brain injury was his initial diagnosis, (2) Ta'mar's chance for survival was almost non-existent, (3) the injuries were almost everywhere, i.e., the brain and skull had been virtually destroyed, (4) violent force, similar to the force when someone is thrown through the windshield in a car crash or falls from a third floor window, was required to inflict the type of injuries that Ta'mar had sustained to his head, and (5) such violent blows would have rendered Ta'mar immediately unconscious so as to make him incapable of crying or drinking formula. Dr. Walker also described the rest of Ta'mar's stay at Hopkins, explaining that for a couple of days he was maintained on a number of medications and a ventilator because he could not breathe for himself, and that, during that time, his brain died.

During cross-examination, Dr. Walker testified, with the assistance of hospital records, that Ta'mar had been delivered prematurely, requiring assistance with breathing, and that Ta'mar's mother had a sexually transmitted disease when Ta'mar was delivered. He also testified that Ta'mar was brought into the Hopkins Pediatric Emergency Department when he was three months old for pneumonia and was treated with IV antibiotics and sent home. Finally, Dr. Walker testified that the autopsy revealed that there was a healing rib fracture at the time of his death from an injury suffered prior to November 27, 1999.

Shawntel Rice, Ta'mar's mother, testified for the State about the events of November 25, when her sons were picked up by appellant and Larry Hamilton, Sr., and about how she learned that Ta'mar had been admitted to Hopkins. She also testified about Ta'mar's demeanor generally and his behavior prior to being picked up on the 25th.

In addition to testifying about the specific events that occurred between November 25 and 27, 1999, Ms. Pinkney testified generally about the parenting skills of her son and Shawntel Rice. She explained that her son and Ms. Rice, as well as the two boys, had lived in her home for a period of time just after Ta'mar was born. She also explained that, after they left her home, she and appellant continued to watch the two children on a daily basis for a while, but that arrangement ended a few weeks prior to the Thanksgiving weekend visit. According to Ms. Pinkney, Ms. Rice asked her if she and appellant would watch the children for the weekend. Ms. Pinkney reluctantly agreed after Ms. Rice promised to provide a place for Davon to sleep.

Ms. Pinkney further testified that the reason she asked her son and Ms. Rice to leave her home was because they used drugs and did not take good care of their children, neglecting to feed them or play with them. She further testified that they cursed at Ta'mar and Davon and that she witnessed them hit both boys on several occasions. The prosecutor challenged Ms. Pinkney's assertions by pointing out that she had never mentioned any past abuse to anyone prior to her testimony in court.

Finally, Dr. Joseph Pestaner, an expert in forensic and pediatric pathology, was called by the State to testify regarding the autopsy he performed on Ta'mar. His testimony was substantially similar to that of Dr. Walker but was more detailed. He was able to discount other incidents, such as older injuries or being tossed in his car seat, as possible causes of Ta'mar's fatal injuries, reinforcing what Dr. Walker said about the amount of force that would have been required to cause such serious damage to Ta'mar's brain and skull. Dr. Pestaner also echoed Dr. Walker's opinion that Ta'mar would have been rendered unconscious almost immediately after being struck, such that crying and drinking from a bottle would not have been possible.

Larry Hamilton, Sr. and Sheena Watkins were called for the defense and testified generally regarding the events on November 25, 1999, when Ta'mar was brought to the home of Ms. Pinkney and appellant. Larry Hamilton, Sr. also testified that he observed his son, Larry Hamilton, Jr., strike Ta'mar in the head on several occasions between September 11, 1999, and the week prior to Thanksgiving of 1999.

Appellant testified in his own defense, describing the events of November 25-27, emphasizing Ta'mar's continuous crying, as well as his efforts to calm him by walking him, patting his back, attempting to feed him a bottle, and changing his diaper. He also described how Ta'mar stopped breathing and how he immediately called 911 for assistance and tried to resuscitate him by performing CPR.

During cross-examination, the prosecutor asked appellant about his admission during his December 3 statement to Detective Peckoo that he may have accidentally hit Ta'mar's head when he was shaking him to revive him. Acknowledging that admission, appellant went on to say that after thinking about it for some time after talking to Detective Peckoo, he knew that Ta'mar did not hit his head. In response to the prosecutor's questions about whether, by Saturday morning, he was tired and frustrated by Ta'mar's constant crying and crankiness, appellant admitted to being tired from the sleepless nights, but denied that he was frustrated by his failed attempts to quiet the baby. Finally, the prosecutor reviewed with appellant another part of his statement to Detective Peckoo, in which appellant described Ta'mar's cries as sounding like a child who had been hit, and explained that when he touched Ta'mar's head, he cried out like someone was beating him. Appellant admitted that he told Detective Peckoo that his first response was to think to himself, "What did I do?"

On the same day that closing arguments were delivered, the jury returned a verdict of guilty on both the first degree murder and child abuse counts. On December 4, 2000, the court sentenced appellant to life imprisonment for the first degree murder conviction, and 30 years incarceration for the child abuse conviction, to be served consecutively.

Appellant filed an appeal to this Court on December 21, 2000. Counsel for both parties argued before a three-judge panel of this Court on February 11, 2002. Following that argument, by order dated March 10, 2003, this Court, on its own motion, ordered that an *en banc* hearing be held on April 29, 2003, to consider whether the theory of the case that the State argued to the jury precluded the jury from convicting appellant of first degree murder. Specifically, this Court asked the parties to address whether the State argued that appellant's intent was to stop Ta'mar from crying as distinguished from arguing that appellant's intent was to kill Ta'mar, with the desire to stop the crying as a motive for the intent, and if so, the legal effect of the State's argument. After reviewing the record and considering the arguments, we are satisfied that the State argued that appellant intended to kill Ta'mar. Consequently, we need not address the legal issue raised by the Court and will address only the issues raised by appellant.

Additional facts will be set forth as relevant to our resolution of the issues.

Discussion

* * *

Sufficiency of the Evidence

Given our rejection of both of appellant's evidentiary challenges, we turn to appellant's main argument — that the evidence was insufficient to sustain a conviction of first degree murder. Specifically, appellant argues that the evidence failed to establish (1) that appellant was the individual who inflicted the fatal injuries upon Ta'mar Hamilton, or (2) that, if appellant did in fact inflict those injuries, he did so with malice or with the premeditation or deliberation necessary for a finding of first degree murder. In support of his second argument, appellant first turns to cases discussing Maryland's statutory elements for first degree murder, arguing that the evidence does not satisfy the statute's strict requirements. In addition, appellant reviews other Maryland cases involving abuse inflicted upon a child resulting in death, suggesting that when the fatal act is the result of an emotionally charged situation involving a baby, the accused is, at most, found guilty of second degree murder. Finally, appellant urges us to consider the fact that other jurisdictions have been hesitant to convict a defendant of first degree murder for the death of a child.

In response to appellant's sufficiency of the evidence argument, the State first argues that appellant's challenge is not preserved for appellate review. Pointing to Maryland Rule 4-324, which governs motions for judgment of acquittal, the State argues that appellant is bound by the reasons stated when he renewed the motion at the end of appellant's case, when defense counsel stated: "I renew my Motion for Judgment of Acquittal because there has been no evidence introduced beyond a reasonable doubt to prove Mr. Pinkney guilty." *See* Md. Rule 4-324(a) ("A defendant may move for judgment of acquittal . . . in a jury trial, at the close of all the evidence. The defendant shall state with particularity all reasons why the motion should be granted."). Consequently, the State contends that appellant's claims are not preserved for review because they were not articulated as the basis for his motion for judgment of acquittal at the close of all of the evidence. On the merits, the State argues that, when applying the deferential standard of review for sufficiency challenges, it is clear that there was ample evidence from which the jury could properly conclude that appellant was guilty of first degree murder.

While there is some merit to the State's preservation argument, because we conclude that the evidence was legally sufficient and appellant's conviction will not be disturbed, we shall resolve the uncertainty as to preservation in favor of appellant and reach the merits. Accordingly, we begin by reviewing the standard of review for sufficiency of the evidence challenges. Most recently, the Court of Appeals, in *State v. Smith* discussed the standard of review in great depth, stating:

> The standard for appellate review of evidentiary sufficiency is whether, after viewing the evidence in the light most favorable to the prosecution, any rational trier of fact could have found the essential elements of the crime beyond a reasonable doubt. "Weighing the credibility of witnesses and resolving any conflicts in the evidence are tasks proper for the fact finder." "We give 'due regard to the [fact finder's] findings of facts, its resolution of conflicting evidence, and, significantly, its opportunity to observe and assess the credibility of witnesses.' " We do not re-weigh the evidence, but "we do determine whether the verdict was supported by sufficient evidence, direct or circumstantial, which could convince a rational trier of fact of the defendant's guilt of the offenses charged beyond a reasonable doubt." A valid conviction may be based solely on circumstantial evidence. The

same standard applies to all criminal cases, including those resting upon circumstantial evidence, since, generally, proof of guilt based in whole or in part on circumstantial evidence is no different from proof of guilt based on direct eyewitness accounts.

Noting some confusion regarding the amount of deference that an appellate court should give to the fact finders' ability to draw inferences from the evidence, the Court went on to explain:

> The following cases further emphasize a trial judge's or a jury's ability to choose among differing inferences that might possibly be made from a factual situation and the deference we must give in that regard to the inferences a fact-finder may draw. *Jackson* (noting the responsibility of the trier of fact to fairly resolve conflicts in testimony, to weigh the evidence, and to draw reasonable inferences from basic facts to ultimate facts); *Jones* (Involving a probable cause issue the Court stated "it is the trier of fact that must draw the inferences. . . . Consequently, absent clear error in its fact-finding, an appellate court is required, in deference to the trial court, to accept those findings of fact."); *In re Timothy F.*(in criminal cases the appropriate inquiry is not whether the reviewing court believes that the evidence established guilt beyond a reasonable doubt, but, rather, whether, after viewing the evidence in the light most favorable to the prosecution, any rational trier of fact could have found the essential elements of the crime beyond a reasonable doubt); *McMillian* (stating that "The trial court's findings as to disputed facts are accepted by this Court unless found to be clearly erroneous").

In *State v. Raines*, the Court stated:

> This analysis indicates that the Court of Special Appeals credited the Raines's version of the events, one that necessarily mitigated his culpability. Of course, the credibility of the witnesses was a matter for the trial court, as fact finder, not the appellate court, to resolve. Furthermore, the determination of an accused's intention is, in the first instance, for the trial judge, when sitting without a jury, and this determination will not be disturbed on appeal unless clearly erroneous. As noted, the trial court discounted Raines's version of the events. Instead, the court drew an inference based on other evidence offered at trial that the killing was intentional, deliberate and premeditated. This, the trial court, as fact finder, has the exclusive right to do. The Court of Special Appeals erred in conducting its own independent credibility analysis and in rejecting the trial court's finding of facts.

> This Court has noted that the trier of fact may infer the intent to kill from the surrounding circumstances: "[S]ince intent is subjective and, without the cooperation of the accused, cannot be directly and

objectively proven, its presence must be shown by established facts which permit a proper inference of its existence."

* * *

Raines's actions in directing the gun at the window, and therefore at the driver's head on the other side of the window, permitted an inference that Raines shot the gun with the intent to kill. Relying upon that inference, the trial judge could rationally find, beyond a reasonable doubt, that the killing was wilful, deliberate and premeditated so as to render Raines guilty of first degree murder.

Although a different trier of fact may have viewed the evidence as establishing second degree murder instead of first degree murder, the trial court's decision was not clearly erroneous. The Court of Special Appeals erred in substituting its judgment for that of the trial court on the evidence.

While in *Raines*, and in some of the other cases, the exact issues relate to the proof of intent in respect to the type of homicide, we, and the Court of Special Appeals, have held that even in murder cases, intent may be established by the use of rational inferences from the underlying evidentiary facts.

The Court's articulation and explanation of the standard emphasizes three important principles: (1) we must give great deference to the trier of facts' opportunity to assess the credibility of witnesses, weigh the evidence, and resolve conflicts in the evidence, (2) circumstantial evidence alone can provide a sufficient basis upon which a trier of fact can rest its determination of guilt, even for first degree murder, and (3) we do not re-weigh the evidence or substitute our own judgment, but only determine whether the verdict was supported by sufficient evidence to convince the trier of fact of the defendant's guilt beyond a reasonable doubt. These principles were summarized by the *Smith* Court when it stated:

> The primary appellate function in respect to evidentiary inferences is to determine whether the trial court made reasonable, *i.e.*, rational, inferences from extant facts. Generally, if there are evidentiary facts sufficiently supporting the inference made by the trial court, the appellate court defers to the fact-finder instead of examining the record for additional facts upon which a conflicting inference could have been made, and then conducting its own weighing of the conflicting inferences to resolve independently any conflicts it perceives to exist. The resolving of the conflicting evidentiary inferences is for the fact-finder.

Appellant's sufficiency argument presents two separate issues; first, whether there was sufficient evidence to prove that appellant was the individual who caused the fatal injuries suffered by Ta'mar; and second, whether there was sufficient evidence to demonstrate that appellant killed Ta'mar wilfully, deliberately, and with premeditation. Appellant's first claim is primarily premised on his theory that evidence that was both admitted and excluded tended to show that Ta'mar's father, Larry Hamilton, Jr., may have been the responsible party. We previously held that the court did not abuse its discretion by excluding certain evidence regarding Larry Hamilton, Jr. In addition, we do not think that any of the evidence that was admitted precluded the jury from finding that appellant was the individual who inflicted the fatal injuries to Ta'mar's head.

In *Deese*, a case with similar facts to ours, the Court of Appeals affirmed the defendant's second degree murder conviction based on its application of the rule that "[i]t is well settled that a conviction may be sustained on the basis of circumstantial evidence." Applying the above rule to the facts of the case, the Court explained that

> the evidence most favorable to the State is that (1) Kyle was alive on the morning of February 8, (2) Kyle was under Deese's exclusive supervision for a period of time on that day, (3) Kyle was found dead a few hours after that period, (4) death was due to blunt force injuries to the head [caused by force of a magnitude at work in car crashes and falls from significant heights] and possibly due to shaking, and (5) no one had contact with Kyle after the period described in (2) and before the event described in (3). From these circumstances, a rational jury could have inferred, beyond a reasonable doubt, that Deese inflicted the fatal injuries.

The similarity between the facts in *Deese* and those in the present case support our application of the *Deese* Court's reasoning to hold that there was sufficient evidence from which the jury could have concluded beyond a reasonable doubt that appellant was the individual who inflicted the fatal blows to Ta'mar's head.

Appellant was convicted under section 407 of Article 27 of the Maryland Code, which provides that "[a]ll murder which shall be perpetrated . . . by any kind of wilful, deliberate and premeditated killing shall be murder in the first degree." As appellant properly recognized, the State has the burden of proving each element of the crime beyond a reasonable doubt. We are reminded that, on appellate review, we are not asked to re-weigh the evidence or substitute our judgment for that of the jury, but instead, we must simply determine "whether, after viewing the evidence in the light most favorable to the prosecution, [the jury] could have found the essential elements of the crime beyond a reasonable doubt."

Having determined that there was sufficient evidence upon which the jury could have found that appellant caused Ta'mar's death, we turn our focus to the additional three elements of first degree murder — wilfulness, deliberation, and premeditation. The Maryland Criminal Pattern Jury Instructions 4:17 (2001), which were used by the trial judge in this case, define those three elements by stating:

> Wilful means that the defendant actually intended to kill the victim. Deliberate means that the defendant was conscious of the intent to kill. Premeditated means that the defendant thought about the killing and that there was enough time before the killing, though it may have only been brief, for the defendant to consider the decision whether or not to kill and enough time to weigh the reasons for and against the choice. The premeditated intent to kill must be formed before the killing.

The Court of Appeals has reinforced the application of those definitions by stating that first degree murder requires "that the defendant possess the intent to kill (willful), that the defendant have conscious knowledge of the intent to kill (deliberate), and that there be time enough for the defendant to deliberate, *i.e.*, time enough to have thought about that intent (premeditate)."

Despite these seemingly clear definitions, we are mindful that it is often difficult to understand these concepts in the abstract, and even more difficult to determine whether each is satisfied when faced with a specific set of facts. Fortunately, a body of case law has developed to guide our interpretation and application of these definitions.

First, examining the wilfulness requirement, we have stated that "[f]or a killing to be 'wilful' there must be a specific purpose and intent to kill [.]" Given the fact that most defendants do not announce their intent to kill to witnesses or other third parties, we are forced to look to other factors as reflecting the defendant's intent to kill.

For example, in *Cummings v. State*, the Court of Appeals reasoned that the trial judge was justified in finding that the defendant had "a specific purpose and design to kill," based on the fact that "he shot the deceased seven times with a deadly weapon at point-blank range, and then, calmly, laid the pistol on her dead body, stating: 'I might go to jail, but I am glad I done it.' " Even if Cummings had not made the statement after shooting his victim, his actions reflected those of an individual who intended to bring about her death. The Court's reasoning, therefore, demonstrates that the circumstances of the death, i.e., the defendant's actions, often speak for themselves when they so clearly involve actions that are likely to bring about death.

So, too, was the situation in the present case. Even though appellant did not use a deadly weapon like the pistol in *Cummings*, the fragile nature of the victim, a six-month-old baby, transformed appellant's hands, and other ordinary objects in the room, into potential deadly weapons given the likelihood of harm that they could cause to the victim. The jury, therefore, could have rationally concluded that appellant's use of his hands or other objects to deliver the fatal blows to Ta'mar's head reflected a "specific purpose and intent to kill."

Similarly, in *Dunn v. State* (involving a man who bludgeoned to death his wife and 18-month-old baby and was tried for the murder of his wife), the Court of Appeals, in determining whether there was sufficient evidence to demonstrate that Dunn had a wilful design to murder, considered the fact that the evidence reflected a clear motivation on Dunn's part for the murder of his wife. Noting that Dunn was involved with another woman whom he planned to marry, the Court reasoned that it was reasonable for the trier of fact to have concluded that Dunn intended to kill his wife.

Although perhaps not as strong a motivation as that involved in *Dunn*, here, the State argued, and appellant concedes in his brief, that appellant's actions could have been motivated by his desire "to quiet the baby." While appellant argues that this phraseology reflects an innocent or innocuous goal on the part of appellant, the jury could have rationally inferred that appellant was tired and frustrated by the sleepless nights and continuous crying, such that he wanted to quiet Ta'mar permanently, *i.e.*, kill Ta'mar.

Finally, in *Faulcon v. State*, in which the defendant ran over the victim with a car and dragged him eight blocks to his death, the Court of Appeals affirmed Faulcon's first degree murder conviction, reasoning that the intent to kill could be inferred in part from the fact that the defendant's version of events was contradicted by other witnesses. In *Faulcon*, the contradiction centered on whether the defendant had been threatened by the victim before he ran over him. The Court concluded that if the trial judge discredited the defendant's version, the existence of legal justification vanished.

Like the Court in *Faulcon*, we think that it would have been reasonable for the jury to consider the fact that appellant's story contradicted the other evidence. In the present case, if the jurors disbelieved appellant's version of events, they could have rationally concluded, based on the medical evidence, that the only possible explanation was that appellant intended to kill Ta'mar when he inflicted the four fatal blows to his head.

The task of demonstrating that appellant acted deliberately and with premeditation is often treated as a single endeavor. Summarizing the principles espoused in earlier cases, the Court of Appeals, in *Willey v. State*, explained that, "[i]f the killing results from a choice made as the result of thought, however short the struggle between the intention and the act, it is sufficient to characterize the crime as deliberate and premeditated murder." Deliberation and premeditation have also been clarified by the principle that

> in order to justify a conviction of murder in the first degree, the trier of facts must find the actual intent, the fully formed purpose to kill with enough time for deliberation and premeditation to convince the trier of facts that this purpose is not the immediate offspring of rashness and impetuous temper, but that the mind has become fully conscious of its own design.

A review of other cases provides support for the conclusion that the evidence presented in this case justifies a finding of deliberation and premeditation, as well as the element of wilfulness. For example, in *Mitchell v. State*, the Court of Appeals, discussing the difference between first and second degree murder, explained:

> Although it is true that a murder committed solely on impulse — the "immediate offspring of rashness and impetuous temper" — is not one committed with deliberation and premeditation, the law does not require that deliberation and premeditation be the product of clear and rational thought; it may well result from anger or impulse. The test for first degree murder is whether there was the deliberation and premeditation — sufficient time to reflect — not the quality or rationality of the reflection or whether it may have been emotionally based.

While appellant argues that the killing, at best, reflects the actions of an emotionally drained and sleep deprived care giver, whose only goal was to have the crying cease, *Mitchell* teaches us that the jury could still have found that appellant acted deliberately and with premeditation despite the fact that he may not have been thinking clearly or rationally because of a lack of sleep and emotional stress, as long as he had time to reflect on his actions.

Another helpful tool for making this determination comes from this Court's review of a first degree murder conviction in *Hounshell v. State*. In *Hounshell*, in which the defendant strangled his victim to death, we expressly recognized that "[p]remeditation may be established circumstantially from the facts of a particular murder." This principle is especially important given the fact that, "[o]rdinarily, premeditation is not established by direct evidence. Rather, it is usually inferred from the facts and surrounding circumstances."

More specifically, *Hounshell* teaches us that "the brutality of the murder act may, in and of itself, provide sufficient evidence to convict for first degree murder." Pointing out that "death by strangulation does not in and of itself establish first degree murder," the *Hounshell* Court emphasized that the "jury . . . may consider that some time element is necessarily involved between the onset of squeezing the throat and death resulting therefrom." Ultimately, the Court affirmed the defendant's first degree murder conviction, reasoning that "[t]he time period in which the strangulation of [the victim] must have occurred, and the brutality with which the act was committed, were such that a reasonable juror could have concluded that appellant committed the act with premeditation and deliberation."

In addition to considering the type of actions involved in committing the murder, it is well established in Maryland that "the firing of two or more shots separated by an interval of time may be viewed as evidence of premeditation." In *Braxton v. State*, we clarified this rule by applying it to a specific set of facts, stating:

Appellant complains that the evidence of four bullet wounds, including a wound to the head, "cannot standing alone, support a reasoned decision to kill." This assertion is refuted by several cases, including *State v. Raines*. . . . The case of is also instructive. There, the Court observed "that the delay between firing a first and a second shot was enough time for reflection and decision to justify a finding of premeditation and deliberation."

In noticeable contrast to *Raines*, in which only one shot was fired at the victim's head, three out of the four shots fired at Mr. Alexander were directed to a vital part of the body. Thus, the jury could easily infer premeditation and deliberation. The jury also was entitled to consider appellant's fingerprint on the outside of the victim's car door, and ballistic tests showing that the bullets recovered from the victim's body were fired from the gun found in appellant's bedroom.

In essence, Braxton's complaint is that "the jury did not draw the inferences that he wished it to draw." He overlooks that it is the function of the jury to decide what inferences to draw from proven facts. The jury was certainly entitled to infer from the facts that "the defendant possessed the intent to kill (wilful), that the defendant [had a] conscious knowledge of that intent (deliberate), and that there [was] time enough for the defendant to deliberate, i.e., time enough to have thought about that intent (premeditate)."

Our discussion in *Braxton* reminds us that our task is not to determine whether there were other permissible inferences that the jury could have made. Instead, we must ensure that the evidence supports a finding that the elements of the crime existed beyond a reasonable doubt.

Before applying these rules to the facts of the present case, we are mindful of one final guiding principle, that being that the existence of the three elements necessary to support a first degree murder conviction must be "discerned from the facts of the case."

Applying these principles to the facts of this case leads us to hold that there was sufficient evidence presented from which the jury reasonably could conclude that appellant acted with deliberation and premeditation in killing Ta'mar. The jury was not required to accept appellant's version of events, especially given that much of the evidence presented by the State demonstrated how his story was inconsistent with the medical evidence. Nor was the jury obligated to conclude from the testimony of other witnesses and from the medical evidence that appellant's actions could not have been done with the deliberation and premeditation necessary to support a conviction for first degree murder.

Like the defendant in *Braxton*, appellant argues that evidence about the nature of the injury suffered by the victim is insufficient to support his first degree murder conviction. We disagree. The medical testimony presented by Dr. Walker and Dr. Pestano clearly established that Ta'mar suffered four fatal blows to his head, involving violent force similar to the force involved when a person is thrown through the windshield in a car crash or falls from a third floor window. Both doctors also discounted other possible causes of his fatal injuries, emphasizing that such injuries were not likely to be the result of an accidental knock on the head during attempts to resuscitate or even the alleged mishandling of Ta'mar by his father when he arrived at Ms. Pinkney's home in his car seat.

Accepting that it was permissible for the jury to use circumstantial evidence to establish the elements of first degree murder, the nature and number of the deadly blows to Ta'mar's head, in the context of all other evidence, supports a finding of deliberation and premeditation. Like the Court of Appeals in *Hyde v. State*, we believe that the evidence supports the jury's conclusion that appellant possessed the necessary mental state and amount of time to reflect on his actions in a manner consistent with a deliberate and premeditated killing.

Even though our decision to affirm rests on our application of case law discussing Maryland's first degree murder statute, we take a moment to briefly address appellant's alternative argument that his first degree murder conviction should be reversed because there is no Maryland case in which an otherwise caring, responsible care giver has been convicted of the premeditated, deliberate, first degree murder of a child, when death resulted from a single incident. Appellant attempts to support his argument by highlighting cases involving child abuse death in which the defendants were convicted of second degree murder, at worst, suggesting that second degree murder was the appropriate verdict here given that the killing of Ta'mar was no worse than those murders where the defendant was convicted of second degree murder.

Appellant does acknowledge at least one first degree murder conviction stemming form the physical abuse of a child but tries to distinguish it from the present case on its facts. Appellant's discussion of *White v. State*, a case in which a mother was convicted of first degree murder and child abuse after she and her boyfriend caused the death of her four-year-old daughter by beating her over a five-day period, resulting in 40 to 50 separate blows to her body, focuses solely on the fact that the death did not result from a single incident. The case does not have precedential effect in any event because the defendant in White did not challenge the murder conviction in the Court of Appeals but only argued that the child abuse conviction should have merged into the murder conviction. This Court, in an unreported opinion, affirmed both convictions.

We also note that there are at least two other examples in which Maryland appellate courts affirmed first degree murder convictions for parents' murder of their children. Both of the cases involved a single, violent episode resulting in the child's death. In neither case was sufficiency of the evidence raised and addressed in a reported opinion, however. As previously discussed, we reach our conclusion that the evidence in this case was legally sufficient by applying the elements of the crime to the evidence. The cases just discussed are by no means authority to support a contrary conclusion.

Finally, we comment on appellant's attempts to argue for reversal of the first degree murder conviction by attempting to demonstrate that courts in other jurisdictions have been hesitant to convict a defendant of first degree murder in the death of a child. For the following reasons, we do not find appellant's argument to be persuasive.

Appellant's conviction was based on Maryland's first degree murder statute, just as our review is governed by Maryland cases interpreting that statute. Courts from other jurisdictions are not bound by our statutes or case law, and thus, their analyses of similar issues may vary based on those differences. Additionally, with respect to legal sufficiency, cases turn on their facts. We have made no attempt to research and compare cases from other jurisdictions because we believe Maryland case law supports our conclusion. We are always cognizant of the fact that every jury is different, and that, in the end, it is our job, "after viewing the evidence in the light most favorable to the prosecution, [to determine whether] any rational trier of fact could have found the essential elements of the crime beyond a reasonable doubt." That is exactly what we have done here, and we conclude that there was sufficient evidence from which the jury could have determined that appellant was guilty of first degree murder. We reach this conclusion based on the totality of the evidence, including permissible inferences.

We expressly do not adopt a bright line rule of legal sufficiency for first degree murder, based solely on the number of blows delivered. We merely hold that the evidence was legally sufficient to convict appellant of first degree murder for the death of a six-month-old child based on the totality of the evidence, including evidence as to the number, severity, and brutality of the blows, the circumstances leading up to the beatings, and appellant's version of events.

Concurring Opinion by Davis, J. joined by Bloom, Theodore G., J. (retired, specially assigned).

I concur in the result reached by the majority only because I perceive no error of law in the charge to the jury or in the verdict rendered by the jury under Maryland law as presently constituted. I write separately, however, because, in my view, appellant's conviction resulted from an obfuscation which has developed in the law between first degree and second degree murder and the likely failure of the jury to comprehend the concept that an intent to prevent the infant from crying is insufficient to sustain a verdict of murder in the first degree.

Six-month old Ta'mar Hamilton certainly deserved better. As the majority points out, his birth was premature, requiring medical assistance to facilitate breathing; he was treated with antibiotics for pneumonia when he was three months old; autopsy results revealed a healing rib fracture indicating injuries sustained prior to his fatal injuries; and the force employed in causing his ultimate death was so violent that it was the equivalent of that which occurs when one is thrown through the windshield in a car crash or falls from a third floor window. There was no serious contest, at trial, regarding criminal agency. It can be fairly said that appellant was not well served by his failure to be forthcoming and a defense strategy that, in hindsight, appears to have been disingenuous and strained credulity.

To be sure, on the evidence presented, a finding of guilt of at least murder in the second degree and imposition of a severe sentence were clearly warranted in this case. Moreover, I recognize that, given the present state of Maryland law on felonious homicide, it was within the province of the jury, armed with the ability to consider inferences and the circumstances surrounding the death of young Ta'mar to conclude that, exasperated at his inability to force the young child to stop crying, he would kill young Ta'mar as the only means to achieve the desired end. The majority quotes from *State v. Smith*, in which the Court of Appeals observed that "the following cases further emphasize a trial judge's or a jury's ability to choose among differing inferences that might possibly be made from a factual situation and the deference we must give in that regard to the inferences a fact[ ]finder may draw."

Consequently, absent clear error in its fact-finding, an appellate court is required, in deference to the fact finder, to accept those findings of fact. I wholeheartedly subscribe to the proposition espoused in *Smith* because it would be improper for this Court to engage in appellate fact-finding when a *possible* ultimate decision was, in fact, supported by evidence or inferences and circumstances properly deducible from that evidence. The majority opinion, with great clarity, makes the point.

All of the foregoing having been said, we must not lose sight of the principal focus in any criminal prosecution, i.e., the *mens rea* or mental state that determines the degree of culpability, except in those offenses as to which the requirement of proof of *scienter* is expressly obviated by statute. The heart-rending circumstances surrounding the short life and death of young Ta'mar have the tendency of causing the jury to shift the focus from the culpability and accountability of the criminal agent to the well-settled inference that the fact finder may take into account the nature of the injuries in determining the intent of the actor.

Although the proceedings in the lower court may not have run afoul of Maryland law as presently constituted, the extent and heinous nature of the injuries would naturally tend to inflame the passions of the jury and permit it to discern intent solely from the evidence of those injuries, totally disregarding other circumstances consistent with the theory that appellant may have acted in a wild, frenetic state, rather than a state of mind which is rational, cool, and reflective. My second concern is that, on the facts of this case, the jury may have been confused in its deliberations, as a result of the emphasis on appellant's stated goal, i.e., to make the infant stop crying, and thereby rendered a verdict of first degree murder without determining that appellant's conduct was "willful" in the sense of intending to kill the child.

The expansive definition of the nature and character of the reflection of one who kills renders virtually all homicides, when there is any period of time prior to the killing, murder in the first degree in the absence of excuse, justification, or mitigating circumstances. With respect to the evidence of intent to kill, I am constrained to conclude that, because under Maryland law, intent may be inferred almost exclusively from the nature of the injuries inflicted, it was within the province of the jury in the case *sub judice* to return a verdict of murder in the first degree. A fully formed intent to kill and evidence of *true* reflection — that one made the decision (even in a split second) between the choice to kill or not to kill — in my view, are incompatible with circumstances which establish that the killer did not act rationally, i.e., he or she was robbed of his or her mental faculties such that he or she was incapable of forming the intent to kill.

The jurors, in the case at hand, deliberating under the current state of Maryland law, could properly find that appellant "reflected" even if they believed his actions were not the product of a rational thought process, i.e., appellant was robbed of the ability to form the requisite intent. Consequently, although the majority opinion accurately sets forth the law as presently constituted and the jury returned its verdict pursuant to the law as instructed, appellant's conviction of first degree murder, in my judgment, resulted from the blurred demarcation between first and second degree murder which has developed in Maryland over the past three decades. Impulsive and rash behavior evidencing lack of ability to formulate the requisite specific intent should not be recognized as the basis for a conviction of murder in the first degree.

With respect to the extensive injuries sustained by Ta'mar, the majority opinion relies principally on *Hounshell v. State*, in which the victim was strangled to death and *Kier v. State*, in which the Court of Appeals had characterized the victim as having been beaten in a "brutal manner" about the face and head with objects that indicated a protracted period during which the assault continued. Noting that the assailant had procured a butcher knife and plunged it twice into the body of the victim, the Court concluded, in *Kier*, that there was ample evidence to justify the jury in its conclusion that the action of the appellant was willful, deliberate, and premeditated. *Kier*, a bench trial, considered the proof of premeditation and deliberation in a case in which the victim had been found by her husband with many lacerations and bruises about her face, the back of her head, and other parts of her body. The most serious wounds, apparently inflicted by a butcher knife, were one in her throat and another in her chest extending some seven inches through the chest cavity to the heart.

Kier and *Hounshell* — as is true with virtually all of the cases cited by the majority — involve the slaying of victims wherein the nature of the injuries are not juxtaposed to circumstances which are inconsistent. Appellant, in his written submission to this Court, refers us to *People v. Anderson*, in which the Supreme Court of California, discussing proof of the elements of first degree murder, concluded:

> The type of evidence which this court found sufficient to sustain a finding of premeditation and deliberation falls into three basic categories: (1) facts about how and what defendant did *prior* to the actual killing which show that the defendant was engaged in activity directed toward, and explicable as intended to result in, the killing — what may be characterized as "planning" activity; (2) facts about the defendant's *prior* relationship and/or conduct with the victim from which the jury could reasonably infer a "motive" to kill the victim, which inference of motive, together with facts of type (1) or (3), would in turn support an inference that the killing "was the result of pre-existing reflection" and "careful thought and weighing of considerations" rather than "mere unconsidered or rash impulse hastily executed"[;] (3) facts about the nature of the killing from which the jury could infer *[The m]anner of killing was so particular and exacting that the defendant must have intentionally killed according to a "preconceived design" to take his victim's life in a particular way for a "reason" which the jury can reasonably infer from facts of type (1) or (2).*

More to the point, it is stated in the treatise of W. LaFave & A. Scott, *Criminal Law* § 7.7(a) at 645 (2d ed.1986), that "[t]he mere fact that the killing was attended by much violence or that a great many wounds were inflicted is not relevant in this regard [establishing premeditation], as such a killing is just as likely (or perhaps more likely) to have been on impulse." The majority makes the point, citing *Mitchell v. State*, that the test for first degree murder is not the quality or rationality of the reflection in determining deliberation and premeditation or *whether it may have been emotionally based.* The discussion in *Mitchell* centered on whether the elements of premeditation and deliberation were established by the agreement in a conspiracy to commit murder in the first degree as to the non-shooter. The Court of Appeals concluded:

> We are unable to follow the metaphysical analysis of [*United States v.Chagra*] or the intermediate appellate court in this case, that spontaneity or acting on impulse can, at the same time, suffice to establish an agreement to murder but not suffice to constitute the deliberation and premeditation that distinguishes first [degree murder] from this form of second degree murder, as we have defined those concepts.

The cases cited by the majority for the proposition that appellant's emotional state does not preclude a finding that he acted deliberately and with premeditation involve homicides in which the circumstances do not provide an alternative theory that not only is more plausible, but which, from the point of view of the lay jury, could reasonably have been endorsed by the State. In that regard, the State, in its closing argument said:

> Now the last form of homicide that the judge instructed you on is first degree murder. It's basically second degree murder with two additional element[s], were the defendant's actions deliberate and were they premeditated[?]

> Deliberate means, was the defendant conscious of his intent to kill[?] Well let's look at this [sic] actions, *he had tried so many different things to get Ta'mar to stop crying and he couldn't do it, and he was frustrated and he was tired. And he wanted to do something that would stop his crying.* He didn't do something that didn't coincide with what his goals were. *So he was conscious of his goal, his goal was to quiet the baby.* So he took Baby Ta'mar and slammed his head into a bed rail. He knew exactly what he was doing, he was conscious of his intent.

> The last element is premeditation. Now people tend to think of premeditation as laying in wait, as plans that go in [sic] for weeks in advance, conspiracy, and all of those things are premeditation. But you don't need time, a significant amount of time for premeditation. You don't need a plan, you don't write out a list [of] things to do. You just need a small amount of time so that you can make the decision whether or not to kill.

> *One, two, three, four. (Indicating.) Between any of those blows the defendant had the opportunity to decide, stop or continue. He chose to continue, he premeditated to kill Ta'mar Hamilton and intended to kill him.*

> Ladies and gentlemen, *what this case really comes down to, the key issue of this case is did [appellant] kill Ta'mar Hamilton . . . .*

At the *in banc* hearing before this Court, it was elicited that the prosecutor, at one point, argued to the jury that the evidence supported the State's theory that it was appellant's intent to kill young Ta'mar, rather than simply to stop him from crying. A review of the prosecutor's argument reveals that its principal thrust was that appellant was attempting to stop the young child from crying and death ensued from acts that were wanton and demonstrated a disregard for human life. Such a finding would be quintessentially depraved heart second degree murder under Maryland law.

Judge Wilner, writing for the Court of Special Appeals in *Simpkins v. State,* explained:

> A depraved heart murder is often described as a wanton and wilful killing. The term "depraved heart" means something more than conduct

amounting to a high or unreasonable risk to human life. The perpetrator must [or reasonably should] realize the risk his [or her] behavior has created to the extent that his [or her] conduct may be termed wilful. Moreover, the conduct must contain an element of viciousness or contemptuous disregard for the value of human life which conduct characterizes that behavior as wanton.

The *Simpkins* Court, discussing the element of intent, further explained:

But intent again will be found to resolve itself into two things; foresight that certain consequences will follow from an act, and the wish for those consequences working as a motive which induces the act. The question then is, whether intent, in its turn, cannot be reduced to a lower term. Sir James Stephen's statement shows that it can be, and that knowledge that the act will probably cause death, that is, foresight of the consequences of the act, is enough in murder as in tort.

The *Simpkins* Court traced the development of English and American decisions that involved the withholding of sustenance from a young child and under what circumstances an intent may be found to elevate the offense from manslaughter to depraved heart second degree murder or first degree intent-to-kill murder. In the cases cited, when the actor intended the act, the natural consequences of which subjected the victim to a high or unreasonable risk to human life, although death was not intended, the cases generally hold that the defendant is guilty of depraved heart second degree murder. When the defendant intended for the withholding of sustenance to result in death, the offense committed is clearly first degree murder.

From the above, establishing that appellant intending for death to occur is indispensable to a finding of first degree murder. For that reason, emphasis should have been placed on the distinction between intending an act, the natural consequence of which involved a risk of death and intending that death occur as a means of causing young Ta'mar to stop crying, notwithstanding that the trial court properly instructed the jury that "willful means that the defendant actually intended to kill the victim." Ordinarily, this instruction would have sufficed to inform the jury as to how to determine whether the evidence supported a finding of first degree murder.

The prosecutor, however, took great pains to make the point that appellant "wanted to do something that would stop his crying" and "he was conscious of his goal, his goal was to quiet the baby." The prosecutor then told the jury that appellant "slammed Ta'mar's head into the bed rail and that he knew exactly what he was doing, he was conscious of his intent." At that point in the prosecutor's argument, the intent to which she referred is to stop young Ta'mar from crying. The jury could have very easily been misled if it believed that appellant acted only with the intent to prevent young Ta'mar from crying, but that he did not intend for the baby to die. Under such circumstances, the appropriate verdict should have been depraved heart second degree murder.

It is certainly within the province of the jury to come to its own conclusions as to what the circumstances reveal about appellant's mental state; however, the emphasis by the prosecutor on what appellant's "goal" was enhances the likelihood that the jury was confused because, notwithstanding dissembling by appellant, there were no circumstances extrinsic to the criminal act itself that indicated that appellant wished the baby dead. The only motive ascribed to appellant is that he wanted the baby to stop crying. The possibility existed that appellant intended to kill the young victim as a means to prevent him from crying. The more plausible explanation, however, is that, in a frenetic state, appellant applied force with little thought of the consequences. Great pains, in my view, should have been taken when such emphasis was placed on stopping the baby from crying as the stated "goal" in order that it be crystal clear that the jury must find that the "goal" was to kill the infant, not merely to stop him from crying. It was incumbent on the court to insure that there was no confusion as to the point.

As I have acknowledged, it was within the province of the jury, based on the evidence, direct and circumstantial, and inferences deducible therefrom, to conclude that appellant *possibly* intended to kill young Ta'mar. My concern is whether, in a case when there had been articulated (and the prosecutor had reinforced) an intent other than to kill the young child, the distinction between an intent to kill and the intentional commission of an act, the nature of which is likely to cause death, may very well have become blurred.

Judge Charles E. Moylan, Jr., formerly of this Court, in his treatise, *Criminal Homicide Law*, traces the definitions of "willful," "deliberate," and "premeditated" to Hochheimer who, in turn, based his definitions on the Pennsylvania Act of 1794. For "interpretive guidance," according to Judge Moylan, Hochheimer looked to a single Pennsylvania decision, *Commonwealth v. Drum*. In delineating the distinction between first degree and second degree murder, the *Drum* decision concluded:

> A learned judge (Judge Rush, in *Commonwealth v. Richard Smith*) has said: "It is equally true both in fact and from experience, that *no* time is too short for a wicked man to frame in his mind his scheme of murder, and to contrive the means of accomplishing it." But this expression must be qualified, lest it mislead. It is true that such is the swiftness of human thought, that no time is so short in which a wicked man may not form a design to kill, and frame the means of executing his purpose; yet this suddenness is opposed to premeditation, and a jury must be well convinced upon the evidence that there was time to deliberate and premeditate. The law regards, and the jury must find, the actual intent; that to say, the fully formed purpose to kill, with so much time for deliberation and premeditation, as to convince them that this purpose is

not the immediate offspring of rashness and impetuous temper, and that the mind has become fully conscious of its own design. If there be time to frame in the mind, fully and consciously, the intention to kill, and to select the weapon or means of death, and to think and know beforehand, though the time be short, the use to be made of it, there is time to deliberate and to premeditate.

The *Drum* decision, as is true with much of the scholarship regarding the law of first and second degree murder, discusses the time required for there to be the fully-formed purpose to kill and for deliberation and premeditation. In the case at hand, my position, unlike the dissent which focuses on the element of premeditation, is that the length of time, standing alone, should not be determinative of whether the jury could find from the facts and circumstances "the actual intent . . . the fully formed purpose to kill. . . ." An act evidencing a non-homicidal intent may be sustained over an extended period of time, despite the fact that it demonstrates a wanton disregard for human life. Appellant's actions were more likely "the immediate offspring of rashness and impetuous temper, . . ." and the mind has not "become fully conscious of its own design." In other words, the instant case, I believe, is devoid of the qualitative, rather than the quantitative, element of reflection. Aside from the extensive injuries inflicted, all of the extrinsic circumstances tend to belie a contention that appellant harbored an intent to kill Ta'mar.

With respect to the requisite elements of first degree intent-to-kill murder, Judge Chasanow, writing for the Court of Appeals in *Willey v. State* explained:

> For a killing to be "wilful" there must be a specific purpose and intent to kill; to be "deliberate" there must be a full and conscious knowledge of the purpose to kill; and to be "premeditated" the design to kill must have preceded the killing by an appreciable length of time, that is, time enough to be deliberate. It is unnecessary that the deliberation or premeditation shall have existed for any particular length of time.

In discussing a homicide scheme similar to that in Maryland, Leo Romero at 18 N.M. L.Rev. 73 (1988), observed at 74:

> An intentional homicide includes only those killings where the actor desires the death of another human being; it does not include a killing where the actor acts intentionally but without the purpose of bringing about death. For example, a person who intentionally shoots at the victim to scare him [or her], but without intending the result of death, does not commit an intentional homicide if the discharge should hit the victim and the victim should die. Even though the act causing death, the shooting, was intentional, the killing amounts to an unintentional homicide because the person did not intend the consequence of death. Hence, it is important to distinguish between intentional shooting and intentional killing.

The author speaks to a further concern presented by the case at bar:

> . . . The more reprehensible the homicide, the greater the punishment the killing should warrant. The grading of homicides on the basis of relative seriousness also reflects differences in stigma and moral wrongdoing.
>
> Although all homicides are in some sense different, the division of homicides into categories should be based on principled, clear, and workable distinctions. Distinctions are principled in the sense that first degree murder includes killings that are more heinous than those killings encompassed by second degree murder. Distinctions are clear to the extent that they meaningfully differentiate the two degrees of murder; for example the line between murder in the first degree and murder in the second degree should be clearly recognizable. *Finally, distinctions are workable if the lines between the different classifications are understandable by a jury of lay people in applying the distinctions and determining the degree of homicide.* Because the different classifications of homicides should reflect differences in culpability, culpability terms should he defined precisely to clarify the distinctions.

The above quotation is clearly a plea for some sense of moral relativism in the law of homicide. Currently, one can act almost spontaneously in an emotional or frenzied state and nevertheless be subjected to a conviction for first degree murder based solely on a theoretical instantaneous period of reflection and the nature of the injuries inflicted. At the same time, one whose actions are more calculating may be deemed to be guilty only of second degree murder as a consequence of the number and nature of the injuries sustained.

Apropos the instant case, no difference in culpability or moral accountability is imputed to appellant, who admittedly committed a heinous act, than to one who commits a murder for hire or one who murders in the course of conducting a criminal enterprise. As despicable as appellant's conduct was, it cannot be equated with that of a professional killer or, for that matter, one who conceives of a calculated scheme to murder a child.

The majority dismisses appellant's argument that no Maryland case in which an otherwise caring, responsible care giver has been convicted of the premeditated, deliberate first degree murder of a child when death resulted from a single incident. The majority notes that appellant cites three cases, as cases in which heinous injuries were suffered by the child victims, but in which the defendants were convicted of either second degree depraved heart murder or manslaughter. Because each case must be decided on its own facts, I do not accept appellant's argument that reversal is warranted simply because there is a paucity of cases that are factually similar in which a first degree murder conviction was rendered. Often, it is the prosecutor's office that decides to pursue only second degree depraved heart murder as the flagship count in the indictment.

Although the distinction between murder and manslaughter is generally discernible by a jury with the aid of instructions from the court, the distinction between second degree and first degree premeditated murder often confounds juries. As a result, a defendant is subject to the vagaries of the charging process as well as confusion by lay persons on the jury.

Judge Chasanow, writing for the Court of Appeals in *Willey*, referred to the confusion resulting from the lack of clarity as to the definition of premeditation:

> [I]t would be preferable, especially *where the distinction is clearly at issue*, for the trial court to emphasize that in order for the jury to conclude that the defendant premeditated the killing it must find that the defendant had sufficient time to consider the decision whether or not to kill and weigh the reasons for or against such a choice. Movement in this direction would be consistent with the developing trend of courts and commentators to focus more attention upon, and more clearly define, the distinct mental states involved in first versus second degree murder.

Although I agree with the observation by the *Willey* Court that there needs to be greater clarity with respect to the distinct mental states involved in first versus second degree murder, my concern in the case *sub judice* does not pertain, principally, to whether there was sufficient time to premeditate but, rather, only whether the jury was confused as to the character of the reflection required and its mandate to return a first degree verdict only if it found from the evidence an intent to kill. I recognize that the time it took to inflict the injuries in this case is more than sufficient to satisfy the element of premeditation as to length of time. Whether the killing was deliberate is intertwined with the intent to kill because one certainly cannot be conscious of an intent to kill if there is no intent to kill. Thus, although the potential jury confusion to which I address my concern is the intent to kill, it logically follows that, if there is jury confusion as to the evidence of intent to kill, then there also can be no consciousness of that intent and, *ergo*, the killing cannot be deliberate.

Judge Moylan, writing for this Court, discusses the interrelationship of the requisite elements of first degree murder in *Smith v. State*:

> Do the three adjectives "wilful," "deliberate" and "premeditated" describe three distinct aspects of the mental state we are searching for or are they, as a rhetorical device for purposes of emphasis, simply three synonyms for the same mental state? Do the second and third adjectives add anything whatsoever to the first? Can there be "a specific purpose and design to kill" without "a full and conscious knowledge of the purpose to kill"? How does one have purpose without being conscious of that purpose? To wit, can an act be "wilful" and not "deliberate"? By the

same token, does the third adjective add anything to the second? How can one be "deliberate" without having had "time enough to be deliberate"?

I acknowledge, as I must, that although the more plausible explanation for appellant's actions is that, exacerbated and in a frenetic state, he engaged in conduct that evidenced a contemptuous disregard of the value of human life, the jury was entitled to find from the direct and circumstantial evidence and the inferences properly deducible therefrom that appellant employed lethal force to kill the infant as a means to stop him from crying. The potential for confusion by the jury, in my judgment, could only have been addressed by drawing its attention specifically to the fact that a *mens rea* simply bent on stopping the baby from crying is insufficient to sustain a conviction for murder in the first degree. As to punishment, a sentence of thirty years' imprisonment, consecutive to the life imprisonment sentence for first degree murder, was imposed for child abuse. Had the jury returned a verdict of murder in the second degree, appellant's exposure would have been in the aggregate, assuming consecutive sentences, sixty years' imprisonment. The sentence for second degree murder would have differentiated appellant's punishment from that reserved for killers who clearly intend to kill their victims pursuant to a discernible design.

SONNER, J., dissenting.

For better or worse, our law separates first degree murder from other killings based on the decision to kill in advance of the act. It is a separation for judges and lawyers to examine, understand, and explain to the jury. And when any evidence of first degree murder is presented, the trial judge, in the first instance, and as a matter of law, must determine whether the evidence could persuade a jury to convict. The judge cannot let a case go to the jury if there is only a morsel of evidence; there must be enough to allow a jury to jump the hurdle of reasonable doubt. The jury, on the other hand, is the sole judge of facts. But just because juries have that power does not permit them to evaluate murders to determine which are the worst and then pick the degree of crime. This delegation of a judicial responsibility to a jury is exactly what the majority condones, and what causes me to dissent.

First, let me make clear that I agree with the majority's opinion concluding that Pinkney barely preserved the sufficiency issue. He was vague as to just how the State's evidence failed. I also agree that we would be mistaken to use that shortcoming to evade deciding the important issue presented. Moreover, I understand that the State can prove all of the elements of first degree murder with circumstantial evidence, and I accept the majority's definition of first degree murder. Lastly, I have no quarrel with the conclusion that sufficient evidence existed to show Pinkney was the perpetrator. My concern, instead, is that we have affirmed a conviction for first degree murder when there has been no showing, indeed, no real focus at trial, of Pinkney's premeditation to commit the fatal acts.

The tortuous history of the law of homicide in Maryland, and throughout the United States, can cause present day confusion and can lead to inconsistent application. This dissent is not the proper place to describe that history, or even to describe the apparent confusion. For my purposes, it is sufficient to work with accepted definitions of the crime:

For a killing to be "wilful" there must be a specific purpose and intent to kill; to be "deliberate" there must be a full and conscious knowledge of the purpose to kill; and to be "premeditated" the design to kill must have preceded the killing by an appreciable length of time, that is, time enough to be deliberate.

To sustain a guilty verdict of first degree murder, there must be some evidence from which the jurors could have found *beyond a reasonable doubt* "the actual intent, the fully formed purpose to kill, with so much time for deliberation and premeditation as to convince them, that this purpose [wa]s not the immediate offspring of rashness and impetuous temper and that the mind ha [d] become fully conscious of its own design." The presence of deliberation and premeditation must be judged from the facts of each case because there is no particular length of time during which they "shall have been conceived or have existed."

I agree that there was sufficient evidence to show Pinkney's intent to kill; Ta'mar's head injuries supply that. But the State produced nothing at trial to show that Pinkney's mind had become "conscious of its own design," that there was "a choice made as the result of thought." There is nothing in the record to show that there was deliberation for any period, long or short, any struggle, that is, between the intention to kill and the act.

As Judge Rodowsky explained in *Ferrell v. State*:

[U]nder the Maryland statute and this Court's decisions premeditation is something more than forming an intent to kill. . . . Professor Perkins goes so far as to say that "[t]he notion that a fully formed intent is always deliberate and premeditated, no matter how short the time between the first thought of the matter and the execution of the plan, is preposterous."

The State's theory of the case at trial, as expressed in its closing argument, bears out the absence of premeditation. As the concurring opinion recognizes, the State proceeded on the implicit theory that the killing was of the depraved heart variety. Its approach was not that Pinkney planned the murder, or even thought about it in advance, but, rather, that he carried it out in a rage that burst forth from utter frustration. Essentially, the State asked the jury to return a verdict based upon facts that would support a depraved heart murder, as if those facts supported first degree murder.

Pinkney, for his part, asserted a defense that he did not inflict the fatal injuries, not that he was guilty only of a lesser degree of homicide. That was certainly an understandable strategy. The double defense of having Pinkney maintain that he did not inflict the injuries, while simultaneously defending that he did not deliberate before inflicting the same injuries would not carry much chance of success with a jury. Each defense would weaken the other. Using the defense that someone else injured Ta'mar meant that he, like the State, did not inject an issue of premeditation into the case. Nonetheless, in affirming the conviction, the majority, working backwards and with hindsight, reads the record and declares that there was enough evidence to support a finding of first degree murder. I cannot agree.

The majority, and to some degree the concurring opinion, relies upon the appellate review of the facts in *Hounshell v. State*, in which the accused contended that the State's evidence failed because there was nothing introduced to show the length of time it would take to strangle a victim. We held that the jury could understand what was involved in strangulation, and so it could find the time necessary to kill by strangulation was sufficient to show premeditation. Speaking for this Court, however, Judge Getty observed that "the autopsy report does not reflect that death resulted from a fracture or sudden blow to the throat." To hold that the time necessary to give a powerful destructive blow to an infant is equivalent to the time necessary to "kill by squeezing the throat so as to shut off the breath," wrongly expands first degree murder beyond its separate sphere.

Even more misleading, the majority quotes *Hounshell* that "the brutality of the murder act may, in and of itself, provide sufficient evidence to convict for first degree murder." But the killing in *Hounshell* required a concentrated effort by the murderer to create the brutality, so premeditation was clearly present. Read literally and independently of the facts in *Hounshell*, and applied reflexively in appeals of murder cases, the quotation may come to mean that any and all brutal killings qualify for first degree murder, with the brutality serving as a substitute for competent evidence of premeditation.

So, too, in *Fuller v. State*, we affirmed a husband's first degree murder conviction for the stabbing death of his wife, and noted the particularly brutal nature of the crime. The multiple stab wounds in that case, however, which stretched the length and width of the victim's body, showed a "protracted and brutal assault." Protracted means an extended period of time — time enough to deliberate and support a finding of premeditation. Ta'mar's death is a tragedy; the injuries he suffered were horrific and brutal, but they do not show the kind of premeditation that the injuries in *Hounshell* and *Fuller* did.

The majority also draws a parallel between Pinkney's two blows and the defendant in *Tichnell*, who fired two shots from a gun. Tichnell's first degree conviction, however, did not rest only on the firing of the two shots, but on the circumstances surrounding his confrontation with arresting law enforcement. A shallow comparison of the two cases invites the use of acts that show an intent to kill as a substitute for proof that the defendant premeditated.

Ultimately, the majority reiterates its deference for the jury function, and the concurrence is optimistic that, notwithstanding the very real problems with the evidence, the jury successfully waded through the confusion presented to it. I emphasize that the State must prove *every* element of a crime beyond a reasonable doubt. Neither the trial judge, nor this Court, can ease this burden for the State.

> [T]he reasonable-doubt standard is indispensable to command the respect and confidence of the community in applications of the criminal law. It is critical that the moral force of the criminal law not be diluted by a standard of proof that leaves people in doubt whether innocent men are being condemned. It is also important in our free society that every individual going about his ordinary affairs have confidence that his government cannot adjudge him guilty of a criminal offense without convincing a proper fact finder of his guilt with utmost certainty.

Moreover, the reasonable doubt standard is "more than simply a trial ritual." When a properly instructed jury in a state trial convicts, "even when it can be said that no rational trier of fact could find guilt beyond a reasonable doubt," the conviction violates Fourteenth Amendment due process and cannot stand.

We respected these constitutional principles in *Rasnick v. State*, in which we reversed a first degree felony murder conviction because there was insufficient evidence of the underlying robbery. The State had put forth evidence that the victim yelled before his death, "He is robbing me." Although we recognized the trial judge's finding that the State's evidence on this point was credible, we did not find the evidence sufficient to allow a jury to conclude that the robbery occurred. There was something to support the required element of robbery, but not enough to sustain a conviction, and we were careful to mark the distinction. We applied the same reasoning and review later in *Robinson v. State*.

In the context of this case, the enumerated principles of law mean that the jury could not have found Pinkney guilty of premeditated murder if there was no evidence from which it could find, beyond a reasonable doubt, that he went through a thought process and chose to act with the intent to murder the baby. The majority would allow juries to take the evidence that supports an intent to kill and use that evidence, if it so wishes, to find premeditation, even though the evidence falls short of showing, as it must, that the defendant deliberated at all. Our law does not permit such a misuse of evidence, such an obscuring of the elements of a crime.

Premeditation is by no means a simple concept. The majority opinion evades the concept of premeditation, at best, or misconstrues it, at worst. It leads us down a path of eliminating the distinction between first and second degree murder and having juries pick the degree as a means of increasing punishment. Indeed, with this decision, we have upheld a jury's verdict of first degree murder without proof of the essential element of premeditation. We, in an overly deferential review, join the jury and the court below in a visceral resolve to punish severely the man accused of a disturbing and horrific crime.

NOTES AND QUESTIONS

1.   The purpose of a dissent is to demonstrate that the majority's result was not inevitable. Did the dissent accomplish that purpose in *Pinkney v. State*?

2.   What type of legal analysis — applying a rule to a set of facts, analogizing, developing a rule from many sets of facts, or espousing a sound policy or philosophy (*see* Chapter Five) — did the majority opinion employ? How about the concurrence and the dissent?

3.   Dissents and concurrences do not create binding authority. What purpose, then, do they serve for litigants? The legal profession?

4.   Which appellate court is stronger, one with regular and vigorous dissenting and concurring opinions, or one in which the judges strive to deliberate and edit until they reach consensus? Judge Ruggero Aldisert suggests "that no separate opinion should ever be written unless there has been a collegial effort toward consensus." Ruggero J. Aldisert, Opinion Writing 195 (AuthorHouse 2d ed. 2010). Do you agree? Judge Patricia Wald noted that in the course of her tenure on the D.C. Circuit Court of Appeals, she came to dissent less often.

> [W]hile still refusing to vote in any case against my best judgment of law, I became more selective, declining to write a dissent in those cases where there was sufficient ambiguity that the law could go either way and a dissent was unlikely to accomplish anything beyond personal satisfaction. A steady dissenter loses leverage with colleagues in negotiating an opinion; sometimes a concurrence with the majority which secures a few important point will do more for the law.

Patricia M. Wald, *Six Not-So-Easy Pieces: One Woman Judge's Journey to the Bench and Beyond*, 36 U. Tol. L. Rev. 979, 988 (2005). Is anything lost when a judge disagrees with the majority's result, but chooses not to issue a dissent?

III.   SUGGESTED FURTHER READING

Ruggero J. Aldisert, Opinion Writing (AuthorHouse 2d ed. 2010).

Joyce J. George, Judicial Opinion Writing Handbook (5th ed. 2007).

Mark Tushnet, I Dissent: Great Opposing Opinions in Landmark Supreme Court Cases (2008).

Patricia M. Wald, *Rhetoric and Results*, 62 U. CHI. L. REV. 1371 (1995).

Chapter 7

CLERKING: THE BEAUTY IS IN THE DETAILS

I. INTRODUCTION

After the judge and law clerk have written, revised, and edited an appellate opinion, the opinion must be checked for accuracy before it is released to the other judges deciding the case. This check for accuracy is known as clerking. The process entails a slow, careful reading of every sentence and citation in the opinion. It attends to the substantive assertions made in the opinion, as well as less consequential things, such as the form of citations. Clerking requires concentration and an equal appreciation for large and small details.

Clerking is the exclusive responsibility of appellate law clerks. Whereas judges may differ in the degree of opinion-drafting that they delegate to their clerks, they all expect their law clerks to clerk well. It is wrong, therefore, to begin a clerkship without having learned the citation form that governs in your jurisdiction, or where to place a comma, or how to offer constructive criticism to another writer. To be sure, you will improve all of these skills in the course of an appellate clerkship, but you should begin the job with a solid foundation already in place. To that end, this chapter explains the clerking process and offers several practice exercises.

II. STEP-BY-STEP CLERKING

In chambers with two or more law clerks, the clerk who did not draft the opinion usually clerks it, because we are more likely to catch other people's mistakes than our own mistakes. Plus, this clerk will have a fresh perspective and can offer a spontaneous and detached reaction to the opinion. But even for chambers with one clerk, the process described below will ensure proficient clerking. Speak with your judge about whether you should mark your edits on a hard copy of the opinion or electronically.

Step One: Read the opinion once through for comprehension.

Step Two: Check every fact stated in the opinion against the record or record extract.

Look for proof in the record for every fact included in the opinion. You may use the citations in the briefs to find the correct page in the record, but do not rely on the parties' statements of facts without independently checking the record. After all, any factual mistakes in the final opinion will reflect poorly on your judge, not the litigants. You should also check for internal consistency within the opinion. For example, is a party referred to as "Mrs. Jones" in the first two pages, but "Ms. Jones" thereafter? Was the younger brother's name switched by mistake with the older brother's name? Do the dates match up with the timetable for the story of the case?

Step Three: Check every statement of law against its source.

The purpose here is to ensure that the precedent is described accurately. This is exacting work. First, review the historical and procedural facts of the cited precedent and assess whether the opinion that you are clerking mischaracterizes this precedent in any way. Second, confirm the accuracy of all quotations in the opinion you are clerking. You may be surprised at how common misquotations are, even when the author purportedly cut and pasted from electronic sources of law. Likewise, you might discover that the opinion is missing quotation marks. Remember that all material copied verbatim from its original source requires quotation marks; judges are not immune from allegations of plagiarism. *See Matter of Brennan*, 447 N.W.2d 712 (Mich. 1989).

Step Four: Correct citation mistakes.

To correct these kinds of mistakes, you must understand the rules of citation that your judge follows. When in doubt, follow the current edition of THE BLUEBOOK: A UNIFORM SYSTEM OF CITATION. Always use a citator to ensure that the cited material is still good law.

Step Five: Correct grammatical and typographical mistakes.

You might assume that this is a straight-forward step in the process, but actually, there are many instances when there is more than one correct way to write, and all writers, including judges, develop idiosyncratic preferences. The primary goal, therefore, is to distinguish mistakes from choices. Mistakes must be corrected, whereas choices can be accepted without comment or discussed respectfully. If the opinion misspells a party's name, for example, you must correct it. You would also want to include a missing comma before an independent clause. On the other hand, you might accept another writer's use of semi-colons, even if you do not use them in your own writing, or you might suggest a better topic sentence without slashing through what has already been written.

As you read for grammatical mistakes, look out for punctuation mistakes, pronouns that do not agree with their subject nouns, and misuse of the passive voice. Ask your judge what source he or she consults to answer questions of grammar and open your mind to practices that may differ from what you were taught.

EXERCISES

1.   Which statements in the following paragraph would you check against the record?

This case began with Edna Adams's knee replacement in November 2003. Following a brief stay in a rehabilitative center, Adams recuperated in the apartment of her daughter, Patricia Smith, and her son-in-law, Nathan Smith. Her stay there, however, was unhappy, and following an animated disagreement between Adams and her son-in-law, Adams abruptly returned to her home on November 19, 2003, via a taxi service.

2.   Are there any typographical mistakes or inconsistencies in the following paragraph?

On November 20, 2003, Adams met with her attorney. She asked him to revise her Last Will and Testament, dated September 5, 2002. Three days later, on November 24, 2003, Mrs. Adams executed a revised will that divided her assets equally among her sons, Donald and Michael Addams; there was no mention of her daughter, Patricia Smith. Nonetheless, three weeks later, while eating Thanksgiving dinner at Donald's house, she told him that she "loved Patty just the same."

3.   Are the following citations correct according to the Bluebook?

This is a case of statutory interpretation, so our review of the trial court's decision is plenary. *Benson v. Health Plan*, 978 A.2d 33, 36 (Sup. Ct. Vt. 2009). Our ultimate purpose is to effectuate the Legislature's intent. *Id.* We begin by examining the words of the statute, giving "meaning and effect" to all of them. *State v. Ben Mont Corporation*, 652 A.2d 1004, 57(1993). Words and phrases should not be rendered superfluous. *Wright v. Bradley*, 910 A.2d 893 at 896 (Vt. 2006). Moreover, because the statute at issue is remedial, we must consider the wrong that the statute was implemented to combat. *Carter V. Freds Plumbing & Heating, Inc.*, 816 A.2d 490 (Vt. 2002). We will construe the statute liberally to advance the remedy that the Legislature intended. *Id.*

4.   Clerk the following excerpt, noting any mistakes in substance, citation, and grammar.

The Fourth Amendment guarantees the "right of the people to be secure in their persons, houses, papers, and effects, against unreasonable searches and seizures.." U.S. CONST. Amend. IV. If the government obtains an item in violation of the fourth amendment protection, the item is inadmissible as evidence. *Id.* Shendell argues that the canine sniff of the his backyard constituted an unreasonable search so that the trial court should suppressed the contraband extracted from his backyard, following the canine sniff. Our review of the precedent leads us to a contrary conclusion.

A canine sniff is *"sui generis* because unlike other investigative techniques, it is "limited both in the manner in which the information is obtained and in the content of the information revealed by the procedure." *U. S. v. Place*, 462 U.S. 696, at 708 (1983). Indeed, the cannine sniff "is less intrusive than a typical search," as it "discloses only the presence or absence of narcotics, a contraband item." *Id.*. There is no Fourth Amendment protection for the possession of contraband. *See United States v. Jaccobson*, 466 U.S. 109, 123 (1984). "Governmental conduct that only reveals the possession of contraband "compromises no legitimate privacy interest." " *Caballes*, 543 U.S. at 408. A canine sniff then is not per se an unreasonable search.

Courts have upheld canine sniffs of luggage at airports. *See, e.g. United State V. Place*, 462 U.S. 696 (1983) (noting that a canine sniff is performed on sealed luggage, protecting from public view the lawful items inside the luggage); *United States v. Jacobsen*, 466 U.S. 109 (1984); *Kyllo v. United States*, 533 U.S. 27 (2001). Additionally, canine sniffs of automobiles are not unreasonable searches. *See, e.g., Illinois v. Caballes*, 543 U.S. 405 (2005); *City of Indianapolis v. Edmond*, 531 U.S. 32 (2000).

III. SUGGESTED FURTHER READING

THE BLUEBOOK: A UNIFORM SYSTEM OF CITATION (19th ed. 2010).

IAN GALLACHER, A FORM AND STYLE MANUAL FOR LAWYERS (2007).

Hon. Gerald Lebovits & Lucero Ramirez Hidalgo, *Advice to Law Clerks: How to Draft Your First Judicial Opinion*, 36 WESTCHESTER B.J. 29 (2009).

WILLIAM STRUNK JR. & E.B. WHITE, THE ELEMENTS OF STYLE (4th ed. 2000).

PART III

FOUNDATIONAL PRINCIPLES FOR TRIAL COURT LAW CLERKS

Chapter 8

A PRIMER ON LAW AND FACT

I. INTRODUCTION

Of course you know what the words fact and law mean, but can you define them and explain the differences between them? Distinguishing fact from law is a fundamental skill for trial court law clerks, because although trial judges answer questions of law, questions of fact are reserved exclusively for the fact-finder. The following summary clarifies the meaning of fact, inference, finding of fact, law, and conclusion of law. Admittedly, this terminology is tricky even for seasoned attorneys, because it is not always easy to articulate the concepts underlying the words. But this section should provide you with a sound understanding that you certainly will revisit if you become a law clerk or litigator.

A. Fact

A fact is something that happened. It can be observed or documented. It relies on at least one of the five senses. Here are three examples of facts: (1) the police officer extended the leash of the drug-sniffing dog; (2) an inch of ice covered the sidewalk; and (3) plaintiff left the household three times in July. These kinds of facts are often called "historical facts" or "narrative facts." You may also see them described as "first-level facts" or "basic facts."

B. Inference

An inference is a conclusion built upon facts. It is sometimes referred to as a "second-level" fact. Consider these examples: (1) the officer accidentally discovered the marijuana plants; (2) the defendant knew that the sidewalk in front of her house was slippery; (3) plaintiff was not worried about his children's safety when he left the household. You could imagine facts that would support these inferences, just as you could imagine facts that would refute them. An inference, therefore, is not absolute. It is only as strong as the facts that support it.

C. Finding of Fact

With testimony or documents, litigants present facts and inferences to tell their version of the events leading up to the dispute. The fact-finder will wade through these evidentiary facts, judging the credibility of the witnesses and the influence of the presented documents. The fact-finder may accept all, none, or some of the evidence presented, and based on the governing law, the fact-finder also will determine which of these evidentiary facts are material. The conclusions flowing from this deliberative process are the official findings of fact.

How do we know what the fact-finder has found? The jury is the fact-finder in a jury trial, and we must rely on its verdict to divine what facts it found to be true. There are two basic types of verdict forms. First, a jury may be given a verdict form that requires it to answer specific questions of fact before stating its verdict. In a slip-and-fall case, for example, the verdict form might include questions, such as: "Was the floor slippery on the day of the fall?" and "Did the slippery floor cause plaintiff's injuries?" before the ultimate question of "Was defendant negligent?" Alternatively, the jury might be asked to provide only its verdict. In a prosecution for criminal assault, for example, the jury might return a guilty verdict, without articulating what it found as fact.

In a bench trial, the trial judge serves as the fact-finder. The judge ordinarily must state his or her findings of fact on the record or include them in a written document. These findings of fact are essential because fact-finding can only be done in the trial court. Appellate courts do not hear live testimony or admit documentary evidence. They derive their understanding of the case from reading the trial transcript and scrutinizing the trial court's findings of fact. As Chapter Three details, appellate courts self-consciously restrain themselves from usurping the fact-finder's mission.

D. Law

The trial judge is solely responsible for deciding the law that governs a controversy. Law is general and applies to more than one set of facts. It sets the rights and responsibilities of societal relationships. Law falls squarely on the shoulders of the trial court and cannot be delegated to the fact-finder.

Questions about the governing law arise before, during, and after trials. These may be questions of substantive law, such as tort law, criminal law, or labor law, or they may be questions of procedural law or evidentiary law. Trial judges are also responsible for the management of the proceedings. They decide, for example, whether to sequester a witness or postpone a trial. These questions of law — substantive, procedural, evidentiary — may arise in written or oral motions, or by objection. And a judge may ask a law clerk to assist in answering any one of them. You will understand, then, why trial court law clerks are destined to learn a lot of law in a short amount of time and why employers are keen on hiring them following the clerkships.

E.   Conclusion of Law

You might think that because the phrase "conclusion of law" includes the word law, it also falls in the province of the trial court. But ordinarily, that is not so. A conclusion of law is the application of the governing law to the found facts and inferences. It "expresses a legal deduction . . . naturally arising from the found facts and carrying with it some form of legal consequence." J.J. George, Judicial Opinion Writing Handbook 231 (5th ed. 2007). As a conclusion based on facts and inferences, it ordinarily falls in the fact-finder's purview.

Here are three examples: (1) the defendant was negligent; (2) plaintiff breached the contract; and (3) counsel provided ineffective assistance. Notice how all three of these conclusions depend on facts and inferences. Also notice how these conclusions include a legal concept — negligence, breach of contract, ineffective assistance of counsel — that was applied to the specific facts of the case. These conclusions do not, however, speak generally about the relevant legal concepts; they are not the kind of law statements reserved for courts.

Think of a claim in the trial court as a sketched drawing. Law outlines the sketched image, directing attention to what matters in the case. Fact colors the image, providing detail to the case. Together, they create the conclusion of law, a complete image that settles the controversy, at least until an appeal is taken.

F.   Appellate Review: Connecting the Dots

Chapter Three discussed the three most common standards of appellate review: *de novo*, abuse of discretion, and clearly erroneous. How do these standards relate to the definitions provided above?

Evidentiary facts and inferences lead to the jury's or trial judge's findings of fact. Appellate courts give these findings of fact great deference under the clearly erroneous standard of review. On the other hand, a trial judge's statement of substantive law is afforded little deference under the *de novo* standard of review, and, ordinarily, a trial judge's ruling on evidentiary or procedural matters is subject to medium scrutiny under the abuse of discretion standard of review. The cases included in Chapter Three show how these standards of review operate to uphold or reverse the actions of the trial court.

That leaves conclusions of law, which appellate courts often refer to as "mixed questions of fact and law." This category has caused considerable difficulty for appellate courts. Some jurisdictions categorically apply *de novo* review to mixed questions, while others apply the clearly erroneous standard. The Ninth Circuit applies a "functional analysis," described below:

The appropriate standard of review for a district judge's application of law to fact may be determined, in our view, by reference to the sound principles which underlie the settled rules of appellate review just discussed. If the concerns of judicial administration — efficiency, accuracy, and precedential weight — make it more appropriate for a district judge to determine whether the established facts fall within the relevant legal definition, we should subject his determination to deferential, clearly erroneous review. If, on the other hand, the concerns of judicial administration favor the appellate court, we should subject the district judge's finding to de novo review. Thus, in each case, the pivotal question is do the concerns of judicial administration favor the district court or do they favor the appellate court.

In our view, the key to the resolution of this question is the nature of the inquiry that is required to decide "whether the rule of law as applied to the established facts is or is not violated." If application of the rule of law to the facts requires an inquiry that is "essentially factual," — one that is founded "on the application of the fact-finding tribunal's experience with the mainsprings of human conduct," — the concerns of judicial administration will favor the district court, and the district court's determination should be classified as one of fact reviewable under the clearly erroneous standard. If, on the other hand, the question requires us to consider legal concepts in the mix of fact and law and to exercise judgment about the values that animate legal principles, then the concerns of judicial administration will favor the appellate court, and the question should be classified as one of law and reviewed de novo.

United States v. McConney, 728 F.2d 1195, 1202 (9th Cir. 1984).

NOTES AND QUESTIONS

1. How do burdens of proof relate to the discussion of fact and law? A burden of proof establishes the degree of evidence necessary to satisfy a claim. In a civil case, for example, the burden of proof ordinarily is preponderance of the evidence. This means that to prove the claim, a greater part of the credible evidence must support the claim, not deny it. The law also determines which party carries the burden of proof. Ordinarily, in a civil case the burden rests on plaintiff, and in a criminal case, the burden rests on the government. Once the fact-finder has sifted through the facts and inferences presented, it considers the burden of proof and who is responsible to the carry the burden of proof, to reach its conclusions of law.

2. Consider this proposition:

As noted, *de novo* review is typically associated with the review of legal questions. While this characterization is largely accurate, it is misleading. It implicitly suggests that all legal questions are equivalent. In reality, the line between questions of "fact" and questions of "law" is to a significant degree illusory. It is better to imagine a spectrum running from questions of "historical fact" on the one end to questions about the content of a legal rule on the other, with a large zone involving the application of legal rules to particular factual situations in the middle.

Chad M. Oldfather, *Universal De Novo Review*, 77 GEO. WASH. L. REV. 308, 314-15 (2009).

3. As this chapter and Chapter Three emphasize, appellate courts respect the fact-finding of trial courts because they experience the evidence first-hand. What happens when appellate courts are able to view the same evidence as the trial courts? In *Scott v. Harris*, 550 U.S. 372 (2007), the police conducted a high-speed chase that injured the person they were chasing. A video recorder in the police cruiser captured the entire chase. The injured person sued the officer for excessive force under 42 U.S.C. § 1983, and the officer moved for summary judgment, arguing that the chase was necessary to protect area bystanders.

The trial court and intermediate appellate court viewed the video and concluded that the propriety of the chase was a jury question. The U.S. Supreme Court, however, also viewed the video, disagreed with the lower courts, and concluded that the chase was clearly justified. It reasoned that "[t]he videotape quite clearly contradicts the version of the story told by respondent and adopted by the Court of Appeals." *Id.* at 378. Justice Stevens dissented, explaining:

> Relying on a *de novo* review of a videotape of a portion of a nighttime chase on a lightly traveled road in Georgia where no pedestrians or other "bystanders" were present, buttressed by uninformed speculation about the possible consequences of discontinuing the chase, eight of the jurors on this Court reach a verdict that differs from the views of the judges on both the District Court and the Court of Appeals who are surely more familiar with the hazards of driving on Georgia roads than we are.

Id. at 389 (Stevens, J., dissenting). What is your reaction?

EXERCISE

Frank and David were roommates at college. During a fight, Frank slugged David in the face, causing injury. David sued Frank and the College in negligence, and the case went to trial. Define whether the following statements are facts, inferences, law, or conclusions of law.

1. Frank hit David's chin.

2. Ordinarily, a person has no duty to protect another person from a third person.

3. The college disciplined Frank three weeks before his fight with David because Frank initiated a food fight in a campus cafeteria.

4. The college did not cause Frank's injuries.

5. The college knew that Frank could become violent.

6. The college was not negligent.

II. SUMMARY JUDGMENT

Once you understand fact, law, and the sum of their parts, you can reason your way through motions for summary judgment, which are prevalent in trial courts and demand careful analysis. Summary judgment is granted if there is no genuine issue as to any material fact and the movant is entitled to judgment as a matter of law." Fed. R. Civ. P. 56(a). Thus, to end a case without a trial, the moving party must show that there is no real dispute about the important facts and the law is on the moving party's side. The following case exemplifies these principles.

TEDONE v. H.J. HEINZ CO.
686 F. Supp. 2d 300 (S.D. N.Y. 2009)

James S. Gwin, J.

* * *

I. Background

This case arises out of personal injuries sustained by Plaintiff Eleanor Tedone when she attempted to open a glass bottle of ketchup. Although the parties dispute the cause, the bottle broke in its neck area and shards of glass drove into her hand, injuring her. Defendant Owens-Brockway manufactured the glass bottle, Defendant H.J. Heinz filled the bottle with ketchup, and Defendant Borgata Hotel Casino & Spa served the bottle to the Plaintiff with her room-service meal.

A. The Incident at the Borgata

Plaintiff Tedone says that the Defendants each produced, marketed, or damaged a ketchup bottle that broke in her hands. She also says that, with knowledge that she had been injured by the broken bottle, Defendants Borgata and Owens destroyed crucial evidence — initially major pieces of the broken bottle and ultimately the entire bottle itself.

In February 2005, Plaintiff Tedone and her friend Margarete Foley went to Atlantic City, New Jersey, for a weekend at the Borgata Hotel Casino & Spa. On February 20, 2005, a Sunday afternoon, Tedone and Foley ordered room service. During the meal, Plaintiff Tedone wanted ketchup with her scrambled eggs and picked up the 2.25 oz. glass bottle of Heinz ketchup that the Borgata had provided with the meal. After removing the protective plastic seal from the bottle, Tedone attempted to twist off the cap. Before she could open it, however, the bottle broke apart, cutting her hands.

Specifically, Plaintiff Tedone held the bottle in her left hand and attempted to screw off the cap with her right. She did not use any utensils in an attempt to pry the cap off nor did she strike the bottle against the table to loosen it. Instead, she twisted the cap and the bottle in opposite directions and the bottle broke within seconds.

After the bottle broke, Tedone got up and went to the bathroom to wash her hands, tossing a fragment of the bottle toward a nearby chair. Other pieces of the bottle fell to the floor. At the sink, Plaintiff Tedone tended to cuts to fingers on both her right and left hands.

After several minutes, Borgata security officer Carl Crossman arrived in the room and listened to the women's story. Crossman then took Tedone and Foley to the hotel nurse. There, the nurse cleaned Tedone's cuts, placing a butterfly bandage on the small finger of her left hand and a band-aid on the right hand. The nurse also informed Tedone that she would need stitches to the small finger of her left hand. While Tedone received treatment, Foley filled out a Customer Injury Report that Tedone later corrected and signed.

Plaintiff Tedone and Foley then returned to their room with a disposable camera. Finding the room just as they had left it, Foley began taking pictures of the floor, bottle fragments, Tedone's hands, and the sink. Once they had finished, Tedone and Foley took a taxi to the nearby Atlantic City Medical Center. At the Medical Center, Plaintiff Tedone received four stitches to the small finger of her left hand and three stitches on her right middle finger.

While Tedone and Foley were at the hospital, the staff of the Borgata cleaned her room and removed all the fragments of the broken bottle. After returning to the hotel, Tedone and Foley remained at the hotel overnight and left for home the next day as scheduled. While driving home, the fingers on Tedone's left hand began tingling, with the sensation migrating through her hand and up to her elbow. As a result, Plaintiff Tedone saw a hand surgeon and underwent physical therapy for nerve damage in her left hand. Despite this therapy, Tedone says that her hand still tingles, gets numb, and ultimately causes her pain and difficulty working.

* * *

C. From Main Street Brockway to "American's Favorite Playground": A Bottle's Journey

Defendant Owens-Illinois d/b/a Owens-Brockway Glass Containers designed the 2.25 oz. glass bottle specifically for Defendant H.J. Heinz, beginning production in 1990 and continuing today. Owens makes the bottles from a proprietary mold and sells only to Heinz. Owens manufactured the bottle in this case at its Crenshaw, Pennsylvania, facility.

Relevant to this motion, after an automated machine forms the glass ketchup bottles and places them on the production line, the bottles enter a large long tunnel called an annealing lehr. Using a computer-controlled system, the annealing lehr reheats several thousand bottles at a time to above 1050 degrees Fahrenheit. Annealing allows the glass to relax and eliminates any thermally-induced stresses that the formation process may have caused. For annealing to work properly, the bottles must reach this high relaxation temperature and then cool at a fairly constant rate. The large lehr accomplishes these tasks by moving the bottles through various temperature-controlled sections, ultimately producing room-temperature bottles. Afterwards, Owens inspects every bottle produced.

After production and packing, Owens ships the pallets of bottles to an H.J. Heinz filling facility located in Fremont, Ohio. Here the bottles are cleaned and then move to a filler where the machine's pockets grip the side walls of each bottle while a small tube fills it with cold ketchup.

The bottles next move to an automatic capping machine. This machine sets a cap on the top of each bottle then sends the bottle into two waiting belts. The top belt holds the cap flat on the bottle while the side belt grips the side wall of the bottle. Together, these belts spin the bottle and torque the cap onto the threads of the bottle opening. Finally, the machine places a date code on the cap of the sealed bottle.

After capping and coding, the conveyor moves the bottles through the sealing process. Then, the conveyor moves the bottles to an accumulation laner, where an employee uses a vacuum head to lift sixty bottles at a time and pack them into cases for shipment to distributors. Because the filling process can sometime cause breakage, Heinz conducts various inspections of the bottles. On January 25, 2005, Heinz recorded no bottles as cracked, chipped, broken or otherwise defective.

Once inspected, Heinz ships the 2.25 oz. bottles to various distributors and retailers. In this case Defendant Borgata, purchased the bottle from U.S. Foodservice in Bridgeport, New Jersey. U.S. Foodservice employees generally unload the shipment while Borgata employees transport it to an in-house warehouse.

When Borgata's in-room dining department needs more bottles, a warehouse employee delivers them in small cardboard cases. The department then stores some bottles on the shelves and places others on food trays in groups of 120. When a food order requiring ketchup comes into the department, an employee removes the necessary bottles from the tray and places them on the room service dining cart. After the meal, the Borgata disposes of any opened bottles but recycles those that still have an intact plastic safety seal.

In summary, Defendant Owens manufactured the offending bottle at its Crenshaw, Pennsylvania facility. On January 25, 2005, Defendant Heinz filled and capped the bottle in Fremont, Ohio. Sometime between January 25, 2005, and February 20, 2005, Defendant Borgata purchased the bottle from U.S. Foodservices in Bridgeport, New Jersey. When the Borgata served the ketchup bottle to the Plaintiff with her room service meal, the bottle broke in her hands, cutting her. After the injury, Plaintiff Tedone filed a five-count complaint, alleging negligence and strict liability as to all three Defendants.

II. Legal Standard

Summary judgment is appropriate when "there is no genuine issue as to any material fact and that the movant is entitled to judgment as a matter of law."

A defendant moving for summary judgment has the initial burden of showing the absence of a genuine factual issue with respect to one or more essential elements of the plaintiff's claim. The moving defendant meets his burden by "informing the district court of the basis for its motion, and identifying those portions of 'the pleadings, depositions, answers to interrogatories, and admissions on file, together with the affidavits, if any,' which [he] believes demonstrate the absence of a genuine issue of material fact." However, the moving defendant is under no "express or implied" duty to "support [his] motion with affidavits or other similar materials negating the opponent's claim."

Once the moving defendant satisfies his burden, the burden shifts to the nonmoving plaintiff to set forth specific facts showing a triable issue. The nonmoving plaintiff may not defeat the summary judgment motion merely by showing some existence of doubt as to the material facts. Nor can the nonmoving plaintiff rely upon the mere allegations or denials of her pleadings.

In deciding a motion for summary judgment, the Court views the factual evidence and draws all reasonable inferences in favor of the nonmoving plaintiff. To be sure, the Court need not conclusively resolve an allegedly disputed issue in favor of the nonmoving plaintiff; rather, the plaintiff must present "sufficient evidence supporting the claimed factual dispute . . . to require a jury or judge to resolve the parties' differing versions of the truth at trial." Ultimately the

Court must decide "whether the evidence presents sufficient disagreement to require submission to a jury or whether it is so one-sided that one party must prevail as a matter of law."

III. Analysis

* * *

C. Summary Judgment

In their various motions for summary judgment, the parties essentially present two substantive questions to the Court: (1) whether the Plaintiff may proceed against any or all three of the Defendants on a theory of strict products liability, and (2) whether the Plaintiff may proceed against Heinz or Borgata on a theory of negligence.

In ruling on the motions, the Court first examines whether the parties have met their respective burdens on proving a defect or lack thereof for purposes of strict liability. If the Plaintiff has produced sufficient evidence, the Court then considers which Defendants can be held strictly liable. Finally, the Court examines whether the Plaintiff has provided sufficient evidence of negligence to preclude summary judgment.

1. Strict Liability

As to strict liability, the Defendants say that the Plaintiff has failed to meet her burden of demonstrating a triable issue of fact as to the existence of a manufacturing defect in the bottle. In addition, Defendant Borgata argues that strict liability does not apply to it because it is not a "seller" of ketchup bottles. Responding, the Plaintiff says that she has in fact produced direct evidence of a manufacturing defect and that Defendant Borgata "sells" ketchup bottles for purposes of strict liability.

A defendant seeking dismissal of a strict products liability claim on summary judgment must "submit proof in admissible form establishing that plaintiff's injuries were not caused by a manufacturing defect in the product." Defendants can meet this burden by submitting evidence of tests, mechanical processes, and inspections, among others.

Once the defendant has established as a matter of law that the product was not defective, the burden shifts to the plaintiff to demonstrate a triable issue of fact as to whether a defect nevertheless existed. In order to do so, the plaintiff "cannot rely solely upon the occurrence of the accident, but must submit some direct evidence that a defect existed."

In support of its argument that the Plaintiff here has failed to show a defect, Defendant Owens cites *Preston v. Peter Luger Enters., Inc.* In *Preston*, the court affirmed summary judgment for the defendant bottle manufacturer on a strict products liability claim. First, the court held that the manufacturer's detailed evidence of its bottle inspection process satisfied its burden to show that the bottle was not defective. The court then found that the plaintiff had not met her burden to show a triable issue because her expert:

> [F]ailed to explain the significance of [his] findings and did not cite to any industry standards or data to support a conclusion that such disconti- nuities in the glass bottle were irregular or otherwise affected the structural integrity of the bottle. More importantly, [the expert] equivo- cally concluded that there were *potentially* manufacturing defects in this bottle that caused it to fail, thus rendering his opinion as to a specific defect wholly speculative.

The Court finds the instant case distinguishable from *Preston*. Here, even assuming that Defendant Owens offers evidence that the ketchup bottle was not defective when it left its manufacturing facility, Plaintiff Tedone has demon- strated that a triable issue exists as to a defect in the bottle. Specifically, by her expert's report and testimony, Plaintiff has produced direct evidence that the bottle failed as a result of improper annealing during the manufacturing process. Unlike the *Preston* expert, Lerman has identified specific properties of the bottle fragments that he contends support a specific theory of failure: improper annealing.

Although Defendant Owens disputes this theory, arguing that such an isolated failure simply could not occur, this dispute is one of material fact that must be resolved at trial. Accordingly, the Court **DENIES** Defendant Owens's motion for summary judgment.

As to Defendant Heinz, "Distributors and retailers may be held strictly liable to injured parties, even though they may be innocent conduits in the sale of the product . . . ." In fact, "It is well settled that strict products liability extends to retailers and distributors in the chain of distribution even if they never inspected, controlled, installed or serviced the product."

Defendant Heinz does not dispute this proposition of law. Instead, it argues that the Plaintiff fails to meet her burden on the issue of a manufacturing defect. Because the Court holds that Plaintiff Tedone has shown a triable issue of fact as to the existence of a defect, the Court **DENIES** Defendant Heinz's motion for summary judgment.

Finally, as to Defendant Borgata's potential strict liability, Borgata says that the Plaintiff fails to show a manufacturing defect — an argument this Court has already rejected — and that strict liability cannot be extended to it because it is a non-seller or mere "casual seller" of ketchup bottles. This Court finds, however, that Borgata can be subject to strict liability.

"One engaged in the business of selling or otherwise distributing products who sells or distributes a defective product is subject to liability for harm to persons or property caused by the defect." Moreover, "Whether a defendant is a commercial seller or distributor within the meaning of this Section is usually a question of law to be determined by the court."

In this case, Defendant Borgata makes two arguments to support its improbable claim that it is not a seller or distributor of the arguably defective product. First, Borgata says that it did not in fact "sell" the ketchup bottle to Plaintiff Tedone but provided it as a free part of a room service meal. Second, the Borgata says that any "sale" of ketchup is incidental to its true business of running a casino and operating a hotel.

As to the first argument, the Defendant cites no authority requiring that a technical, isolated "sale" occur before a party may be subject to strict products liability for distributing a defective product. In fact, existing case law counsels against such a restrictive understanding of the doctrine. Having sold Plaintiff a meal — a meal that included ketchup — Defendant Borgata cannot plausibly claim that the sale of the ketchup was not part of its regular business practices. As noted below, Borgata admits it purchases and stocks caseloads of ketchup.

In support of its second argument, Defendant Borgata relies primarily upon *Gobhai v. KLM Royal Dutch Airlines*. In *Gobhai*, the plaintiff alleged strict products liability against the defendant airline company after she slipped and fell in her son's apartment while wearing a pair of slippers the airline had given her son on a transatlantic flight. The court dismissed the claim, finding that KLM "is not in the business of manufacturing or selling slippers but is in the business of providing air transportation for passengers and cargo." The court reasoned further, "Distribution of these goods by KLM was incidental to the basic service provided and the slippers were for in-flight use by defendant's first class passengers."

In this case, however, Defendant Borgata's provision of the ketchup bottle was not merely incidental to its business as a hotel and casino. According to Borgata's own manager of in-room dining, his staff serves approximately 30,000 guests per month. Thus, unlike the occasional pair of slippers provided to first class passengers in *Gobhai*, here the Defendant regularly provides condiments with its room service meals, potentially serving as many as 300 bottles of ketchup per day. In fact, the in-room dining staff keeps two separate trays of 120 bottles each on standby for delivery to guest rooms with appropriate meals.

Moreover, *Gunning v. Small Feast Caterers, Inc.* supports this Court's conclusion. In *Gunning*, the court held that a patron could sue the defendant restaurant when he was injured by shards from a broken water glass. The court reasoned, "[T]his product is not merely an amenity, like slippers given to an airline passenger, but is an important component of the meal. As such, strict liability may be imposed upon the defendant." Similarly here, the ketchup bottle automatically provided to the Plaintiff with her lunch was an integral part of her room service meal.

In addition, the public policies underlying strict liability support extending it to Defendant Borgata. As the court in *Sukljian* summarized:

> [S]ellers, by reason of their continuing relationships with manufacturers, are most often in a position to exert pressure for the improved safety of products and can recover increased costs within their commercial dealings, or through contribution or indemnification in litigation; additionally, by marketing the products as a regular part of their business such sellers may be said to have assumed a special responsibility to the public, which has come to expect them to stand behind their goods.

In this case, Defendant Borgata cannot claim that it lacks the opportunity or incentive to ensure that the approximately 5,000 ketchup bottles it serves each month are safe.

Accordingly, this Court **DENIES** Defendant Borgata's motion for summary judgment as to strict liability.

For the same reasons articulated *supra*, the Court finds summary judgment in Plaintiff Tedone's favor similarly unwarranted. Although the Plaintiff's expert opines that the bottle failed due to improper annealing, the Defendant's expert disagrees and concludes that based on the manufacturing process, quality controls, and anecdotal evidence, the bottle failed because of some later impact. These conflicting conclusions present a dispute of a fact essential to determining the potential strict liability of all three Defendants. Accordingly, the Court **DENIES** Plaintiff Tedone's motion for summary judgment on her strict liability claim.

2. Negligence

In its motion for summary judgment, Defendant Heinz says this Court must dismiss Plaintiff Tedone's negligence claim against it as a matter of law because, "[P]laintiff has simply failed to provide any evidence that Heinz breached any duty it might have owed her." Defendant Borgata similarly says that there is no evidence that it created or had notice of any defect in the bottle prior to serving it to the Plaintiff. In response, Plaintiff Tedone says that the theory of res ipsa loquitur defeats summary judgment for Heinz and Borgata and in fact entitles to her to summary judgment against all three Defendants.

As an initial matter, "[T]he doctrine of res ipsa loquitur does not entitle a plaintiff to summary judgment." "Res ipsa loquitur is a rule of evidence, which merely provides a permissible inference of negligence, rather than a presumption. Thus, application of the doctrine as a basis for awarding summary judgment is inappropriate." Accordingly, the Court **DENIES** Plaintiff's motion for summary judgment on the theory of res ipsa loquitur.[11]

Generally, to make out a negligence claim, a plaintiff must show: "1) the existence of a duty flowing from defendant to plaintiff; 2) a breach of this duty; 3) a reasonably close causal connection between the contact and the resulting injury; and 4) actual loss, harm or damage." As to the duty owed, "Manufacturers and suppliers are not obliged to supply merchandise that is accident proof but are held to the same standard applied in negligence cases generally, reasonable care." Applying New York law, however, courts in the Second Circuit have cautioned against granting summary judgment to defendants on the issue of breach of this duty. *See Ferguson v. Lion Holding, Inc.* ("Summary judgement is inappropriate where there exists in the record *any* evidence that could reasonably support a finding in favor of the non-movant.").

Although the question is close in this case, the Court finds that Plaintiff Tedone has provided sufficient evidence to support an inference of Heinz's and Borgata's negligence. Specifically, Defendant Owens's expert Kilpatrick concluded that the ketchup bottle broke because of a preexisting flaw — most likely damage from a hard impact or some other mishandling. As to the source of the impact, Kilpatrick opined: "The incident bottle could have been damaged by the improper handling of the full case of bottles in which it was packed and shipped," and, "This type of full case handling damage could have occurred in the warehouse where filled goods were stored prior to being shipped."

In addition, Kilpatrick agreed that the Heinz safety seal and product label "could have prevented [the bottle] from failing immediately at the time the damage occurred . . . and could have held the bottle together." In fact, Borgata's in-room dining manager testified that his staff recycles bottles that are delivered to guests but unused.

Again, although the Court recognizes the issue is close, it nevertheless concludes that a jury could infer that Heinz and Borgata negligently handled the bottle, reused it, or failed to properly inspect it before it reached the Plaintiff.

Accordingly, this Court **DENIES** Defendants Heinz's and Borgata's motions for summary judgment.

---

[11] Although some New York courts have recognized that summary judgment based on the theory of res ipsa loquitur might be appropriate where "the prima facie proof is so convincing that the inference of negligence arising therefrom is inescapable and unrebutted," this is simply not the case here.

* * *

NOTES AND QUESTIONS

1. *Tedone v. H.J. Heinz Co.* discusses seven motions for summary judgment. Exactly why did the court deny each motion, based on a factual dispute or as a matter of law?

2. As *Tedone v. H.J. Heinz Co.* notes, upon deciding a motion for summary judgment, the trial judge considers the facts presented in a light most favorable to the party that did not bring the motion. Why? What injustice does this principle safeguard against?

3. What proof could be so convincing that a court should grant summary judgment based on the theory of *res ipsa loquitur*?

EXERCISE

Determine whether summary judgment would be appropriate in the following scenarios. Is there a dispute about a material fact? Is there a dispute about the governing law?

1. A woman dies, leaving a will that gives one-third of her estate to her son and two-thirds to her daughter. The son files suit, claiming the will is invalid. He claims his mother suffered from dementia and was not competent when she signed the will. He submits medical records, documenting a neurosurgeon's treatment of his mother in the months prior to her signing the will. The daughter disputes this claim of incompetence and submits to the court a letter written by the mother, explaining the unequal distribution. The governing statute provides that any adult of sound mind and memory may create a will. The son moves for summary judgment that the will is invalid. Is he entitled to summary judgment?

2. Same hypothetical as above, but now imagine that the daughter moves for summary judgment, claiming that the governing law is the state where the mother's property lies, rather than the state where the mother executed her will. Is she entitled to summary judgment on this issue?

3. A homeowner finds a dead black bear in his backyard. He claims ownership of the bear, but the local department of resources confiscates it and issues a citation against the homeowner for illegal possession of a wild animal. The governing law defines wild animals as "all living creatures, not human, wild by nature, endowed with sensation and power of voluntary motion." The homeowner moves for summary judgment that he did not violate the statute. Is summary judgment appropriate?

4. Same hypothetical as above, but now imagine that six months before this case, the highest court in the jurisdiction held that the a dead coyote, found on

a farm, was not a wild animal under the governing law because it was not a living creature. Would the homeowner be entitled to summary judgment?

III. SUGGESTED FURTHER READING

RUGGERO J. ALDISERT, OPINION WRITING (AuthorHouse 2d ed. 2010).

John J. Brunetti, *Searching for Methods of Trial Court Fact-Finding and Decision-Making*, 49 HASTINGS L.J. 1491 (1998).

JOYCE J. GEORGE, JUDICIAL OPINION WRITING HANDBOOK (5th ed. 2007).

Chris Guthrie et. al., *Blinking on the Bench: How Judges Decide Cases*, 93 CORNELL L. REV. 1, 10 (2007).

Chad M. Oldfather, *Universal De Novo Review*, 77 GEO. WASH. L. REV. 308 (2009).

Chapter 9

WORKING WITH STATUTES

I. INTRODUCTION

Much of our governing law is statutory. In law school, you may have examined a small portion of a statute to learn a discreet principle of law. But controversies between people are rarely so tidy. Instead, judges and lawyers work with entire statutory schemes, and they must integrate various provisions to reach a legal answer. Proficiency in reading, understanding, and integrating statutory law is a fundamental skill for a trial court law clerk. This chapter exemplifies the kind of statutory analysis that trial court judges and law clerks complete.

II. PRACTICE

Imagine that you are a trial court law clerk and the judge has asked you to assist her with the following two cases using the three statutes provided below.

Case One: Parents have three children, ages 20, 18, and 16. Their parental income is $125,425.

1. What is the parents' annual child support obligation?

2. Father's yearly income is $58,425, and Mother's yearly income is $67,000. What is Father's pro-rata share of the child support obligation?

3. Imagine that the oldest child is a freshman in college, and Father paid all of the tuition, which cost $18,000. Should he receive a credit for this contribution?

Case Two: Father and mother signed a separation agreement that obligated Father to pay child support until their two children were 21 years old, but if they attended college, until they were 23 years old. When their oldest child became 21, Father petitioned the trial court to terminate his child support obligation. Which provisions governs resolution of his petition?

PARENTS DUTY TO SUPPORT CHILD
N.Y. Family Law § 413 (McKinney 2010)

1. (a) Except as provided in subdivision two of this section, the parents of a child under the age of twenty-one years are chargeable with the support of such child and, if possessed of sufficient means or able to earn such means, shall be required to pay for child support a fair and reasonable sum as the court may determine. The court shall make its award for child support pursuant to the provisions of this subdivision. The court may vary from the amount of the basic child support obligation determined pursuant to paragraph (c) of this subdivision only in accordance with paragraph (f) of this subdivision.

(b) For purposes of this subdivision, the following definitions shall be used:

(1) "Basic child support obligation" shall mean the sum derived by adding the amounts determined by the application of subparagraphs two and three of paragraph (c) of this subdivision except as increased pursuant to subparagraphs four, five, six and seven of such paragraph.

(2) "Child support" shall mean a sum to be paid pursuant to court order or decree by either or both parents or pursuant to a valid agreement between the parties for care, maintenance and education of any unemancipated child under the age of twenty-one years.

(3) "Child support percentage" shall mean:

(i) seventeen percent of the combined parental income for one child;

(ii) twenty-five percent of the combined parental income for two children;

(iii) twenty-nine percent of the combined parental income for three children;

(iv) thirty-one percent of the combined parental income for four children; and

(v) no less than thirty-five percent of the combined parental income for five or more children.

(4) "Combined parental income" shall mean the sum of the income of both parents.

* * *

(c) The amount of the basic child support obligation shall be determined in accordance with the provision of this paragraph:

(1) The court shall determine the combined parental income.

(2) The court shall multiply the combined parental income up to the amount set forth in paragraph (b) of subdivision two of section one hundred eleven-i of the social services law by the appropriate child support percentage and such amount

shall be prorated in the same proportion as each parent's income is to the combined parental income.

(3) Where the combined parental income exceeds the dollar amount set forth in subparagraph two of this paragraph, the court shall determine the amount of child support for the amount of the combined parental income in excess of such dollar amount through consideration of the factors set forth in paragraph (f) of this subdivision and/or the child support percentage.

(4) Where the custodial parent is working, or receiving elementary or secondary education, or higher education or vocational training which the court determines will lead to employment, and incurs child care expenses as a result thereof, the court shall determine reasonable child care expenses and such child care expenses, where incurred, shall be prorated in the same proportion as each parent's income is to the combined parental income. Each parent's pro rata share of the child care expenses shall be separately stated and added to the sum of subparagraphs two and three of this paragraph.

(5) The court shall determine the parties' obligation to provide health insurance benefits pursuant to section four hundred sixteen of this part and to pay cash medical support as provided under this subparagraph.

* * *

(6) Where the court determines that the custodial parent is seeking work and incurs child care expenses as a result thereof, the court may determine reasonable child care expenses and may apportion the same between the custodial and non-custodial parent. The non-custodial parent's share of such expenses shall be separately stated and paid in a manner determined by the court.

(7) Where the court determines, having regard for the circumstances of the case and of the respective parties and in the best interests of the child, and as justice requires, that the present or future provision of post-secondary, private, special, or enriched education for the child is appropriate, the court may award educational expenses. The non-custodial parent shall pay educational expenses, as awarded, in a manner determined by the court, including direct payment to the educational provider.

(d) Notwithstanding the provisions of paragraph (c) of this subdivision, where the annual amount of the basic child support obligation would reduce the non-custodial parent's income below the poverty income guidelines amount for a single person as reported by the federal department of health and human services, the basic child support obligation shall be twenty-five dollars per month or the difference between the non-custodial parent's income and the self-support reserve, whichever is greater. Notwithstanding the provisions of paragraph (c) of this subdivision, where the annual amount of the basic child support obligation would reduce the non-custodial parent's income below the self-support reserve but not below the poverty income guidelines amount for a single person as reported by the federal department of health and human services, the basic child support obligation shall be fifty dollars per month or the difference between the non-custodial parent's income and the self-support reserve, whichever is greater.

* * *

(f) The court shall calculate the basic child support obligation, and the non-custodial parent's pro rata share of the basic child support obligation. Unless the court finds that the non-custodial parents's pro-rata share of the basic child support obligation is unjust or inappropriate, which finding shall be based upon consideration of the following factors:

(1) The financial resources of the custodial and non-custodial parent, and those of the child;

(2) The physical and emotional health of the child and his/her special needs and aptitudes;

(3) The standard of living the child would have enjoyed had the marriage or household not been dissolved;

(4) The tax consequences to the parties;

(5) The non-monetary contributions that the parents will make toward the care and well-being of the child;

(6) The educational needs of either parent;

(7) A determination that the gross income of one parent is substantially less than the other parent's gross income;

(8) The needs of the children of the non-custodial parent for whom the non-custodial parent is providing support who are not subject to the instant action and whose support has not been deducted from income pursuant to subclause (D) of clause (vii) of subparagraph five of paragraph (b) of this subdivision, and the financial resources of any person obligated to support such children, provided, however, that this factor may apply only if the resources available to support such children are less than the resources available to support the children who are subject to the instant action;

(9) Provided that the child is not on public assistance (i) extraordinary expenses incurred by the non-custodial parent in exercising visitation, or (ii) expenses incurred by the non-custodial parent in extended visitation provided that the custodial parent's expenses are substantially reduced as a result thereof; and

(10) Any other factors the court determines are relevant in each case, the court

shall order the non-custodial parent to pay his or her pro rata share of the basic child support obligation, and may order the non-custodial parent to pay an amount pursuant to paragraph (e) of this subdivision.

(g) Where the court finds that the non-custodial parent's pro rata share of the basic child support obligation is unjust or inappropriate, the court shall order the non-custodial parent to pay such amount of child support as the court finds just and appropriate, and the court shall set forth, in a written order, the factors it considered; the amount of each party's pro rata share of the basic child support obligation; and the reasons that the court did not order the basic child support obligation. Such written order may not be waived by either party or counsel; provided however, and notwithstanding any other provision of law, including but not limited to section four hundred fifteen of this act, the court shall not find that the non-custodial parent's pro rata share of such obligation is unjust or inappropriate on the basis that such share exceeds the portion of a public assistance grant which is attributable to a child or children. In no instance shall the court order child support below twenty-five dollars per month. Where the non-custodial parent's income is less than or equal to the poverty income guidelines amount for a single person as reported by the federal department of health and human services, unpaid child support arrears in excess of five hundred dollars shall not accrue.

(h) A validly executed agreement or stipulation voluntarily entered into between the parties after the effective date of this subdivision presented to the court for incorporation in an order or judgment shall include a provision stating that the parties have been advised of the provisions of this subdivision and that the basic child support obligation provided for therein would presumptively result in the correct amount of child support to be awarded. In the event that such agreement or stipulation deviates from the basic child support obligation, the agreement or stipulation must specify the amount that such basic child support obligation would have been and the reason or reasons that such agreement or stipulation does not provide for payment of that amount. Such provision may not be waived by either party or counsel. Nothing contained in this subdivision shall be construed to alter the rights of the parties to voluntarily enter into validly executed agreements or stipulations which deviate from the basic child support obligation provided such agreements or stipulations comply with the provisions of this paragraph. The court shall, however, retain discretion with respect to child support pursuant to this section. Any court order or judgment incorporating a validly executed agreement or stipulation which deviates from the basic child support obligation shall set forth the court's reasons for such deviation.

* * *

CHILD SUPPORT STANDARDS
N.Y. Social Services Law § 111-i. (McKinney 2010)

1. Each social services district shall ascertain the ability of an absent parent to support or contribute to the support of his or her children, in accordance with the statewide child support standards as set forth in subdivision one of section four hundred thirteen of the family court act.

2. (a) The commissioner shall publish annually a child support standards chart. The child support standards chart shall include: (i) the revised poverty income guideline for a single person as reported by the federal department of health and human services; (ii) the revised self-support reserved as defined in section two hundred forty of the domestic relations law; (iii) the dollar amounts yielded through application of the child support percentage as defined in section two hundred forty of the domestic relations law and section four hundred thirteen of the family court act; and (iv) the combined parental income amount.

(b) The combined parental income amount to be reported in the child support standards chart and utilized in calculating orders of child support in accordance with subparagraph two of paragraph (c) of subdivision one of section four hundred thirteen of the family court act and subparagraph two of paragraph (c) of subdivision one-b of section two hundred forty of the domestic relations law shall be one hundred thirty thousand dollars; provided, however, beginning January thirty-first, two thousand twelve and every two years thereafter, the combined parental income amount shall increase by the product of the average annual percentage changes in the consumer price index for all urban consumers (CPI-U) as published by the United States department of labor bureau of labor statistics for the two year period rounded to the nearest one thousand dollars.

* * *

CHILD SUPPORT STANDARDS CHART 2010

Number of Children

Annual Income		1	2	3	4	5+
FROM	THRU		Annual Obligation Amount			
125,000	125,099	21,250	31,250	36,250	38,750	43,750
125,100	125,199	21,267	31,275	36,279	38,781	43,785
125,200	125,299	21,284	31,300	36,308	38,812	43,820
125,300	125,399	21,301	31,325	36,337	38,843	43,855
125,400	125,499	21,318	31,350	36,366	38,874	43,890
125,500	125,599	21,335	31,375	36,395	38,905	43,925
125,600	125,699	21,352	31,400	36,424	38,936	43,960

Chapter 10

DRAFTING IN THE TRIAL COURTS: THE LONG AND SHORT OF IT

I. INTRODUCTION

All courts, appellate and trial, are abuzz with questions that need answering. Unlike appellate courts, which answer questions in written opinions, trial courts may choose to answer questions orally or in written form. In fact, trial courts accomplish much of their decision-making orally, so you can expect to write less in a trial court clerkship than in an appellate court clerkship. This is not to say, however, that you will work less. Managing your judge's docket and communicating with all the courtroom players makes for a demanding job. And when a written decision is required, trial judges will turn to their law clerks for a useful draft.

Trial courts render two kinds of decisions, orders and judgments. Orders resolve an issue in the case, for example, whether to allow a continuance, but do not fully adjudicate the underlying claim. Judgments, on the other hand, fully adjudicate the claim, stating, for example, that the defendant is liable in negligence for $18,000. Beyond orders and judgments, following a bench trial in a civil case, trial courts produce a third kind of writing that sets out findings of fact and conclusions of law. Each of these documents — orders, judgments, and "findings and conclusions" — is discussed below.

Keep in mind that the lessons about legal analysis in Chapter Five apply equally to the written work of trial courts. The *mise en place* of accuracy and clarity continue to be the twin goals of a legal analysis, whether you are drafting an appellate opinion or a trial order. Accordingly, you should review Chapter Five before you draft any trial court documents.

II. ORDERS

A. Three Examples

Trial courts issue orders, also known as rulings, for every kind of motion or objection that litigants raise, as well as for matters that the court addresses *sua sponte*. Courts usually have the choice of whether to issue an order orally, or in writing. Moreover, the length of orders varies widely, from a few sentences for a routine discovery matter to triple-digit page numbers for a complex, multi-issue controversy. Medium-length or long orders are often titled "memorandum," "decision," or "opinion."

Naturally, the rules and customs in your chambers will dictate the form and length of the orders you draft. Some trial judges equate the word "order" with a short, signed document that states the court's resolution. These judges may append a document to the order that spells out their reasons for the decision, similar to an opinion in the appellate courts. Other judges will include their reasoning and the resolution of the controversy in a single document. Consider the following two examples.

PELLEGRINI v. L A FITNESS SPORTS CLUB LLC
No. CV 2008-002245, 2010 WL 6615162 (Super. Ct. Ariz. Dec. 8, 2009.)

EDWARD O. BURKE, JUDGE.

The Court has received and reviewed Defendants' Motion for Reconsideration of the Court's Order Dated October 27, 2009 Concerning Plaintiffs' Motion for Leave to Amend Complaint to Add a Punitive Damages Claim which the Court previously granted, a copy of Plaintiffs' Response to Defendant Brunswick Corporation's Response in Opposition to Plaintiffs' Motion for Leave to Amend Complaint to Add a Punitive Damages Claim and Plaintiffs' Reply in Support of Their Motion for Leave to Amend Complaint to Add a Punitive Damages Claim.

Having carefully reviewed the Response and the Plaintiff's Reply thereto, the Court affirms the granting of its motion to allow Plaintiff to add a punitive damages claim. To deny the motion would require the Court to make a significant finding of fact based on an incomplete record which, obviously, the Court cannot do.

LIPS v. UNIV. OF CINCINNATI COLL. OF MED.
No. 2009-01115, 2010 WL 2937463 (Ohio Ct. Cl., July 9, 2010)

JOSEPH T. CLARK, JUDGE.

{ ¶ 1} An evidentiary hearing was conducted in this matter to determine whether R. Bruce Bracken, M.D., is entitled to civil immunity pursuant to R.C. 2743.02(F) and 9.86. Upon review of evidence presented at the hearing, the court makes the following determination.

{ ¶ 2} R.C. 2743.02(F) states, in part: "A civil action against an officer or employee, as defined in section 109.36 of the Revised Code, that alleges that the officer's or employee's conduct was manifestly outside the scope of the officer's or employee's employment or official responsibilities, or that the officer or employee acted with malicious purpose, in bad faith, or in a wanton or reckless manner shall first be filed against the state in the court of claims, which has exclusive, original jurisdiction to determine, initially, whether the officer or employee is entitled to personal immunity under section 9.86 of the Revised Code and whether the courts of common pleas have jurisdiction over the civil action."

{¶ 3} R.C. 9.86 states, in part:

{¶ 4} "[N]o officer or employee [of the state] shall be liable in any civil action that arises under the law of this state for damage or injury caused in the performance of his duties, unless the officer's or employee's actions were manifestly outside the scope of his employment or official responsibilities or unless the officer or employee acted with malicious purpose, in bad faith, or in a wanton or reckless manner."

{¶ 5} Plaintiff's decedent, James A. Lips, was diagnosed with prostatic carcinoma in September 2007. Lips subsequently conducted extensive research about the various treatment options available to him and the physicians who were qualified to perform such treatments. On December 31, 2007, Lips underwent a robot-assisted radical prostatectomy at University Hospital in Cincinnati, Ohio. The procedure was performed by Dr. Bracken, a member of defendant's faculty. Dr. Bracken testified that certain complications arose during surgery which resulted in the procedure lasting approximately eight hours. Lips never recovered from the surgery and died on January 6, 2008.

{¶ 6} The parties agree that Dr. Bracken is a member of defendant's faculty and that resident physicians were present in the operating room when the surgery was performed. Plaintiff concedes in her post-hearing brief that immunity should be granted for any negligence that occurred during the surgery and post-operative care. Indeed, the testimony at the hearing establishes that Dr. Bracken's duties included meeting with prospective patients, explaining treatment methods, and disclosing his personal experience. Thus, the court finds that he was acting within the scope of his state employment at all times relevant hereto. Plaintiff contends, however, that Dr. Bracken acted in bad faith when he intentionally misled plaintiff and her husband regarding both the details of the surgical procedure and the extent of his surgical experience.

{¶ 7} At the hearing, plaintiff testified that her husband had interviewed many physicians in the area and that several had recommended Dr. Bracken due to his experience in his field. Plaintiff also testified that her husband discussed with Dr. Bracken the advantages and disadvantages of undergoing the procedure at a regional facility rather than a local hospital. Plaintiff testified that the convenience of follow-up appointments was a consideration that led her husband to choose to undergo the surgery at a local hospital.

{ ¶ 8} Dr. Bracken testified that he met with Lips and plaintiff and engaged them in a thorough discussion about the procedure. He has no recollection of giving Lips an estimate on the length of time the procedure would take, as it tends to vary based upon many factors, including the ease at which he can surgically connect the bladder to the urethra. According to Dr. Bracken, ten days prior to surgery he received a letter from Lips wherein Lips stated that he wanted his lymph nodes to be removed during surgery and to have them tested for cancerous cells. Dr. Bracken stated that he had previously informed Lips that removal of the lymph nodes during surgery would increase the probability of complications.

{ ¶ 9} Plaintiff alleges that Dr. Bracken erroneously informed plaintiff and Lips that he had participated in approximately 200 similar procedures when, in fact, he had performed only 26 such procedures. Plaintiff also alleges that Dr. Bracken guaranteed both her and Lips that the procedure would not exceed two to three hours when, in fact, it lasted approximately eight hours. Finally, plaintiff states that Dr. Bracken exaggerated the benefits of undergoing the procedure at a local hospital as compared to a regional facility. According to plaintiff, Dr. Bracken was motivated to "overstate his experience," in order to secure Lips as a patient because Lips was a friend and neighbor of Dr. Tew, head of University Hospital's neurosurgical department, and that Dr. Bracken believed it would impress Dr. Tew if Lips were his patient.

{ ¶ 10} The court finds that there is sufficient evidence to conclude that Dr. Bracken made the aforementioned representations to plaintiff and her husband. The question becomes whether Dr. Bracken made such representations in bad faith. "Bad faith" has been defined as "dishonesty of belief or purpose." Black's Law Dictionary (9 Ed. 2004)159.

{ ¶ 11} Dr. Bracken testified that he had, in fact, "participated in the approximately 200 cases" in which a radical prostatectomy was performed and that he had not misrepresented his experience to Mr. and Mrs. Lips. Indeed, the evidence convinces the court that Dr. Bracken participated to some degree in approximately 200 cases where the procedure was performed. Although other surgeons performed the surgical procedure in many of those cases, the court finds that Dr. Bracken did not intentionally mislead plaintiff or her husband regarding his surgical experience.

{ ¶ 12} Similarly, while Dr. Bracken has no recollection of estimating the duration of the procedure for Lips, the court finds that Dr. Bracken's representation regarding time was simply an estimate, not a guarantee. Moreover, Dr. Bracken did caution plaintiff and her husband that their decision to have Lips' lymph nodes removed during the procedure would increase the possibility of complications. In short, plaintiff has not convinced the court that the statement was made with a dishonest belief or purpose.

{ ¶ 13} With regard to plaintiff's contention that Dr. Bracken acted in bad faith when he recommended a local surgical facility rather than a regional facility, the court finds Dr. Bracken simply related the relative benefits and disadvantages of the facilities for Lips to consider, and that Lips used that information along with the advice of other physicians to reach his own conclusion. As such, Dr. Bracken's representations in this regard were not made in bad faith.

{ ¶ 14} Based upon the totality of the evidence presented, the court finds that Dr. Bracken acted within the scope of his employment with defendant at all times relevant hereto. The court further finds that Dr. Bracken did not act with malicious purpose, in bad faith, or in a wanton or reckless manner toward plaintiff or plaintiff's decedent. Consequently, Dr. Bracken is entitled to civil immunity pursuant to R.C. 9.86 and R.C. 2743.02(F). Therefore, the courts of common pleas do not have jurisdiction over any civil actions that may be filed against him based upon the allegations in this case.

JUDGMENT ENTRY

The court held an evidentiary hearing to determine civil immunity pursuant to R.C. 9.86 and 2743.02(F). Upon hearing all the evidence and for the reasons set forth in the decision filed concurrently herewith, the court finds that R. Bruce Bracken, M.D., is entitled to immunity pursuant to R.C. 9.86 and 2743.02(F) and that the courts of common pleas do not have jurisdiction over any civil actions that may be filed against him based upon the allegations in this case.

NOTES AND QUESTIONS

1.   Compare the two orders above with *Tedone v. H.J. Heinz Co.* in Chapter Eight. Why do the orders take different forms? Do you prefer one of the orders over the others?

2.   Imagine that the decision in *Lips v. Univ. of Cincinnati Coll. of Med.* is appealed. How would an appellate court opinion for this controversy differ from the trial court's order? Specifically, how would the legal analysis change?

B.   Drafting Guidelines

You learned in Chapter Five that an appellate opinion ordinarily has four elements: (1) an introductory paragraph; (2) a review of the facts; (3) a legal analysis; and (4) a mandate. An involved order should include the first three elements, though there are some differences between opinions and orders that are explained below. Moreover, instead of a mandate, an order has a disposition that states the court's resolution. A short order may have only a legal analysis and a disposition, or even just a disposition. Let us take a closer look at each of the elements.

1.   Introductory Paragraph

The introductory paragraph(s) of a trial order should identify the question(s) before the court and state the ruling as simply as possible. Consider the introductory paragraphs from *Tedone v. H.J. Heinz Co.*, 686 F. Supp.2d 300, 303-04 (S.D. N.Y. 2009), as follows:

> In this personal injury case, Defendants H.J. Heinz Co. ("Heinz"), Owens-Brockway. ("Owens"), and Borgata Hotel Casino Spa ("Borgata") each move this Court for summary judgment. [Doc. 25, 28, 35.] In addition, Defendant Owens moves this Court to exclude Plaintiff Eleanor Tedone's expert witness Steven Lerman. [Doc. 25.]

> Plaintiff Tedone opposes these motions and also moves this Court for summary judgment. [Doc. 34.] Moreover, Plaintiff Tedone asks this Court to exclude Defendant Owens's expert witness William Kilpatrick. [Doc. 34.] Finally, Plaintiff Tedone seeks a remedy for the Defendants' alleged spoliation of evidence. [Doc. 34.]

> For the following reasons, the Court: **DENIES** the Defendant's motion to exclude the Plaintiff's expert Lerman and **DENIES** the Plaintiff's motion to exclude the Defendant's expert Kilpatrick; **DEFERS** consideration of the issue of spoliation until trial; **DENIES** Defendant Owens's motion for summary judgment; **DENIES** Defendant Borgata's motion for summary judgment; **DENIES** Defendant Heinz's motion for summary judgment; and **DENIES** Plaintiff Tedone's motion for summary judgment.

2.   Review of the Facts

The second element, a review of the facts, should set out the material facts for the dispute, as well as its procedural posture. It is customary to include citations to the record. Be thorough, accurate, and neutral. Remember that the factual record is developed in the trial court only, so the facts stated in the order will carry through the entire history of the case. Indeed, as Judge George has remarked, "[a]n improper factual recitation can result in an irreversible miscarriage of justice because an appellate court, free to question to the legal reasoning and procedure of the trial court but not the facts it sends forward, cannot effectively cure it." J. J. GEORGE, JUDICIAL OPINION WRITING HANDBOOK 164 (5th ed. 2007).

To achieve a thorough, accurate, and neutral recording of the facts, you might have to sacrifice a flowing narrative of the dispute. In other words, the utilitarian purpose of a trial order trumps creative storytelling. But if you can meet the purpose of a trial order in an interesting way, by all means, do so. Moreover, Chapter Five's guidance for organizing the facts of an appellate opinion applies equally to a trial order.

3.   Legal Analysis

As for the third element, legal analysis, a trial order answers the question presented by applying the governing law to the found facts. Begin the legal analysis of an order with a summary of the statute or case that governs the dispute. This summary should be logical and specific. Keep it simple. After setting out the governing law, apply it to the facts before the court. This application may be simple and short or complicated and long. What you do not want is a long explanation of a simple application, or a short explanation of a complicated application. Answer the question presented and no more.

Trial courts are not designed to create new law or to reject precedent. Instead, they are tasked with applying the law — as it stands — to the current controversy. Admittedly, the line between application of law and creation of law may slack and meander, but as a law clerk, you should strive to meet the designated purpose of your court. Ordinarily, for example, you should not include a history of the governing law or a summary of the law in other jurisdictions. Nor should you explain principles of law that relate only tangentially to the dispute at hand. Such analytical techniques may be appropriate in an appellate opinion, but they are gratuitous in a trial order.

4.   Disposition

The final element, a disposition, is a concluding statement of the court's ruling. Having explained its reasons beforehand, the court writes the disposition to clarify the outcome of the dispute. Think of it as a final score. The disposition may be as simple as saying, "Plaintiff's motion for summary judgment is denied." Can you locate the dispositions in the two sample orders above?

NOTES AND QUESTIONS

1.   Imagine the trial judge is denying a motion for summary judgment because there is a dispute of material fact. How would such a ruling affect your drafting of a review of the facts? Should you resolve the factual dispute in your review?

2.   Other than the litigants in a case, who else reads trial orders? What are those readers looking for in the orders?

III.   JUDGMENTS

A judgment, also known as the decree, fully resolves the claim filed in the trial court. *See* FED. R. CIV. P. 54. Unlike orders, which courts may issue orally, judgments must be written, signed by the presiding judge, and filed with the clerk of the court. *See* FED. R. CIV. P. 58.

A judgment is usually a short document of a few sentences that states the ultimate disposition of the claim, sets the monetary award, and assigns court costs. In its simplicity it is similar to the disposition of an order, described above. Any explanation for the judgment, meaning, any statement of the court's reasoning for the judgment, should be attached as a separate document. And as with appeals, the losing party ordinarily pays the court costs. Consider the following judgment below.

SERRANO v. AUSTIN
No. PLCV 2007-01393B, 2010 WL 3001693
(Super. Ct. Mass., July 9, 2010)

RICHARD J. CHIN, JUDGE.

This action came on for trial before the Court and a jury, Richard J. Chin, Justice, presiding, the issues having been duly tried and the jury having rendered its verdict,

It is ORDERED and ADJUDGED:

That the plaintiff, Renee Serrano recover of the defendant, Raymond Hadley Austin, the sum of $1,905.00 with interest thereon from 10/26/2007 to 07/09/2010 in the sum of $618.16 as provided by law, and its costs of action.

IV. FINDINGS OF FACT AND CONCLUSIONS OF LAW

Judges produce "findings and conclusions" after civil bench trials. This document serves a similar purpose to the litigants as a jury verdict. It provides the litigants with a clear delineation of the court's findings of fact and conclusions of law, so they understand the basis of the court's judgment. That way, litigants may intelligently challenge any findings or conclusions on appeal. Return to Chapter Eight for definitions of "facts" and "conclusions of law."

In drafting this document, strive for a disciplined separation of the findings of fact from the conclusions of law. Also, it is customary to list the findings of fact in numbered paragraphs. In the example below, notice how the court identifies some of the evidentiary sources for the findings of fact and how it weaves the findings of fact into its conclusions of law.

CARTER v. UNITED STATES
725 F. Supp. 2d 346 (E.D. N.Y. 2010)

MEMORANDUM AND ORDER

BLOCK, SENIOR DISTRICT JUDGE:

In the early morning hours of February 25, 2004, armed law enforcement officers invaded plaintiffs' home based on what turned out to be incorrect information that a suspect named Kinte Carter lived there. Plaintiffs thereupon sued the individual officers under *Bivens v. Six Unknown Named Agents of Federal Bureau of Narcotics* and the United States of America under the Federal Tort Claims Act ("FTCA").

The *Bivens* claim was tried to a jury, which found the individual defendants not liable. The FTCA claim was then tried to the Court. For the reasons explained in the following findings of fact and conclusions of law, the Court awards plaintiff Lillian Carter ("Lillian") $300,000 for past and future emotional distress suffered because an employee of the United States Postal Service negligently misinformed law enforcement that Kinte Carter resided in Lillian's home.

FINDINGS OF FACT

A. Background

In 2004, Lillian lived with her husband Russell, her sons Chad Carter and Terrance Wilson, and her younger cousin Virgil Williams at 525 Cary Avenue, in the Port Richmond neighborhood of Staten Island. Between late 2002 and early 2004, Special Agent Jon Ellwanger of the Bureau of Alcohol, Tobacco, Firearms, and Explosives ("ATF") was investigating narcotics activity and violent crime in the neighborhood.

By February 2004, Ellwanger's investigation had yielded indictments and arrest warrants for twenty-eight suspected members of two rival drug gangs in the area. One of those suspects was Kinte Carter, who was considered by law enforcement to be armed and dangerous.

B. The Investigation into Kinte Carter's Address

On separate occasions, two confidential informants pointed out to Ellwanger three or four houses in the 500 block of Cary Avenue and stated that Kinte Carter may have lived in one of them. Ellwanger eventually identified 526 and 471 Cary Avenue as possible addresses for Kinte Carter. He also identified 35

Holland Avenue, Apt. 5E, as a third possible address.

On February 17, 2004, a member of Ellwanger's team, Special Agent Tom Shelton ("Shelton") faxed a request to the Postal Inspection Service to verify the three possible addresses for Kinte Carter (along with possible addresses for several other suspects). The Postal Inspection Service is the law-enforcement arm of the United States Postal Service; one of its primary functions is to verify addresses at the request of law-enforcement agencies.

Shelton's request was processed by several Inspection Service Operation Technicians, including Wilhelmina Corley ("Corley"). Corley has worked at the Postal Inspection Service for over ten years. Although her training was brief and informal, she understood that requesting agencies expected her to provide reliable information to be used to "track people down." Trial Tr. at 1025.

Corley was responsible for verifying the possible addresses for Kinte Carter. In that regard, she contacted the postal carrier responsible for the 500 block of Cary Avenue. Neither Corley nor the carrier remembered any conversation regarding Kinte Carter. Based, however, on the carrier's testimony that he did not recall Kinte Carter ever receiving mail at 525 Cary Avenue, the Court finds that he told Corley only that a Carter *family* received mail at 525 Cary Avenue.

Following her usual procedure, Corley made handwritten notes of her investigation on the fax from Shelton. Her note-taking method invited confusion regarding names: As she learned who received mail at each address, she would sometimes write a first and last name, sometimes just a last name, and sometimes a last name with the notation "FNU" ("first name unknown"). Next to the entry for 526 Cary Avenue, she wrote "Vasquez fam.," Pls.' Ex. 30. Above it, she wrote "525 Carter (good)." *Id.*

Corley later typed out her notes on another copy of Shelton's fax; she had no recollection of how much time passed before she transcribed her handwritten notes. Since she received Shelton's fax on February 17th and sent her response on February 20th, there could have been as much as a three-day delay. During that time, Corley was responding to "numerous, if not hundreds of" other address verification requests. Trial Tr. at 1041-42.

For 526 Cary Avenue, Corley's handwritten notes became "KINTE CARTER IS GOOD AT 525 CARY AVE. 526 CARY AVENUE — VASQUEZ FAMILY IS GOOD." Pls.' Ex. 29. In other words, Corley incorrectly assumed that the reference to "Carter" in her handwritten notes referred to Kinte Carter. By comparison, Corley transcribed her handwritten note "Viola (FNU)" as "VIOLA FAMILY," and her handwritten note "Edmond" as "EDMOND FAMILY." Pls.' Exs. 28-30. Kinte Carter was the only subject whose first name did not appear in Corley's handwritten notes but was included in her response to ATF. In sum, the Court finds that Corley failed to use due care in transcribing her handwritten notes and, as a result, erroneously reported to ATF that Lillian's home was a "good" address for Kinte Carter.

Corley's fax caused Ellwanger to change his focus from 526 to 525 Cary Avenue. At Ellwanger's request, one of the confidential informants returned to the 500 block and reported back that 525 Cary Avenue was one of the houses where Kinte Carter might have lived. Ellwanger then confirmed with Consolidated Edison ("ConEd") that someone with the last name "Carter" received utility service at 525 Cary Avenue; however, the name "Kinte" did not appear in ConEd's records. Finally, Ellwanger asked a New York City Police Department detective in the 120th Precinct if Kinte Carter was "associated" with 525 Cary Avenue; the detective (whose name Ellwanger could not remember) said he was. Trial Tr. at 510. Ellwanger would not have approved a search of 525 Cary Avenue had Corley not reported it as a "good" address for Kinte Carter.

C. Execution of the Search Warrant

The arrest warrants for Kinte Carter and 27 others were executed simultaneously in the early morning of February 25, 2004, by hundreds of agents from multiple law enforcement agencies. The executing officers had not participated in the investigation.

The four officers executing the arrest warrant for Kinte Carter went to 525 Cary Avenue. They knocked loudly on the door and Lillian let them in. At that time, she was the only occupant who was awake: Russell was not at home, while Chad, Terrance and Virgil were asleep in their bedrooms.

The officers told Lillian that they were looking for Kinte Carter and proceeded to search each room in the house, with their guns drawn for at least part of the search. Lillian accompanied some of the officers, going with them to the bedrooms and the basement. She honestly — although incorrectly — believed that one of the officers held a gun to her back throughout the search because she felt something cold touch her neck and back, though she never saw what it was.

The search took approximately 30 minutes. Kinte Carter was not found. The Court credits Lillian's testimony that Kinte Carter was unknown to her and her family and had never been in their home.

D. Lillian's Injuries

Lillian was terrified that she or one of her family members might be killed during the search. Moreover, she began to think that the suspect the officers were seeking might have broken into her home, and that she would be killed in a firefight between him and the officers. Following the search, Lillian had nightmares about alternate versions of the incident in which members of her family were killed, and flashback hallucinations in which she felt a gun on her neck.

In addition, the incident dramatically affected Lillian's ability to enjoy her work or the company of her family. Her relationships with her sons and the younger cousin for whom she was caring deteriorated. Her fear of having her house invaded motivated her to install security cameras on the exterior of her home and watch the attached video monitor constantly. She eventually moved upstate — temporarily abandoning her family — because of the fear she associated with her house on Cary Avenue.

Two days after the incident, Lillian saw her primary-care physician, Dr. Salvator Prainito. He prescribed Xanax, a tranquilizer that Lillian had previously taken to reduce anxiety. As of the time of trial, Lillian was still taking Xanax.

Dr. Prainito referred Lillian to Dr. Santapuri Rao, a psychiatrist. Dr. Rao treated Lillian between June of 2004 and June of 2005. He diagnosed her as suffering from Post-Traumatic Stress Disorder ("PTSD") and, in addition to continuing Lillian on Xanax, prescribed Paxil, another anti-anxiety medication that Lillian had been taking prior to the incident; he eventually quadrupled Lillian's dosage of Paxil from her pre-incident prescription.

When Lillian moved upstate, she began treatment at an outpatient mental-health clinic in Monticello, New York. Psychiatrists there confirmed the diagnosis of PTSD and, over time, moved Lillian from Paxil to a combination of medications to manage her continuing anxiety. As of the time of trial, Lillian was still receiving treatment and continuing her medication regimen.

At trial, the medical experts proffered by both Lillian and the United States agreed that Lillian suffered from PTSD as a result of the incident; however, they disagreed as to her prognosis and the amount of anxiety attributable to other causes. Having reviewed the evidence in its entirety, the Court finds that Lillian's PTSD, although less pronounced than it was immediately after the incident, is chronic. In addition, the Court finds that other stressors (such as financial and health problems both before and after the incident) have contributed to Lillian's anxiety, but that the incident was, and continues to be, a principal cause of her PTSD and its negative effect on her quality of life.

CONCLUSIONS OF LAW

* * *

B. The Merits

Since the plaintiff's claim is a variant of negligence liability, she must satisfy the conventional elements of negligence, namely "the existence of a duty, a breach of that duty, and that such breach was a proximate cause of the events which produced the injury." In addition, in order to be compensated, a plaintiff must show damages.

1. Duty and Breach

Because Corley was aware of the use to which her information would be put, it was foreseeable that providing incorrect information would lead to a search of an innocent person's home, and that person might suffer physical or emotional injuries as a result.

2. Causation

Corley's negligence was the proximate cause of the mistaken search of the home. "The proximate cause of an event must be held to be that which in a natural sequence, unbroken by any new cause, produces that event and without which that event would not have occurred." Before Corley's fax, Ellwanger had information connecting Kinte Carter to a handful of houses that his informants had pointed out on the 500 block of Cary Avenue, with number 526 being the most promising. By contrast, number 525 did not even appear on Ellwanger's operational plan or the list of addresses he asked the Postal Inspection Service to verify. Thus, as the Court has found, Corley's mistake caused Ellwanger to focus on 525 Cary Avenue instead of 526.

Ellwanger's subsequent acts did not break the chain of causation because they were themselves motivated by Corley's negligence. In any event, his call to ConEd confirmed only that someone with the last name "Carter" lived at number 525, while his conversation with a detective at the 120th Precinct took place only after Ellwanger had decided to include 525 Cary Avenue in the list of locations to be searched.

3. Damages

Lillian seeks damages for the pain and suffering resulting from her emotional distress. "The measure of damages for pain and suffering and emotional distress is fair and reasonable compensation to be fixed by the trier of fact in the light of all the evidence in the case. Unlike pecuniary losses, these damages are, by their nature, not susceptible to mathematical computation." Guidance may be found, however, in prior awards involving similar torts, similar injuries, or both. Having undertaken an exhaustive review of such cases, the Court finds the following most apposite:

In *Sulkowska v. City of New York*, the plaintiff was arrested, removed from her workplace in handcuffs, and detained for several hours in jail. She experienced no physical injury, but was humiliated by the events and suffered PTSD for two-and-a-half years. Finding that "the emotional injury that plaintiff has endured has been severely limiting, even debilitating at times, and will be a significant factor in plaintiff's life for the foreseeable future," the court awarded $275,000 for past and future pain and suffering.

In *DiSorbo v. Hoy*, an excessive force and battery suit, the Second Circuit reduced a $400,000 jury verdict for non-pecuniary damages to $250,000. The court noted that the plaintiff's physical injuries were not severe, but that the experience of being beaten and choked by a police officer while handcuffed was especially mentally traumatic.

In *Bender v. City of New York*, the Second Circuit reduced a $300,000 jury verdict to $150,000 in favor a plaintiff whose injuries consisted of a blow to the mouth, one day of confinement, criminal charges that were pending for six months, and "nightmares and occasional loss of sleep over a period lasting a year and a half."

Finally, in a case not involving a false arrest or similar conduct, a New York State court reduced a jury award to $200,000 for the past and future pain and suffering of a plaintiff who suffered "principally from mild to moderate posttraumatic stress disorder" that did not "appear to be interfering with [her] life in any significant way."

When adjusted for inflation, the awards in these cases fall, in the main, between $200,000 and $300,000. The nature of the harm here — which involved an invasion of the sanctity of the home and, from Lillian's perspective, a risk of serious harm to her or her family — was more traumatic than the stress of a simple false arrest. And, as the Court has found, that trauma had a particularly profound and long-lasting effect on Lillian's mental health and is chronic. For these reasons, the Court concludes that an award at the top of the range — $300,000 — is necessary to fully compensate Lillian for her past and future pain and suffering as a result of the incident.

CONCLUSION

For the foregoing reasons, the Court concludes that it has subject-matter jurisdiction; accordingly, the United States's motion to dismiss is denied. On the merits, the Clerk is directed to enter judgment in favor of Lillian Carter and against the United States, in the amount of $300,000. The award shall bear post-judgment interest, but not pre-judgment interest.

SO ORDERED.

NOTES AND QUESTIONS

1.   Consider this comparison of an order, referred to as a decision, and findings of fact and conclusions of law:

> The difference between a decision and findings of fact and conclusions of law is one in form only. Unlike a decision you may render in another case, the factual findings are required to be separate from the conclusions of law. . . . While the form is different, both types of judicial writings are composed in the same manner. The facts are stated succinctly; the law is set forth, and the law then is applied to the facts to decide the case.

JOYCE J. GEORGE, JUDICIAL OPINION WRITING HANDBOOK 198 (5th ed. 2007).

2.   A court may ask counsel to prepare a draft document of findings of fact and conclusions of law, which the court can then review, amend, and finalize. Could there be any harm in such a practice?

3.   Commentators often recommend that trial judges announce their findings of fact orally, at the conclusion of the hearing, instead of reserving them for a written document.

> The announcement of findings of fact from the bench at the conclusion of a hearing allows the judge to tell the litigants face-to-face who he or she believed and why. This process demonstrates that the court is an independent institution where the judge has no reservations about stating his or her findings in the presence of those he or she chose not to believe.

John J. Brunetti, *Searching for Methods of Trial Court Fact-Finding and Decision-Making*, 49 HASTINGS L.J. 1491, 1505 (1998). Do you agree?

V.   SUGGESTED FURTHER READING

RUGGERO J. ALDISERT, OPINION WRITING (AuthorHouse 2d ed. 2010).

John J. Brunetti, *Searching for Methods of Trial Court Fact-Finding and Decision-Making*, 49 HASTINGS L.J. 1491 (1998).

IAN GALLACHER, A FORM AND STYLE MANUAL FOR LAWYERS (2007).

JOYCE J. GEORGE, JUDICIAL OPINION WRITING HANDBOOK (5th ed. 2007).

Hon. Gerald Lebovits & Lucero Ramirez Hidalgo, *Advice to Law Clerks: How to Draft Your First Judicial Opinion*, 36 WESTCHESTER B.J. 29 (2009).

Jennifer Sheppard, *The "Write" Way: A Judicial Clerk's Guide to Writing for the Court*, 38 U. BALT. L. REV. 73 (2008).